T0129942

Take Two Aspirins,

—— but ——

Don't Call Me in the Morning

M. H. Genraich, MD

iUniverse, Inc.
New York   Bloomington

Take Two Aspirins, but Don't Call Me in the Morning

iUniverse books may be ordered through booksellers or by contacting:

iUniverse
1663 Liberty Drive
Bloomington, IN 47403
www.iuniverse.com
1-800-Authors (1-800-288-4677)

ISBN: 978-1-4502-7114-1 (pbk)
ISBN: 978-1-4502-7117-2 (cloth)
ISBN: 978-1-4502-7115-8 (ebk)

Printed in the United States of America

iUniverse rev. date: 10/21/10

Prologue

This book chronicles one man's thirty-six years of experiences in the medical profession. But, unlike most of today's best selling, non-fiction, medical literature, this work is not in any way a self-help book or the next great weight-loss panacea. Nor is it a famous person's autobiography (ghost written of course,) especially given the fact that I am most definitely not a well known anything, bit it psychologist, fitness expert, diet guru, politician, actor, professional athlete, criminal, terrorist, or anyone even remotely known to the general public. This begs the question, why should I, just another middle-aged family doctor, have any desire to write a memoir? What is so special about me? Do I dare presume that I am the only doctor that has had a terminal itch to write a tell-all novel? Nope. Or am I just that much smarter and more talented a writer than any of my contemporaries. Not necessarily. But, has my life been more eventful and thus more interesting than most others in my profession? Well, YES, as a matter of fact, I think it has. There have been too many twists, turns, and ups and downs to enumerate, setting my store apart from the usual humdrum existence of the average American doc. And who really wants to settle for "humdrum" anyway? Not I!

But what I believe truly puts me in a league of my own, is how many times I have tried, with every resource I could muster, to succeed and yet, still failed. I submit to you that one has to try very hard to fail when you're making a handsome living, and have grudgingly earned the respect of both the public and your peers. Let me explain: for the better part of twenty-nine years, in spite of decent cash flow, I have teetered on the brink of bankruptcy, and, admittedly, have fallen into that abyss twice. Each time I fell, or nearly fell, I came back financially just enough to avoid another disaster. And so it has gone, through divorces, lost jobs, stock market screw ups, and numerous miscellaneous bad decisions. But I'm still here, barely solvent but alive and kicking.

Through all of this financial debauchery, I have unbelievable as it may seem, had some great times with very expensive toys. For example, I have leased or owned at least six Mercedes Benz vehicles, including my present SUV. I've also had four Bimmers, a variety of American luxury vehicles, and I even once owned the most plebian of vehicles, the dreaded Volvo sedan.

I've also been fortunate (and conniving) enough to have lived in some great homes in such great cities as Toronto, Houston, Lubbock, Oklahoma City, Odessa, Monahans, Levelland, and now back in Lubbock, TX. In Amarillo, Texas, I lived in an exclusive country club community right up to, and even after, my second divorce. I remained there for an additional year after marrying my third wife, Debbie. Inevitably, financial constraints compelled me to leave behind that custom-built beauty. I enjoyed it while it lasted, even though I knew full well that I could never really afforded to stay there indefinitely.

Expensive clothes you ask? No problem! Isn't that why God created credit cards? I always had the best and latest in men's fashions, dressing like the true executive I knew I deserved to be. When I walked through the hospital, heads would turn to catch a glimpse of the GQ attired man. My main jewelry accessory was a Rolex (Texas Timex,) but I've also owned Cariter, Brietling and other overpriced timepieces. How, you ask, could I afford all this? Well, I couldn't! But, creative financing, along with well-timed bankruptcy, can achieve material goods otherwise unattainable. I've thought about writing an entire book on the subject, but that may be just a wee bit honest and revealing. I had better stick to the vague generalities.

So why write a book? Well, for one thing, if sales are good, I'm hoping to maintain my quirky, expensive lifestyle. That sill won't guarantee that I can avoid future disaster (bankruptcy,) but it should stave off the inevitable for a few years. Secondly, it's cheap psychotherapy. Psychiatrists are very expensive, while paper and pencil are cheap. It's amazing how much hositility and anger you can exorcize by writing about all the thing that piss you off, past and present. Not to mention, some people deserve a real good pencil-whipping, and they receive just that, in full measure, in these pages. And, by changing names, dates, locations, etc., I've avoided any possible litigation, not that suing me would reap anyone substantial reward. However, being sued is messy business—very unpleasant indeed, and best avoided.

Regardless of any success, or lack thereof, this book may bring, I'll keep plugging away, optimistic to the end. Hopefully, I'll have enough money to have a high time living in the style to which I have become accustomed, and which I so richly deserve.

There's only one thing more to say really, ignore all of the nonsense above. I just thought I'd plant my tongue firmly in my cheek, and have a little fun with y'all. (That's Texas for all of you.) The real motivation behind this work is twofold: firstly, it is, in fact a retrospective of a long career in medicine, including my four year 'sentence' in med school. Also, I've written extensively about the summer I spent in Europe, preceding my senior year. There was much to see and learn back in 1968---many life lessons that are pertinent even today, and important for me to remember, even at my advanced age. The past and the present have melded into on a continuum for me, and I unwittingly miexed the two eras throughout. It wasn't a plan to be clever; it just came out that way.

The second motivating factor was a desire to discuss in the full light of day, the political nonsense, profound greed, and petty rivalries that are all too pervasive today in medicine. Most decisions in today's medical environment are based solely on the bottom line. It is as devious and cruel as any other big business in this country, and I want those aspiring to a medical career to be prepared for a world they weren't necessarily aware of. It's down, it's dirty, and it's mean as hell and one has to be tough to navigate these polluted waters. Much of what goes on behind closed doors is not for consumption by the lay public, but I think everyone is better served knowing the truth. I hold very strong opinions on such matters and am not afraid to state them. Indeed, I am overly opinionated on many topics outside the realm of medicine, and have liberally sprinkled some of these thoughts herein.

If honestly is your thing, this book is for your, because it is one painfully honest rendering of my life as a med student and doctor, with my take on a wide range of topics. However, the main focus is my travels and travail in the medicine world. Medicine is widely known as the 'healing art', but I submit that much of the profession would be well served by some healing of its own. I sincerely hope that you find this book not only entertaining, but enlightening as well.

M. H. G.

Chapter 1

Toronto 1976

"Melvyn, how can any Jew live in a place like Texas? After all, that's the southern part of the United States where all that nasty race stuff goes on, isn't it?" I thought that was a fair question to ask, coming from my parents, two people who hadn't been south of Detroit. To them going to America, especially the South, meant leaving the civilized world as they knew it. Cowboys and guns and violence everywhere, that was their notion of Texas. And, most importantly, there were no Jews!

"You might as well move to the Sahara; at least there aren't any clansmen there" my mother said with great conviction.

"Listen" I said, with my usual level of frustration I experienced in trying to reason with my parents. "Belive it or not, there are civilized people in Houston, and thank God, even a few Jews. Besides the money will be so much better, I work my heart out for so little financial reward here in Canada. Between the office, obstetrics, emergency room moon lighting, surgical assists, and even house calls , you would think that I'd be a man of means; but in seven years I have saved virtually nothing, live in a tiny house with my wife and two children, and don't have money left over a for a decent vacation. Do you call that the good life in Toronto, Canada?"

"But you're a cultured, civilized Jewish man; you'll be lonely, miserable and isolated. Money isn't everything you know," said mom.

My parents are Phillip Roth's worse nightmare come true.

"I take that back," mother continued, " you'll probably be shot before you have a chance to be lonely and miserable."

So went the parental advice and encouragement. What a blessing it is to have such positive, optimistic, and enthusiastic role models who never took a calculated risk in their lives. Thus they find themselves alone and largely forgotten by their former friends and family, living in some high-rise apartment building in the wilds of suburban Toronto. I vowed that I would survive my parents' pessimism and negativity. I was determined to make a better life for myself and my family, and that's exactly what I did. Unfortunately, the definition of better keeps changing for me every time I embark on a new adventure.

Chapter 2

The Luck of the Jewish

I was going to talk a bit about my high school years, but I have trouble remembering even one event that stood out, save for the fact that I managed to graduate and move on. I really didn't have superior grades or standing. But manage to secure a position in the pre-med program at the most prestigious medical school in Canada, The University of Toronto. Back in 1963, U of T was rated one of the top ten medical schools in the world. This accomplishment was a long-shot of epic proportions.

Let me explain: for one year and one year only, the university medical administration decided to engage in a bold new experiment; they would select students for the handful of coveted positions in the pre-medical program, based not only on grades, as in the near and distant past, but also on character. Equal weighting was to be given recommendations given by your high school teachers and administration, as well as personal letters of reference. Strangely enough, no person to person interviews with the University of Toronto staff were arranged as part of this selection process, an oversight on their part in my opinion. This was a radical departure from tradition, and the one year this experiment was undertaken was my graduating year from high school. I had already been accepted to another very good medical school in Ontario, but when I got my acceptance letter from U of T, I felt as if I had won the lottery. Being from a poor family, I couldn't afford to live in residence out of town unless I was to secure significant scholarship funding, which was not bloody likely with my grade point average.

Strangely enough, I knew that my high school years really hadn't gone that well in terms of academics, and furthermore, I felt that I hadn't created that much of a favorable impression with my teachers and the administrative staff. And yet, there I was being accepted into this prestigious medical school. All I can conclude is that I underestimated myself: those that mattered saw something in me that led them to believe I was someone of substance who should be given a chance to fulfill his dream of becoming a doctor. They, as it turns out, had more faith in me than I did, thank God. So, yes, it certainly was dumb, f---ing luck that this was the one year ever that I could achieve my goal with my grades; but I now realize that it wasn't just luck: I did deserve this opportunity. And, ultimately, I believe that I have not let my benefactors down, always striving, even now at my advanced state of life, to be the best physician and person I can be.

Sometimes I wonder what I would have done if I hadn't chosen medicine as a career. I had entertained thoughts of being an English professor, but quickly dismissed that notion when I discovered what a pitiful living they made. Then there was my architect phase, which I thought would suit my left brain, artistic side. I had always enjoyed sketching and painting, but architect was a wholly different matter. This required a certain type of precision and discipline that I came to realize I didn't posses.

For no reason in particular, I sensed that I would be more suited to a career in medicine, and this was a world I could excel in. Besides, every other job or profession I could think of, by comparison, seemed tiresome and even boring. My dad had been an accountant and he pretty much hated it, and I could see why. He felt trapped, chained to a desk, restless as a caged animal. I pitied him his burden and struggles to eke out a decent living from a job that provided little satisfaction. God bless him though for sticking with it for those many years, sustaining our little family through some tough financial times. Watching my father go through that torture, I vowed that I would never have a job that was so boring that it would zap me of any desire to live a well-rounded, fulfilling life.

My mother had been a housewife, a politically incorrect label today I realize, but she was darned good at it, enjoying her little life to the fullest. Her world had always been a little scope, having alienated all her friends and family. Shockingly, later in life I did not know my uncles, aunts and cousins on her side of the family, because of my mother's dysfunctional, hateful, and paranoid personality. I subscribe to the theory that her psyche changed forever when she lost her first-born, my brother Gary, at the tender age of ten. I was seen at the time and really didn't understand the gravitate of this event and the impact it would forever have on all our lives. I had always believed that Gary was the favorite child, being the eldest, and possessing a much more docile, agreeable personality than his younger brother. I was the hell raiser of the two , which didn't sit too well with my folks, especially mother. So, when Gary came down with a rare fatal disease, it was more devastating for mom, it truly was unbearable. His death , after a mercifully short period of suffering, was the watershed event in my parents' lives. I believe tit was the day they really stopped living, and began to just exist, especially my mother. It was just too much for her fragile psyche to handle, and she snapped.

From that point on, mother became increasingly reclusive and, without exaggeration, psychotically paranoid. Also, she became unbearably overprotective of me, not allowing me to participate in normal childhood activities that she deem to "dangerous" for her little boy. This behavior continued right up to her death, when I was already an aging baby- boomer of the sixty. All my relationships, especially with women, have been, to some extent, affected by my parents' fearful approach to life that followed my brother's passing. Somehow I would have to learn how to overcome their attempts to shield me from the real world, and seek out a life for myself. Getting into medical school was the turning point of my life in terms of my journey to become a self-sufficient individual.

So my "dumb f---ing luck" making it into med school in Toronto, was a God-send for many reason. However, I quickly learned that life as a medical student had its own set of problems, leaving me with the main goal of simply surviving the unrelenting pressure and chronic fatigue caused by endless hours of studying for another set of exams just around the corner. But it would all be worth it.

Chapter 3

University Days

I can't say that I have talked much about my course study in pre-med. How much can you say about physics, organic chemistry, physiology, philosophy, and so on. We did what we had to do to pass and move on, at least that was true for most of us. There was still competitive spirit, but it was a far cry from medical school, where the real assassins emerged from their anonymity.

My relationship with the opposite sex usually didn't involve anyone from pre-meds. Perhaps that was because most females pondering a career in medicine were, to be brutally honest, desperately unattractive, in other words, "dogs", the cruelest of terms back in the day. Now, why didn't good looking gals consider medicine as a career choice? Because, ion my opinion, most "lookers", especially Jewish gals, still had a high school mindset: always look your best, date the best looking guys, and eventually marry a professional man, preferably a med student or doctor. She might have to settle for a dental student, or law school candidate, but she was still in the right ballpark. That might sound arrogant coming from your humble narrator, a doctor, but that's just they way I saw it in those days (1963-69.) However, to actually work hard to get into med school and choose that as a career path, well, that was indeed rare thinking for a "looker." Accordingly, in med school, we were "blessed" with no lookers – except for Carol.

Carol Connors had it all, or so it seemed: looks, brains, a great sense of humor; a person just easy to hang out with---- in short, perfect! Sadly she had a boyfriend back home in London, Ontario. She was gentile, and of all the coincidences, he was Jewish. I told you she was perfect. If she had asked me, I would have strongly advised her to not get involved with a Jewish college student. After all, his only goal in this situation was free, gouache (gentile) pussy. No, it should have been me that she chose, not because I was a Jewish med student, but because I was atypical. I would have treated her with respect and kindness for a while, but without putting out sooner or later, (preferably sooner,) I probably would have turned into a real prick like her present beau, Jonathon. Or maybe not, because I could never really be that cruel to a girl, even if she deserved it. So I'll stand by my original statement, and say that I'm atypical.

This girl seemed to have it together all the time. I couldn't detect any hint of ambiguity or deep sadness. In reality, she was far removed from being together---she was just as fucked up as the rest of us; maybe even more so. Rumor had it that she had once tried to commit suicide by slashing her wrists. I couldn't confirm that, especially since she always wore bracelets and long sleeved blouses. Whatever her shortcoming, one things was for certain---Carol was most definitely a "looker." And she was damned smart too. With relative ease, she glided through pre-med into first year med school. If she had really desired it, she could have been ninetieth percentile material. But she wanted something else far different—Him. And when, in the end, she couldn't have Him, she was a med school dropout waiting to happen. As an interested "friend" I tried my best to talk her out of leaving school. What a waste of potential; she'd have made a great doctor for several reasons, chief among them which was that she was in touch with her feelings of compassion for others in distress, like herself. Secondly, she was one of the few decorative and intriguing gals in my year. The other ladies were devoid of personality and boring as shit, not to mention quite unfortunate in appearance. For my own selfish reasons, I couldn't allow Carol to leave me behind in callas so burdened with disastrous looking females. There was only one thing left to do—date her, and hope, beyond all reason, that she could fall for me. Hey, I was Jewish too, wasn't I? That alone should be my ticket for an intimate relationship with her, along with the fact that I am bright, witty beyond words, edgy, and physically, not totally unattractive.

So I tried to arrange the "safe coffee date;" nothing to obvious; you know, the kind of thing friends do. This was very benign way to approach her – the platonic method, with a hope on my part for much more. To my surprise and delight she was fine with that. And so it came to pass one evening that we met at a favorite coffee house haunt of mine, which served up some great live entertainment. This was 1966, and the Yorkville district of Toronto was the folk-singing, espresso drinking, hippy-laden center of

Canada. There was also an abundance of U.S. students, draft dodgers, who had partially taken over Yorkville. Their numbers were swelling rapidly, eventually topping one hundred thousand in Toronto alone. Poor bastards, forced to leave family and friends behind; and for what? I'm not going to let myself get side-tracked here with politics, so back to the matter at hand--my "safe date" with Carol.

The Riverboat was jumping, more than usual on this particular evening, with awall to wall people. Talk about atmosphere, it was as thick as the smoke filling the room, mostly from "grass." One could compare it to a scene out of Woodstock except for the fact that Woodstock didn't occur until 1969. The main reason for the crowd was the headliner for the night, my folk music hero, the great Gordon Lightfoot. Even if the date turned out to be a complete dud, I was going to see and hear Lightfoot live, in a small club, playing just a few feet away from us. How could I not have a memorable night, even if there was no intimate connection between Carol and I by evening's end? At any rate, keeping my expectations low was always a good plan for me and my fragile ego: I never was much for getting a good butt kicking by a woman I lusted either.

We began the evening with polite small talk, but as Carol gained some sense of sincerity and genuine fondness of her, she slowly opened up, and became shockingly frank. Just as she began to detail her relationship with Super Jew in London, Lightfoot hit the stage. I quickly forgot our discussion, as G.L. banged away on his Gibson twelve string, backed up on lead guitar by the great Red Shea. He opened with a rousing rendition of "Steel Rail Blues," and continued on with a dozen or so classics of his that I never got tired of hearing. Such great music---- I was transported ot another universe during his first set. Okay, I'm not writing a music review for the Toronto Daily Star, but he was a special talent. And he was spot on this night. Even today, I listen to that old nostalgic stuff, attempting to play background rhythm on my faithful old Martin twelve string.

Fortunately, Carol loved Lightfoot almost as much as I did, but I could also tell, with an occasional glance, that her thoughts were frequently taking her someplace else. But, after all, I couldn't expect her to forget Him in one night, could I? Ah, but hope springs eternal, even if it is delusional. We left the club after Lightfoot's encore "Canadian Railroad Trilogy," one of my personal favorites. Carol was not particularly talkative on the drive back to the dorm. I, on the other hand, was still riding a musical high after that performance, so Carol's silence didn't bother me at all. Once we arrived, surprisingly, she invited me in for more caffeine. All of a sudden, the night reeked of potential, or so I thought. With some gentle coaxing on my part, she began to talk about herself, which helped me gain some insight into who this person really was. After all, I barely knew her. She was from a little town near London, Ontario, the second of three children. Her father had been a doctor, but a prolonged illness had forced his early retirement. She was obviously crazy about her father; a real daddy's girl. Her two siblings were boys, so naturally, dad dated over his beautiful little girl. Her mother was an English professor at Western University in London. Carol wasn't too close with mom, but still held her in high esteem. I got the feeling, listening to her description of mom, that she was a rather cool, aloof individual with regards to her family, while her daughter yearned for a mother who was warmer and more nurturing. Her mother's favorite was her firstborn, Kenneth, who too was academia, and they had a strong bond. I detected more than a hint of jealousy when Carol spoke of her brother, and the love that came his way from mother.

Not so casually, I asked her how things were going with the boyfriend back home, Mr. Super Jew. The words had barely left my lips, when she began to tear up. I felt awful for having been so bold and rude as to insert myself into her private affairs, but she regrouped and was able to speak calmly about Jonathon. It was readily apparent that he had this girl on a short leash---at his beck and call so to speak. Her life revolved around his feelings towards her at any given point in time. This is a classic tale of self-victimization, obsession, and a total lack of self esteem. She had no sense of herself at all: how warm, smart, and beautiful (inside and out) she was. How odd I thought, I was supposed to be the insecure one here, not the "looker."

Carol went on for quite some time with her Jonathon monologue. Why did her do this, and what did I do wrong, and what if I had said this instead of that, etc… I listened very attentively at first, but as she droned on, my mind wandered, as it was what to do when things got really monotonous. I fantasized about the two of us getting physical. If I had any balls at all I would have shut her up by making a surprise move, like leaning over and kissing her flush on the lips. She would then, of course, melt into my arms and we would make passionate love for the rest of the night. She would forever forget Jonathon because I had the power to change her mind and heart. I just knew that I had this gift of power over women, so why wasn't this possible? I was, after all the deserving recipient of all her affection. What a dumbass bit of whimsy I could conjure up! The question was, being young and horny, how long could I stay in her room, listening to her perseverate about this Jonathon asshole, without wanting her more and more?

So, did I make the big move? Of course not! My style was the furthest thing from bold. In retrospect, I now know that I was passive-aggressive in my approach to women. I realize that now, looking back on many such moments as this. I was benign on the outside—patient and calm; but inside, I was thoroughly pissed off. It was easier to lump all women together and say to myself that they weren't worthy of attention. But the truth I hated to admit about myself was that I was a gutless coward. My romantic notions of myself, when put to the test of real situations, failed to materialize. It was all smoke and mirrors these head games I played.

The date ended as expected: with a whimper, not a bang (forgive for the pun.) I pretended to be a friend, consoling and reassuring her that all would be week between her and Johnboy, even though I knew this was utter nonsense. I knew too many pricks just like him, who treated women like shit. Again, I asked myself, why do the dicks get all the great girls, while the truly decent, genuinely sincere, caring and "deep" guys, like me, get left in the dust? I did kiss Carol good-night, on the cheek. What a coward, but that's all the courage I could muster. Besides, I was exhausted by the Herculean effort I had put forth spending an entire evening listening to a pretty girl's rant about her boyfriend problems. I dragged my butt home, had a coke, showered, gave a passing thought to relieving my sexual frustration, but quickly dismissed that notion given my extreme level of fatigue, and soon fell dead asleep. Ah, another evening well spent.

As for Carol, she did as expected and dropped out of school. I could now fully understand why given our conversation that night. To me, that was such a waste, but perhaps I was one hundred and eighty degrees off that mark. That was the right thing for her. Her dream wasn't to become a doctor. Now, looking back, I realize what a total commitment medical school had to be in order to successfully navigate those four years. It would become one long, tough grind, save for one glorious summer in 1968—my "European Extravaganza."

Chapter 4

Medical School

It felt good to officially be enrolled in medical (not pre-med) school. This as the real McCoy—no soft electives. Oh yes, I forgot to mention that one of my two electived in pre-med was karate! I know, that's just a joke of a course3, but what the hey, it was great exercise, and self-defence training was always useful, especially in fending off unsolicited advances from the opposite sex (I should be so lucky.) Our instructor was a tiny, elderly Japanese gentlemen who happened to be the highest ranked black belt in Canada, all appearances to the contrary. He was tough as nails, and his workouts were so physically demanding, they usually left me nauseated and thoroughly spent. But I learn karate in spite my lack of finess. He must have been a great teacher, for , even now, some thirty-seven years later, I remember most of the moves fairly well. If you werent' properly balanced with your stance, he'd sneak around behind you and give you a pretty good kick in the ass. Natually, you would take a header if your position wasn't correct. Most of us made damned sure that it was. Nope, medical school was totally absent of fun electives, or any fun for that matter. Anatomy, physiology, pathology, histology, embryology, and a few other "ology's," this was the first year menu. When you first descend deep into the bowels of that old and historic medical building in Toronto, the first whiff of formaldehyde is overwhelming. A few students became quite nauseated—and they hadn't even seen their cadavers yet. One student, Miles Hightower (not his real name) a suspiciously effeminate male, fainted dead away, landing on his cadaver. He had to be helped to his feet, and then was escorted to the student lounge for a little lie-down. We tried as hard as we could not to but most of us just had to laugh at this spectacle.

Miels had the last laugh in that he indeed finished medical school with a high ranking. We called him "menopausal Miles" after that incident, well not to his face of course.

The rest of us were divided into groups of four per cadaver, two on each side of the body. That reminds me of the old saw that goes, "Sorry ma'am, I can't help you since your pain is on the right side of your chest; I only dissected the left side in anatomy class." Most of us had nicknames for our specimens, we called our guy "Dead Earnest." Oh, we thought we were ever so witty, but I'll wager we were about the thousandth group to use the same name over the years. But you know what? He did have a pretty earnest look about him, and he certainly was dead. Aside from Miles, the rest of us didn't seem to have any problem acclimatizing to the smell, sights, and sounds of the room. Our anatomy professor was Dr. Charles Duckworth, was a very proper Scotsman, with a brogue as thick as molasses. The professor emeritus was J.C. Boileau Grant, whose anatomy, "Grant's Atlas of Anatomy," was the worldwide standard in anatomy textbooks. Dr. Grant was ninety-three years old, but still gave one lecture per year to the first year students. The lecture was standing room only as usual. After all, he was the supreme living authority in the subject, and his annual visit to the school was a historic occasion. Thinking back on it now, I feel deeply honored to have witnessed his last appearance in that wonderful old building. Hew was still pretty spry, with a needle-sharp wit, and an obvious soft spot in his heart for us fledgling medical students. Hew as quite hard of hearing, and spoke very loudly; but none cared how he spoke. They just wanted to be able to tell heir children and grandchildren someday, that they had seen and heard the "Great Man." If this had occurred in the present time, I'm sure there would have been dozens of digital cameras and camcorders recording this once in a lifetime event.

Chapter 5

As it was in anatomy, our histology professor was another living legend, Dr. Arthur W. Ham. He too had produced the definitive test on the subject, "Ham's Histology." As a matter of fact, when I was in Denmark a couple of years later, I saw med students studying from his book. You could say that I'm very proud of my medical school and its heritage. Did I mention that insulin was discovered at our institution in the 1820's by Dr. Frederick Banting, and Mr. Charles Best, (Best a medical student at the time." We have also been pioneers in orthopedics and cardiology, but I will not bore you with the litany of famous names you won't recognize anyway (unless you attended medical school.) I will say this---American medical students have little or no appreciation for the accomplishments of other medical institutions around the world. Their general belief, in my opinion, is that all modern day advances in medicine came out of American schools and research facilities. Since I'm now an American citizen, I feel free to express my indignation at the egocentricity of Americans as it pertains to the study of medicine; what arrogance!

As I mentioned earlier, Dr. Arthur ham was our histology professor; good fortune smiled on us once again. He would only teach one or two more years, and then retire permanently to his farm in rural Ontario. For a man of such renown, he was self-effacing, soft spoken, and his possession of keen sense of humor. Everyone in class, I'm certain, will always remember his surprise "pop quizzes" whereby we were to identify from what organs the microscopic specimens were derived from. We are failed miserably at first, even the top echelon players in the class of '69. You see, he had substituted slides of monkey tissue instead of human. That was a sly prank that he like to pull occasionally , but not necessarily with every years' new class of students. I think that he would only play this game with a group of folks that felt certain affinity for. Even though it was a joke, sure enough the competitive types were still miffed at their marks. What more is there to say about these humorless androids?

I actually did quite will in my studies the first year, achieving a good standing by year's end. I was overachieving academically but socially I was failing miserably. I can't recall a single girl, aside from Carol, who had even the slightest influence on my life in those first three years of med school. Oh well, three more though years to come, and with them, hopefully, many exciting heterosexual experiences to make those years remotely tolerable.

Chapter 6

I had been at the university for three years and had not seen a sick person yet. I had, however, had an intimate one year relationship with a dead person, but that's not quite the same thing. That all changed upon entering our second year of med school. The class was divided into clinical groups, consisting usually of six students. My group of six couldn't have been more diverse that if I had hand-picked them; six very different personalities indeed. My best friend in the group as it turned out, was Ron Feld – ten years my senior, and a former pharmacist. We were polar opposites, but somehow we clicked. He appreciated my sick sense of humor and I appreciated his calm, rational approach to life. He was married, and I, of course was not. We never, ever bud died up off campus, for there we had nothing in common; not to mention the fact that his wife, Marian, was a strange, moody, borderline hostile individual. She wasn't unpleasant to look at, especially when she stood next to Ron. Sorry Ron, but man you were homely – obese, big old bug-eyes, balding, reminiscent of a bloodhound with an overactive thyroid. I haven't seen him in thirty years. Save for our twentieth class reunion (a real disaster.) If he is still alive, I can't imagine that his looks have improved any. That's not mean-spirited, just factual. Ran was a chain smoker when I first met him three packs a day or more. We studied at the main campus library, and on our coffee breaks we both smoked up a storm, but Ron would smoke three to my one. Then one day he told me that he was quitting for good, which I thought was a pipedream for such a dedicated smoker. To his credit, one day Ron just tossed away his last pack of cigarettes and never picked them up again. Once he put his mind to a goal, he usually achieved it, something that I admired most about him.

All through med school Ron and I studied at the campus library most every night. We were inseparable friends and colleagues; at least during the working day. Without Ron's encouragement and example, I'm really not sure if I would have made it through those intense four years of med school. Unbeknownst to me, that he felt the same about me, as I later found out from a mutual acquaintance. Funny, it seems that the people you help the most are the ones you least feel that you're helping. Maybe that's the true spirit of giving; being totally unaware of you're act of giving. Happily, Ron, in the end, achieved a very high standing in our graduating class, landing in the top twenty out of one hundred and sixty. Unhappily, I didn't fare quite as well, but I was grateful just to have survived the ordeal. Ron has since gone on to specialize in oncology, and has been involved in numerous published research studies. What an over-achiever he was and is! Our one and only encounter, as I mentioned previously, was at our twenty year class reunion. He and his wife were disappointingly aloof, and even arrogant towards me and wife number two. He had changed dramatically, unfortunately for the worse. He was now part of the medical establishment, which, in my opinion, was a bad thing. Peering down from his academic ivory tower, I was just another family doctor peon; one of the "huddled masses." That experience was chilling. It never happened again, thank God, our reunion having been a total disaster. I don't know why I would have expected otherwise, given how wretchedly competitive and back-stabbing people in med school were. These folks hadn't changed one nano-iota. Time had stood still for them – still duking it out for prestige and standing amongst their peers, even after twenty years. My God, can't some people get over their insecurity and just move on?

Chapter 7

Let me describe for you the rest of my clinical gang. I have to mention Imre Fejer first because he was such a memorable figure. Imre was a huge, muscular man -- not obese by any means. He stood about six feet two inches, weighed about two hundred and twenty pounds, and almost always looked menacing and even mean. As it turned out, this was just a put-on, a façade behind which was a really kind, decent, and funny person. When I first met him, I'm not ashamed to admit that he scared the crap out of me. Actually we all met him on our initial day of clinical rounds. We were all gathered around a patient's bed, the curtains drawn of course, as the professor of medicine was discussing the patient's signs and symptoms. Imre was late, a common trait of his and I later discovered; so we had no idea who he was since he didn't come through the pre-med ranks with the rest of us. Suddenly, the curtains parted like Moses parting the Red Sea, and in strolled Imre. He frightened everyone, including I believe, the instructor. Fittingly, he had a deep baritone voice, very authoritarian, and a thick Hungarian accent. He was dressed impeccably in a grey suit with yellow tie, and freshly polished wing top shoes. At first, we didn't know what to think, but we sure didn't want to say or do anything to piss him off.

As I mentioned above, Imre was in fact, a pussycat, a big, Gentle Ben type Hungarian Bear, and he was very funny! A confirmed chain-smoker, Imre had three other things that he loved above all else, wine, women and shooting pool. He was very proficient at the latter, but I was pretty fair with a pool cue as well (misspent youth.) Imre and I had many terrific, closely contested matches. But, when there was money on the line, he became unbeatable -- Minnesota Fats reincarnate. He always had a cigarette dangling from his mouth when he played, and he looked so cool.

I tried that, but the smoke always managed to find its way into my eyes; so much for looking cool while shooting pool. I'm almost ashamed to admit that I missed many a boring biochemistry class because of my love for the game, and of course, the great fun to be had putting my ability against my Hungarian friend's great skill.

Imre had a very dry sense of humor, and he told a joke with impeccable timing. He turned out to be our main source of humor and general nonsense in out little group -- a pleasant surprise for us all. Imre went on to become a family doctor, and married a woman somewhat older than myself, who also had two children. Now that did surprise me. Mr. Playboy of the Western world went and settled down into family life. His present whereabouts are unknown to me, but I m's rue that wherever he is, that is if smoking didn't kill him, he is prosperous and giving everyone around him a good laugh. Seriously speaking, I do hope that he quit smoking, not every big Imre could survive a three pack a day habit for too many more years.

Chapter 8

Compared to Imre, the rest of us in the group were mere boys, and serious nerds. But what males in the class weren't? Well, actually we were a mixture of different types of nerds, subsets if you will. In our group John Carlisle was a legal nerd. His parents were both lawyers, and his goal was to enter law school upon completion of medical school. Medico-legal jurisprudence was coming into its own as a legal specialty, and that's where John was setting his sights. I surmise that he wanted to go through the process of medical school so that he could better understand the mind of the doctor. I'm assuming that he thought that this would make him a more effective litigator against the medical profession. Malpractice cases in Canada didn't fetch much of a settlement for the plaintiff as was the case and still is in the U. S. A., but John was looking to the future and the inevitable legal problems doctors would increasingly face, especially in light of increased governmental regulation of medicine in Ontario. Carlisle was tall and lean, no make that skinny, with short cropped hair, and oversized glasses. Top that off with the same crummy U of T Med School blazer, grey slacks, thin tie and white shirt every damned day of school for four years, and you pretty much know all there is to know about John's very hip presentation. As expected, John was very active politically , helping various Conservative Party (of course) candidates at election time. I can definitely picture him serving in a Conservative government post – Minister of Health for example. In spite of his physical appearance, and conservative right wing leanings, I rather liked John, and never found him to be boring or obnoxious. He was our group's arbitrator if any disagreements arose -- pleasant and accommodating, skillfully unobtrusive. His calm, rational exterior belied, I think, a true competitive fire burning inside; he just wasn't obvious. Truly bright people are like that in my experience, very modest and self-effacing about their abilities and accomplishments. I enjoyed him as did my compares'. John was our rock of Gibraltar through difficult academic times, helping to keep all of us calm and panic-free. To this day, when I think back on the guys, I can really appreciate how much I actually admired and respected John, and I'm confident that he either is or will soon be Minister of Health of Canada.

John's best friend in and outside of our clinical gang, was Richard Isaacs, or Sir Richard as we like to call him, since he had this air of nobility about him. At first I thought he was arrogant and a snob, but I was wrong. In fact he was painfully shy and soft spoken, letting others carry the conversation before he made any little contribution. Richard was quite good looking, but his manner was very—well, effeminate: prim and proper like a real lady, but very likeable. He rarely offered an opinion except on matters legal. Like John, he was also from a legal family background. After med school, the two of them, indeed, did go to law school and graduated cum laude. John and Richard were inseparable, much like Ron and I, but unlike us, their friendship extended beyond school. Their goals and interests were the same: both were single, both were from wealthy families. They had attended a private prep school together, Upper Canada College, which at that time, coast about as much as med school. They came from the true blue-blood, upper crust Toronto society, but they never exhibited that sort of elitism towards us common folk. As long as I knew both gents they never went on dates with the opposite sex, or even kept company with girls around campus. I think John was just too focused and ambitious, whereas Richard just didn't seem to be physically interested. He did have one female friend in our class, a very large, unattractive young lady, who looked like a Russian weightlifter. Richard, however, was perfect for our clinical clan, lending it a touch of class it so desperately needed.

Chapter 9

Now that brings me to one Jack Dubinsky; not that I was that anxious to arrive here. Jack was the dufus, the Kramer if you will, of our little entourage, so far beyond nerd that he made even the rest of us look cool. Jack, like Kramer, was a tall, lanky drink of water. He stood about six foot four inches, weighed no more than one hundred and fifty pounds, and always looked disheveled. His hair reminded me of a briar patch, sprouting out in all directions, and dripping of dandruff, which was always in evidence on his University of Toronto blazer. He always seemed to be leaning forward as if being blown from behind by a strong wind. I think the leaning, hunched over posture was intentional since he was always straining to hear every word that everyone around him was saying, even if it was none of his business. Jack was very paranoid, and with good reason being viewed as the class clown by all. Witnessing nerdom in its purest form was liberating for me, for I could never put myself in the same league as Jack. In Jewish we'd say Jack was a "shlomeele," in genital vernacular, a nauseating creature known as a "dork." I'm betting the ranch that old Jackie got down on all fours for all his gay high school teacher in order to get recommendations for med school. Some people are naturally funny – they think and act in an amusing way, and are thus appreciated for their effortless wit. Jack was funny, but not in that way. You had to laugh at him not with him because he was walking, talking unintentional joke. Nobody could be that naïve, clumsy, inappropriate, and thoroughly annoying; or could they? Yes they could! I know this because Jack Dubinsky does exist. His personality was reminiscent of the old fingernails on a blackboard audio flashback; or the feel of itchy underwear; or, hemorrhoid pain, just getting under your skin all the time, and staying there for four years. Yes, J.D. was man for all seasons, you could despise him any season of the year.

He was such a nauseating suck-up, you could usually find his nose stuck up some professor's ass.

We all made fun of Jack, but maybe, in the end, he got the last laugh. I heard that he had established a family practice in the burgeoning north end of Toronto, and indeed, had prospered. Yes Virginia, a "dufus" can succeed, perhaps because they are frighteningly unaware of just how fucking ridiculous to the rest of the world they really are. It must be swell not to be burdened with self-awareness, or any common sense for that matter. That's it! People like Jack are simply living in another universe wherein, seemingly, none finds them inappropriate, and they wouldn't give a damn if they did. Maybe there's a lesson in that for all dufus about not taking ourselves so seriously or worrying about how other see us? Nah! That's bullshit; Jack was just an obnoxious, unlikeable idiot. The only thing I learned from Jack was to avoid people like him, although there weren't too many folks in that club.

And wouldn't you know it; Jack was one of the first doctors I ever knew who used gimmicks in his practice to generate big bucks. His specialties were weight loss(read diet pills), and hypnosis for smoking cessation, and treatment of anxiety disorders. He was way ahead of his time on the weight loss deal, he should've written a book on charlatanism, "The dufus guide to Rapid Weight Loss and Other Scams I've Perpetrated," Dr. Atkins move over!

If this portrait of J.D. seems mean-spirited and arbitrary, so be it. Jack was certainly no angel: he wished none of us well. You know the kid in grade school who would snitch on you to the teacher for every little thing? That's our Jackie-boy. Whatever he could do to improve his class status at your expense, he would do without a second's though.

Chapter 10

As for me, med school left a deep scar on my psyche, even to this day, some thirty-five years later. The other night, I had a nightmare that I've experienced occasionally in the past. I was walking up the steps of the med school's main entrance, all set to begin writing my final years exams. However, my way was blocked by a giant of a man, a menacing looking creature with a vile temperament. He bellowed at me that I was in legible to sit the finals, and ordered me to leave the building. When I asked why, he ignored me. When I tried to by pass him repeatedly, and repeatedly he brushed me aside. When I awoke I was in the middle of a full-fledged panic attack, hyperventilating and sweating profusely. After a few minutes of this near death feeling, I finally regained my senses, but the bad vibe lasted all day---that sense of impending doom that lingers and leaves you exhausted by the end of the day.

Med school could do this to anyone, and probably did. We were always sweating out the next set of exams upcoming, and worried about the results of the previous tests that hadn't yet been graded. Rationally , we all knew that we'd pass since almost no one had flunked out of med school in decades, you would have either quit or die not to make it. But, as I said earlier, we were all so damned paranoid by senior year that rationality had exited stage left a long time ago. Competition was keener than a razor's edge, spurred on by our professors, and of course, by our fellow students. I had frequent thoughts of assassinating our professors, and of course, my fellow students. If murder were legal, you knew that they would have done just that to their closest rivals---anything for a higher standing.

Personifying the importance of our final class standing, I give you Michael Littman, bridge player extraordinaire. He had his priorities in order, and he didn't deviate from his plan. Mike was the last, but certainly not the least, member of my clinic group that I need to describe. We had in our midst, without appreciating it at the time, a true genius! Not handsome, not a whole lot of personality, not a sharp dresser, but indeed, a genius. A master bridge player, Mike played big tournaments around the country with his regular partner, Sam. He had been doing the bridge circuit for years, all the way through high school as a matter of fact, and he still managed to get into med school. But how could he get through the toughest professional curriculum on earth and still maintain his tournament schedule? Easy---if you have a calculating devious mind. What Mike did, in retrospect, was something we all could have done if we weren't so damned anal about grades and class standing. Each year, unbeknownst to us, Mike would decide which two subjects he would devote virtually no time to that year. He would then go to summer school, cram like a sonofabitch, and pass the two course3s by a whisker, He did this each and every year, including our fourth and final year, which was an achievement of Herculean proportions, given the volume of work involved in each subject. By sticking with this program, Mike was able to participate in all the major bridge tourneys during the school year; and he would win most of them, earning in the process, a ton of money; more than enough to cover his annual expense in med school. None of us geniuses in the group could figure out what Mike was up to when he finally caught on during a fast game of contract bridge that he sat in on with Mike one lunch hour towards the end of our last year in med school. Somewhere in the middle of the game, Ron kiddingly asked Mike what subject he planned to fail this year. Without hesitation, Mike said "Internal Medicine and Ob-Gyn." Ron relayed this information to the rest of us, explaining how Mike had beaten the system all this time. Here's the final irony--Mike ended up in California as a high-dollar shrink to the Hollywood celebs. How does that speak to the importance of our final standing in medical school? Bullshit! Four years of sheer crap, this is unnecessary ill will, infighting, and jealousy. Life outside of medical school hasn't been any picnic either, I'll grant you that. Competition for jobs, or for moonlighting gigs in places like the E.R. for extra cash, will always exist, bit it can never match the intensity and emotional extremes of medical school. Thank God it's over and in the past. Whenever I feel a pang of nostalgia setting in about those old school days, the reality of it all hits me pretty fast, and my thoughts return to the present, grateful to be where I am now in spite of any current problems that may seem impossibly difficult. What, me worry? Not after medical school.

Chapter 11

Medical School was like one long examination, with little else in between, save for one glorious summer night in 1968. Up until then, I had held a succession of summer scud jobs, each one more tedious than its predecessor. I had been a dishwasher in the bowels of Toronto General Hospital, a summer counselor for some real bratty Jewish kids, an orderly, schlepping bedpans in two hospitals, one in Vancouver, the other back at Toronto General. I had worked my way up from the basement at TGH, to the bottom--- of patients' buttocks that is. Now that is what I call a giant leap in status, eh?

But now it was the summer hiatus preceding my fourth and final year of medical school, and I was headed for Europe: Copenhagen, Denmark to by exact. God knows I deserved this good fortune. I had found out about a foreign exchange program for med students, which not only sounded like great fun, but was also dirt cheap. Thanks to the University's contract with a charter airline, the fare was a mere two-hundred and forty dollars return from London to Toronto. What a joke, even in the stone age of 1968. And the timing was perfect for my little excursion from another standpoint. My on-again, off-again girlfriend, Linda, was driving me nuts, exacerbating my usual sate of insanity secondary to my intense educational experience. One day she would show great affection towards me, the next, she wasn't sure how she felt.

When I was really honest with myself, I knew that she must have had another relationship cooking, probably with an out-of-towner. Something was keeping her from making a total commitment to me, I was merely her in-town guy, convenient when Mister Number One was not available. We've all been there before, right? Men and women have been playing this game since time immemorial, so why was I stressing? Because I was in love with the bitch, that's why! Or so I thought.

Boy, did I need a vacation. I needed to get as far away from Linda as possible. Actually, we hadn't seen each other or even spoken on the phone for weeks; it was just getting too painful and confusing for me. Funny, Linda wasn't particularly beautiful, or even pretty, but there was just something about her that drove me crazy—charming, and endearing I suppose, with a good sense of humor. So there was chemistry there, or so I thought. Funny, it wasn't like me to pursue someone who wasn't a "looker," a prize trophy so to speak. Not that I was particularly successful at snaring one; but then again, my batting average was probably no worse than even the studliest studs on campus. But I digress. During my "separation" from L, I began seeing another gal whose name escapes me, probably because she was eminently forgettable. Lets' just call her "LBFH"—Jewish Bitch from Hell. Just kidding, but she was a conniving, deceitful little thing, bent on landing her a doctor. I know it's a cliché, but Jewish girls really did fancy a future as "Dr. and Mrs. Welltodo," at least in the big metropolis of Toronto. What a world apart from West Texas, where a girl's dream guy has a beer-belly, talks perfect hick English, and works either as a farmer or in the oilfield. As for JBFH, she was pretty, not exactly beautiful, but in possession of f---ing magnificent body. My fracture ego needed someone just like her, who found me attractive for whatever reason I could careless. And man did I need to get laid! Okay, there—I admit it: I was young, horny, frustrated by one gal while my testosterone overload was about to kill me. So, did I, in fact, have great sex with JB? Hell, no! I didn't quite get to home plate cause, like all good Jewish females, she was genetically blessed with the ability to tease but not fully please. She lead me to the very edge of bliss, and then bailed out, leaving me so frustrated and wound up that I had to go home and finish the job myself—damn it! But hey, if more young men masturbated when they were bursting for sex, just think how fewer sexually motivated criminal acts there would be. I know—that rationalization is a stretch.

Getting back to my upcoming adventure, the time was drawing near, and I was getting pretty damned excited. I was to fly to Copenhagen via London, and remain there for six weeks. My residence would be in a hospital on the outskirts of the city. I would make rounds with the residents and interns, and attend grand rounds, getting to know how clinical teaching was done in another country. Hopefully this would be a rich cultural and educational experience. After Denmark, I planned to take a train to Paris with my classmate acquaintance, Mike Adams. There, we would rent a car, and explore Europe for the next eight weeks or so.

Strangely enough, I hadn't been that close a friend of Mike's, thus the term acquaintance, but we really seemed to jell when discussions concerning possibly hooking up as travel buds cam up. Somehow I had heard of his interest in the exchange program, and got in touch with him one day after class. He was keen on joining forces to share our car expenses, and to have a familiar face from home along for the ride. One word best describes Mike, agreeable. In planning for the journey, we never once argued about anything--- especially about the itinerary. We were of like mind; have a general idea what countries we wanted to explore, but let the wind blow us any which why it wished. Que sera sera, so to speak--- which was the perfect attitude for this lengthy trip. Mike was a very laid back dude, and I was not; so I guess once again. As the old saying goes, opposites attract. Also, we were quite opposite in physical appearance, not that it mattered. Mike was typically gentile: thin, blue eyes, short-cropped sandy blond hair, and always a hint of a smile---nothing phony about it. Come to thinking of it, we were all a little taller, a hell of a lot thinner, and sadly, more awkward in every way than we would care to admit. At any rate, Mike genuinely liked most people, and they liked him. I needed an easy going companion to help me maintain my composure; I was not "Mr. Affable, Easy Going" personality, but Mike would be there to help smooth out the rough spots that I was sure would pop up sooner or later, knowing me. So we had a pretty good idea of our route once we left Paris. The plan called for covering the most ground in the time allotted before having to return to London, and then home. One side trip that Mike did insist upon, was to small town just outside of Barcelona, where he planned to purchase a hand-made classical guitar. He, in fact, was an excellent guitarist, and that was the only thing about him that really made me jealous since I'd always wanted to play the guitar. Funny, later in life I actually did learn to play rather well, (if I do say so myself), but it came only at a time that I could really stay focused on lessons and practice. It was all I could do to concentrate on my studies--- hobbies would have to wait.

Another acquaintance of mine, Harvey Greenfield, had heard of my travel plans, and offered me some assistance via my stay in Copenhagen. He had been there the year before, also as an exchange student, and he was anxious to hook me up with a native of that city. I don't know whey he was being so considerate towards me since we weren't ever close friends, but I was most appreciative. He told me that the liaison for foreign med student in Copenhagen the year he went over, was a young lady by the name of Suzanne Holke, a first year med student. Apparently they had become good friends during his stay there, and they had continued to communicate through the mail. Naturally, I was more than a little curious about her appearance, I just dove right in and asked Harv that very question. Harv was charming, but, as always, a little evasive.

"I think you'll find her quite attractive, and certainly, a terrific person. She was immensely helpful to me in explaining the way things worked in her country's medical system, and what I could expect in my studies there in Copenhagen. She also gave me some great travel hints for my tour of Scandinavia and parts of Europe. She's well-traveled to say the least."

The only thing I hear him say were the words, "quite attractive," so I pressed on. "So you says she's attractive? Do you mean drop dead gorgeous, or just plain Jane, with a good personality that makes her seem attractive?"

"Mel, I am telling you; she's every easy on the eyes as are most Danish girls, with the added bonus of being friendly and helpful. Is that satisfactory Valentino?"

"Well no, not quite," I said. I had no shame, or, for that matter, good manners. "Now you say, easy on the eyes." Next you'll lower it to "down-to-the-bone-ugly." Come on Harvey, fess up please for God's sake. What's the real story?" I was being a jerk, and Harv let me know it.

"Okay already Mel, just keep your hormones in check for second, alright? Now listen! I'm laying a great opportunity to meet an actual native of Denmark right in your dumb-ass lap, and all you've done so far is give me grief. How about just a little appreciation? You'll meet her and judge her looks for yourself—you won't believe anything I say anyway. I strongly suggest that you call her the instant you touch down in Copenhagen because if you don't, someone else will, and your' have blown something really good. I'll bet it wouldn't be the first time you screwed up on a gift like this, eh?"

"Hey, I am sorry if I offended you Harv, but I'm just expressing a natural male curiosity here."

"No Mel, you're just showing you're a butt! Just go with it, okay?"

"Okay Harvey, you've properly put me in my place, but would you just answer me one more question?"

"Sure, what is it?"

"Do you know if she is unattached at this point?"

"Last time I heard from Suzanne, which was a couple of weeks ago, she was available---sans boyfriend. We still write each other regularly, so that's accurate ok?"

"Harv, tell me, did you do the deed with her?" I stupidly asked.

"Jesus Mel, I told you that we were just good friends so drop it. Now just go over there and have a great time---and call her damn it!!!"

"Thanks a lot Harv, I really mean it, and I'm sorry if I seemed ungrateful. I'll say this though; you've lowered my expectations to the point where I can't possibly be disappointed. Hey, see ya' when I get back buddy."

"You're welcome I think. Bye for now. Oh, and by the way, don't call me, I'll call you."

I don't know exactly what Harvey was trying to tell me or not tell me, but I sure as hell was going to call her asap. Like Harvey said, who the hell did I know over there anyway? Nothing to lose—just go with tit for once in your dumb-ass life, I told myself. Funny, as the day for departure rapidly approached, I didn't give much more thought to this potential Danish jackpot. Go figure the obsessive-compulsive mind!

Chapter 12

Europe Here I Come

Our flight left at ten p.m. and I was at the airport with my folks at nine. Mike was there as well, as were another hundred and twenty or so fellow med students with their respective families and friends. In short, the airport was wall to wall humanity. Seemingly out of nowhere a familiar figure approached me. I'll be damned, it was Linda, my erstwhile girlfriend. She walked right up to me and kissed me on the lips---with tongue! I was dazed and confused, my normal reaction to most events surrounding this relationship.

"What on earth are you doing here?" I asked. "I mean, we haven't even spoken in weeks! My God, what do you want from me?"

"I just wanted to see you off and, before you left, apologize for my callous, insensitive behavior," she replied. " I think I now realize just how much I care for you, and I didn't want you going away for the entire summer without knowing that. Oh, and guess what? I'll be leaving for London myself in two weeks. I wanted you to have my itinerary, and perhaps we could rendezvous in Paris or London. What do you think about that?"

"Are you kidding? I'll tell you what I think, I think I need to sit down for a minute and collect myself before I fall down from the shock of just seeing you. What do you want from me anyhow? I mean, you can't decide how you really feel about us as a couple. You're driving me crazy and I'm getting pretty sick of it. Unfortunately, I still love you, so, in answer to your question, of course I'll hook up with you wherever. Just let me know in advance when you're coming to Paris. You can send a postcard to me care of the nearest American Express office and give me exact dates of arrival and where you'll be staying, okay?"

"That's great Mel—I will write. Just check with American Express at all your major city stops. I promise you I won't let you down this time."

We strolled through the airport hand in hand. I felt lighter than air, I was so happy. Finally the time for departure had arrived. One last kiss for my parents and Linda, and I was on the plane heading east to London. Yahoo!!

The scene inside the airplane was something to behold. Put one hundred and twenty or so university students together with free booze and food, and you've got quite a party at thirty-two thousand feet. Pretty much everyone stayed up all night long drinking and socializing. A few wise individuals actually managed to get some sleep. Although I don't know how they did it in that den. Just after sunrise, we could see the city of London below us, and fatigue or not, we were genuinely excited. We landed at Heathrow Airport at about 8:30 a.m. Some of the passengers had partied a little too hardy, and required assistance disembarking the aircraft. One or two students hadn't quite regained consciousness and had to be carried off. Mike and I, along with several other folks, had to be across town at Gatwick Airport to catch our commuter plane which would take us to Copenhagen. We had less than an hour to get there, and that would be through London rush hour traffic. We hailed a typical oversized London cab, which sat six of us comfortably. The cabbie was an elderly gentleman with white hair and a thick Scottish brogue.

"No problem at all ladies and gentleman. I'll have you there right on the dot," said the cabbie. "Now just hold on and enjoy the ride."

He wasn't kidding when he said, "hold on." He was off and running in a heartbeat, bobbing and weaving through impossible traffic, both city and highways, at unimaginable speeds. I thought New York Cab drivers were nuts: not ever close! I will say this for him though. He got us to Gatwick on time, barely making our connection. The flight over to Denmark was uneventful, especially in comparison to our near-death experience in the cab.

As soon as we touched down, each of us headed off in separate directions to our respective hospitals. I shared another taxi with two tight-assed colleagues from my class, Mike G. and Mark W., who I kenw to be snobby and clannish from back home. Well, not to disappoint, they would be absolutely no different here, perhaps even worse, considering that they were already ignoring me, a fellow traveler from their med school class.

We headed for Bispebjerg Hospital, where was way out in the boonies of North Copenhagen, some twenty kilometers from centre ville. All the way there, Mike and Mark (M&M) were engaged in private chit chat, ignoring me. Typical, I thought, but painful none the less to be treated with such casual disdain. I was deep in thought about how to sabotage these two pricks, when the cab's abrupt stop snapped me out of my daydream. And there we were, standing in front of this beautiful hospital, seemingly in the middle of a park. It looked more like a four star hotel than a hospital. We were greeted by one of the medical residents, and shown to our rooms where were in the basement. When I first entered my digs, I was shocked at how small, and dungeon-like it was. There were no windows, and little furnishings; very stark indeed. A bed, a closet, a bathroom with a shower stall, and a couple of uncomfortable chairs comprised all the amenities therein. If I was claustrophobic, I would have turned right around and left, but I stayed. Besides, where else was I to go? This wasn't New York or Toronto, with a thousand hotels and motels all around.

After just a short while in my room, I came to the conclusion that I had better get busy meeting people fast, or this would turn out to be a disaster. I had regained enough composure to call Harvey's friend, Suzanne. Normally, I would be rather nervous calling a girl for the first time, but necessity is the mother of braver, and I rang her up. Cold calling was not my habit, so I did prepare myself for anything, including total rejection. To my surprise and delight, she couldn't have been nicer. Her English was a bit dicey, but I managed to convey Harvey's message of hello, and introduce myself as his closest and dearest friend. I'm not sure if she bought that one, but she did agree to meet me for dinner the following evening. Also on the agenda, was a tour of downtown Copenhagen, which she thought I would find most interesting. She had a soft, soulful voice which I found very comforting; I was hoping that she would look as good as she sounded. Heck, I would settle for half as good. After our conversation, my curiosity was rapidly peaking, but I didn't want to set my expectation bar too high for fear of a terrible let-down.

It was quite difficult to get to sleep that first night in my little dungeon. For one, the bed sucked, and secondly, I was a little nervous as to what would be expected of me at clinical rounds first thing in the am. Okay, I'll have to admit that I was so obsessing just a tad about my upcoming "date" with Suzanne, conjuring up different images of her just from her telephone voice. I was definitely expecting someone pleasant looking, but not flat out beautiful. She would, of course, be a blonde with blue eyes—after all, this was Scandinavia. Medium height, decent body, but again, nothing spectacular, just a sweet-natured gal with a not too displeasing physical presence, all in keeping with my low expectation mindset.

Chapter 13

Clinical rounds began the next morning, and they would have gone just fine save for one little detail: no one, from professor to intern, made an effort to speak any English during formal teaching sessions. How bloody rude! Here we are, med students from Canada, a long damn way from home, obviously not knowing Danish from Pig Latin , and common courtesy was absent in toto. Now, these folks certainly knew English since it is taught as a second language from grade school on. Add to that the fact that I overheard conversations in English between students and clinical staff alike in more informal settings. I wondered how people k in my own profession no less, could have such callous disregard for their guests. Perhaps, I rationalized, it was just the Danish peoples' negative attitude towards all things American, especially in 1968, with the Vietnam War in full swing. But wait a minute, I wasn't an American; I was Canadian, and we in Canada were generally unsupportive of the war, but the problem with being Canuck, was that we didn't (and still don't) have a national identity whereby other countries would always know where we stood on the major issues of the day. We're like plain vanilla ice cream; it doesn't really matter what brand it is, it all tastes pretty much the same. So, as the de facto fifty-first state, I might just as well say I too was an American, and not create any confusion as to who and what I was about. But I digress….

As I was saying, this was 1968, the year of the Tent Offensive. Those poor, downtrodden North Vietnamese and Viet Cong had risen up to kick American ass, a turn of events that the rest of the world seemed delighted with. This was also the year of two assassinations in the U.S.A., R.F.K. and M. L.K. Let me sum up the attitude of the Danish people I came to know at the hospital: cynical indifference. I was sitting in the physicians' lounge, when the news of Robert Kennedy's death was reported on the TV.

No one in that room expressed event the slightest show at the moment. One of the residents said, "What else would you expect in America, such a violent society—so, big deal!"

After JFK's murder in Dallas in 1963, I believe that most Europeans felt that anything was possible in American political life. Right, and their governments had never known corruption, assassination, dictatorships, and anarchy. What effete snobbery! Nott o mention how quickly and conveniently they forgot who sacrificed the most to free their pathetic continent in World Wars One, and Two; and who helped them get back on the road to economic recovery. Maybe, in reality, the goose step appealed to them more than democracy. Ah, but I wax too political once again. Not to mention, Europeans in general are too easy a target for any like-minded cynic such as myself.

Chapter 14

How Sweet It Is

It was seven pm., and I was standing outside the hospital at a pre-designated post, awaiting the arrival of Suzanne, my new best (and only) friend in Denmark. She was to drive us into town for dinner and then we would play it by ear. Shortly after I left the building, my two classmates, who also had plans to go into town, came outside. I knew of their plans because I had overheard them talking on the ward about that evenings activities. I'm sure that they wanted to share their collegial spirit and invite me along, but they just sort of forgot I was there. These things happen I guess. After ten minutes or so, Mike W. finally asked me what I was up to. I was salivating at the prospect of relating my good fortune, but I still didn't know what this girl looked like, I downplayed the whole thing.

"Just getting a lift into town from a girlfriend of a friend. She's a little late, but the lives quite a ways from here."

"Hey Mel," Mike asked, "do you actually know a girl in this country?"

"Never met her, but Harvey G. said she was a neat person to hang out with' I replied.

"Neat person? That's all you know about her? Haven't you even talked to her on the phone?" Mike inquired.

"Well I have had one brief telephone conversation with her, but that's about it Mike. Say, what are you gents up to tonight?" I was trying hard here to be subtle and understated.

"Oh, we're just heading into town to sample some Copenhagen night life. I don't suppose your friend could give us a ride, eh?" said Mike.

"That's up to her I guess, but I don't see why not?" God I am a nice person.

Just as this brilliant verbal exchange concluded, I caught a glimpse of a female figure about two blocks away at the local kiosk. Then she turned around and began walking towards me. With every step she took, she got better and better looking. My first thought was, no way could I be this fucking lucky; probably just a coincidence. But at a half a block away, I knew that this, indeed, was Suzanne, and she was drop-dead gorgeous! I think my mouth fell open, and I was a little trembly, but I rallied quickly, thank God, and regained some composure. But, standing before me was the single most beautiful female I had ever seen in my entire miserable life. Linda who????? She was classically Scandinavian in appearance, but not in a stereotypical cold way. She was tall, with long, wavy blonde hair (as predicted) that fell over her right eye, deep blue eye, a perfect complexion (naturally), and a body men have probably fought duels over. Even with a long coat on, her physical attributes could not be concealed. And, to top it all off, she was terrific—friendly as could b, with a smile that could melt the hardest heart. It was at that that I knew my days of cynicism and mistrust of all women were over for good. And I also knew now, that there absolutely, positively, unequivocally, had to be a God!!!!

Unbelievable!! I was on a date with Miss Denmark! And, to make the moment even more delicious, my two asshole colleagues were witness to my good fortune. Suzanne and I got into her vehicle, a tidy little Volvo sedan. Oh yes, we did give M&M a lift into town, depositing them on some street corner downtown. Their jealousy was palpable, and, as we drove off, I couldn't control my nasty little laugh. I'm sure Suzanne thought I must have been as crazy as a loon, however, after detailing my relationship with these two jerks, she began to laugh as well, appreciating the wonderful irony of it all. We quickly became friends and confidants, talking non-stop seemingly for hours, even though it was a short drive to the disco/bar. The place was packed, but we managed to find a table away from the dance floor, quiet enough to continue our introductory conversation. She told me that her father was an engineer, and she had two siblings, an older brother, and a sister two years her junior. I asked her if her sister was a as good looking as she, and I'm pretty sure that I made her blush. Modest to a fault was this gal. Continuing on, I learned that she was a first year med student with straight A average. Wouldn't you know it; she was not only gorgeous, but was a perfect student as well. She was a little guarded at first, but she quickly warmed, and kept up her end of the conversation. I'm not sure if she was somewhat of an introvert, or, just being cautions with a stranger. Her English was decent, but at times, difficult to decipher because of imperfect grammar. Well, I guess something had to be imperfect. I caught myself staring at her several times, but I just couldn't help myself. If she notices, she was too polite to call me on it.

As it turns out, this girl loved to travel, and had seen most of Europe. She described in detail some of the places I told her I was planning to visit. Her memory for detail was remarkable. She mad eme feel like I had already been there, but unfortunately, I wouldn't be travelling with her. Suddenly I felt depressed about my future itinerary because I would be with Mike, and not her wonderful self. Now, Mike's a great guy, but hey, let's be realistic here. I 'm acutely in love, no, make that lust. I'm in lust with Suzanne, and I desperately wanted her to be my travel "buddy," not a guy.

Our conversation continued for several hours, and in spite of her broken English, we managed to get to know and understand each other fairly well for a first meeting (date). She, I'm sure, perceived my miserable attempts to come off as a strong, self-assured, worldly man; but if she did, she didn't let on. Conversely, I felt that her shy and self-deprecating exterior concealed a much more confident person who really understood her place in the universe. One thing I'm absolutely sure of: she was compeletly unaffected by her obvious beauty.

The evening concluded with her driving me back to my dungeon at the hospital. We made plans to see each other in a few days, nothing formal. And then, surprisingly, she kissed me goodnight, I, of course, didn't have the guts to make the first move. Thank God she felt no such inhibition. I kissed her back, but afterwards, was speechless. She finally said cheerio, and drove off in to the night, leaving me floating on cloud nine, ten and eleven.

Chapter 15

The remainder of my stay in Copenhagen couldn't have gone better mainly because I saw Suzanne almost every week night and weekend. Spending so much time together, we became close and intimate friends. We shared our life stories, the highs, lows, and in-betweens. We talked about people we had loved and thought loved us back, which was the case more often than not. We talked about everything except the future; there was only the glorious present—why spoil it? Most important to me, was our agreement to rendezvous in Paris the next month. I was already anticipating the singularly most romantic adventure of my young, naïve, life, in, arguably, the world's most romantic city. This trip was getting better with every passing day, and was about to become almost too wonderful indeed.

I can't say that I was sorry to soon be parting company with Bispebjerg Hospital, and its compliment of snotty, rude and inconsiderate staff, including the med students. From a medical education standpoint, it was a total failure. I was grateful when I finished serving my "time" and finally received my parole. It was off to Paris in a few short days, and then on to the rest of Europe—or at least as much of it as we could see in the allotted time. It was depressing to think of this summer ever coming to an end, so I tried to keep myself as much in the moment as possible, savoring every little detail of my great European adventure. Somehow I knew that I probably would never return to these places, nor would I recapture the initial thrill of just being there in that time, with people like Suzanne and Mike, tow of the most exceptional individuals I could ever hope to encounter in my lifetime. Yes, there would be great adventures in the future, and love affairs to be sure; but nothing can capture the feeling of that first moment when you realize that you're the luckiest person on earth, and there's nowhere else, and no one else you'd rather be.

Chapter 16

To Paris and Beyond

Before I talk about my further travels, I must say something about Copenhagen. I'm afraid that I've painted a much too negative picture of the city because of my miserable experience at the hospital, and the description I rendered of those doctors and students way do I mean for that to apply to the rest of this wondrously beautiful, charming town, where coziness is a cherished feeling. Ko/benhaven (Danish for Copenhagen) is an elegant, yet unpretentious capital city. When I wasn't with Suzanne, I would ride the bicycle trails into town, as good a way to experience your surroundings as any. Exploring the city on foot is also a great pleasure. Narrow walking street, with little-bitty shops are abundant, as are kiosks in public squares which wear odd little copper hats. The architecture is a blending of the old, classical style with the more modern additions adding a flavorful oxymoron. Denmark functions as a social democracy, with a constitutional monarchy. Education and medical care are free, or inexpensive. The average working person has five vacation weeks a year. Even a person on unemployment benefits is entitled to a regular vacation. But who pays for all of this? As in many left leaning societies in Europe, it is, of course the taxpayer who is saddled with enormous personal income taxes. The Danish tax starts as forty percent! Now there's a flat tax rate to consider, right Mr. Forbes? Given the generally agreeable nature of most folks in this country, few Danes complain, at least not publically about their taxes. Perhaps the Danish sense of humility, or "janteloven," essentially the idea that you shouldn't think too much of yourself, has much to do with acceptance of the status quo. Yes Virginia, Utopia has a steep price, but the people seem genuinely content. And, what is more, there is almost a total absence of violent crime. The streets, even at night, are safe, and parents don't fear for their child's life if the send him/her to the local convenience store. During my travels throughout the city, I don't think I heard a voice raised in anger, and did not observe there to be any "street people." If drugs were being consumed or injected, it certainly wasn't in public places.

Yes, there was and is so much to admire about Denmark and its capital city, but, for me, it's just a little too sterile. People are, indeed, very pleasant and agreeable, but where's the emotion? Where's the passion? On the emotional scale, I'd experienced nothing but a range of A to B. That is the only thing that troubled me concerning my Danish friend, although she could certainly be affectionate. In retrospect, I overlooked her few shortcomings, as I perceived them at any rate, not only because of her physical beauty, of course, but also because she was a very kind and gentle person. She was, in fact, typical of the Danish personality previously described, and that was not a bad thing at all.

Chapter 17

I bade farewell to Denmark, and hooked up with my new travelling companion and mate, one Michael Adams. We soon found ourselves on the train to Paris, which so packed in with students from everywhere, I managed to fall asleep literally standing up, or should I say, propped up to be more accurate, by this throng of humanity. That was first, and hopefully, a last. It was a lengthy journey that took us through parts of Belgium and Germany before hitting France. As we entered East Germany, the train came to a halt, and several armed soldiers came aboard. Remember, this is 1968, and there were hard feeling by the communist side of Germany towards all things western, especially Americans. Everyone on the train was thoroughly checked for I.D.—passports in particular. The image of millions of Jews being loaded onto trains and taken to their death by the Germans suddenly popped into my paranoid little mind. Perhaps not so paranoid if you could have seen these thugs – they were damned scary and a lot of us felt threatened. It seemed like an eternity for them to check everybody's paper, and finally let us carry on down the road. They finally disembarked the train, and slinked back to their dismal little lives in their dismal country. Good riddance!

We arrived in Paris after a long, very hot, and tiring train ride. Mike and I immediately headed for the Citroen car factory several miles from centre ville, where we were to pick up our brand new vehicle for our jaunt through Europe, the infamous Deux Chaveaux. It was small, noisy, and devoid of much power, but the damned thing never quit on us. This was s new car. Let me explain: essentially we were buying the car for three months, and delivering back to the factory on a set date, whereby the vehicle was bought back from us by the factory less the cost of three months rental fee (ie depreciation) if it warranted damage. Nice arrangement eh?

For me, the only problem was that it was a manual shift, which I was not too familiar with. I did practice on such a car in Toronto before the trip, but alas, my coordination lacking. Accordingly, Mike did most of the driving, while I proudly assumed the role of navigator. I say that proudly in retrospect, because, not once did I get us lost in all our travels. My wife, Debbie, has berated me many times in the past and present for my poor sense of direction, and you know she is partly correct. I say partly because most of the time, my concentration is only a fraction of what is was back in 1968. I had to be super sharp and maintain focus on all our maps, with some help from my trusty compass.

Arriving back in Paris, Mike and I started our search for a place to stay. We confined ourselves to exploring the artsy fartsy Left Back, where all the most pretentious pseudo-intellectuals and wannabe Renoirs and Monet's, hung out. It was, I most confess, very quaint and charming in spite of my usual level of cynicism (which still plagues me to this day). Eventually, we came upon a six story walkup just off Blvd. St. Michael, one of the main thoroughfares through this part of town. Luckily, there was a vacancy, yes you guessed right it was on the sixth floor. What a joke I was. Elevator? This wasn't Manhattan or even Toronto. A very short old woman, with a severe kyphotic hunchback ran the place. After a brief negotiation over price, which of course we acceded to without complaint, she showed us to our suite. I don't know how the hell she made it up those steep six flights of stairs, but she did -- and none the worse for wear I might add. On the other hand, we were breathless and leg weary. Aerobics wasn't very big with me in 1968. I reckon she had been climbing those steps for more years than I had been alive.

Actually, it turned out tot be a great apartment with a decent view of the main intersection of St. Michael and St. Germaine. But what first caught my attention was a mysterious porcelain object almost in the center of the room. Mike and I took turns guessing at the purpose of this mini-toilette, when it finally dawned on us: how brilliant were the French for knowing how weary travelers such as ourselves, would appreciate massaging and soaking our tired, aching feet after walking the streets of Paris all day. A foot bath!? Ha!! What a joke we were, how young, innocent, and naïve – and stupid. This was our first encounter with a bidet for Christ sake. We learned this through our little landlady, who, using a few obscene gestures to get the message across, explained this to us in her native tongue. In my defense, I have to say that I had never seen a bidet before, and nor had Mike. We still thought, however, that soaking our feet in it was still a damn good idea, and that's exactly what we did. Screw convention!

Chapter 18

The best thing to do on the Left Bank of Paris was nothing. Just grab a seat at a local sidewalk cafe, nurse a glass of wine with some cheese, and kick back to watch the parade of interesting people. This non-activity could amuse me for hours. The women especially, were incredible to watch--- their manner, dress and language to me were the epitome of sophistication and chic. And they were beautiful, even exotic00 I had never seen women that even remotely looked like this, at least not all in one town. God I wished I had the nerve to approach just one of these incredible creature—just once. I was just too damned intimidated, that's all there was to it. Even hopeless attempts at rationalizing my important place in the universe as budding physician and world citizen, could not move my butt from the chair. I would have to be content with vivid memories of missed opportunity. Masturbating when I got back to my apartment went a long way to assuage my fractured ego, not to mention, taming my hormonal urges into temporary submission.

Paris turned out to be more than just beautiful and culturally stimulating: it almost succeeded into turning me into a neurotic cripple. Let me explain. I made it a daily ritual to go down to the American Express office to check on any mail or messages. Well, one fine day I was shocked to find two letters and one message from three different Mademoiselles!! Firs, there was the message from Suzanne that she would meet me in Paris in three days, and, for good measure; it was signed "with love." Okay, this is very good I thought, and I'm walking on air again, right? Wrong! The other two letters were from Linda and JBH respectively, essentially saying that they too would arrive in the city of light in three days. What dastardly luck: I rarely had one gal pursuing me, and now I had three---and all in the same city at the same time! Here I was, in the most romantic city on earth, presented with the most unromantic of dilemmas. And, of course, all three ladies would be staying somewhere on the Left Bank. Fucking unbelievable!

My razor-sharp mind had to be up to the task of devising a schedule that worked in this precarious situation. I was playing a reality game like "Survivor," but for real life stakes in the real world. So here was the plan: I would meet Suzanne at the railroad station and get her back to her walkup rental; leaving her, I would hustle over to Café de L'Auberge fro an intimate lunch with Linda. I then grab a little siesta at around four p.m., get up just in time to have dinner with JBH, my least favorite of the three, but oh what a body. Like most men, I'll put up with a lot of shit for one more chance at bedding down with her. The only kink in my plan was the fact that I really wanted to be with just one person—Suzanne, especially on her first evening in Paris. I had to admit to myself that I was falling hard for her, and I didn't want her to think that our time together in Copenhagen was in any way frivolous.

I did manage to have my little siesta in the early afternoon, I had just got up when Miek returned from a walkabout tour of our neighborhood. I explained my three-women-dilemma to him, which prompted a somewhat angry response.

"Do you seriously believe that I am sympathetic about this you jerk? Look, you've got three girls chasing your stupid ass all over Paris, while I am by myself tonight. How about a little perspective here Melvyn? I'll tell you what I CAN do for you--- let me take one of these ladies off your hands. So, who's going to be the lucky one?"

"Thanks for your kind offer friend, but I'll manage. Besides, I think I have the logistics of this thing figured out." I proceeded to explain my plan to Mike, after which he asked how I was going to end up with Suzanne by evening's end. I had a simple answer for that---I would simply feign illness after supper, and politely excuse myself. JBH wasn't a deep thinker, so I believed she would accept me at my word. Mike was skeptical.

"So you really think she'll buy that bullshit, eh boyo?"

"Of course I do Michael. After all, JBH is not all that bright. Hey, she still thinks I have feelings for her aside from physical. How smart does that make her?"

"Okay Mel, good luck. But I think you're in shit up to your eyeballs. Godspeed friend. Oh, and if you pull this off, you're a better man than I. Hell, you'd be a better man than I've ever known!"

In retrospect, Mike was quite right about this situation: why was I stressing about multiple females wanting to be with me in this magnificent, romantic place? And the answer to this rhetorical question is simple: because I'm anal and this is what anal people do—worry themselves to death over everything, even if it's something petty. This is who I am and this is what I've done all my life, perseverate to the point of exhaustion. After a while, I become rational and calm down, realizing that things are not necessarily desperate and unmanageable. In recent times, with my wife's help, I've improved immeasurably, and I am much more laid back. Funny, after all this discussion about me being pursued by women, in the end it was I who did the pursuing; and luckily, I caught the best gal of the bunch in Debbie, the one true love of my life. All my previous relationships may have had the illusion of love, but, being a natural-born romantic, I was kidding myself. I finally learned what the word "love" meant. Thank God it happened before my time was up.

Chapter 19

The next morning, as planned, I went to the railroad station to greet Suzanne. When I saw her get off the train, I became, once again, the happy, content person I'd always hoped I could be. I gave her a hug and we kissed in that romantic movie way. It was like some dream that had become my new reality. We left the station, and hailed a cab to her B&B, a lovely little two-story on the extreme west side of Paris, The lady who ran the place was kind enough to prepare breakfast (really brunch) for the two of us. Madame was a handsome, middle-aged woman who spoke quite good English, and was considerate enough to use it, unlike the boorish staff at the hospital I had just left. I suddenly realized it was time to go and meet Linda for lunch at the aforementioned café, near her hotel. I said my good-byes, told Suzanne I would see her that evening, and made a dash for the subway back to into central Paris.

Linda was waiting for me at the restaurant, and didn't appear to be upset about my late arrival. I kissed her politely on the cheek, prompting her to pull back and say:" What was that—don't I mean more to you than a kiss on the cheek?" I can get that from my dog! What's the matter wit6h you, don't you care anymore?"

Boy was she right on the money. I had just been with someone I did care deeply about, and I just couldn't fake more emotion than I felt at the moment. I mumbled something like, "of course I care Linda, but I'm just so damned tired right now its hard for me to do much more than have a good meal and some conversation. Okay?" I wanted to be completely up-front, but how could I be that cruel. I mean, here we were, a million miles from home, and I'm going to level her with honesty? Not now---it can wait tell we get home.

Fortunately, she sort of forgot about the weight of the moment, and we actually had a pleasant meal together, exchanging small talk and gossip about certain people in Toronto. I felt comfortable with her for the first time in quite a while, and she probably sensed that. Without any romantic feelings, I could be a friend—no other agenda. Being at ease like that, I saw what a terrific person Linda could be, genuine and funny and not altogether bad looking (but not in Miss Denmark's League.) When we were ready to leave, I kissed her again, but this time on the lips. No thinking, just going with instinct and spontaneity. I had to hurry "home," catch a little siesta, and then get ready for my dinner date with JBH.

So, I picked Pauline up that evening, we strolled down the street her b&b was on, arriving at a nearby restaurant which had been recommended to me, ironically, by Suzanne. She had been to Paris many times in her brief lifetime, and knew it like the back of her hand. It was on her ten best lists of places to eat in Paris, not fancy, but exquisite food and great service, something I was finding hard to come by. I wasn't trying to impress my date; I was just very hungry for a good meal. Rather pricey obviously, fracturing my meager budget so carefully plotted out by Mike and I. "Europe on Five Dollars a Day"--- sure, that's possible!!!!

The dinner conversation centered mainly on her (surprise), her moods, feelings, wants and needs, desires, goals, and, oh yes, how she felt about me.

"I think I'm falling in love with you" she said, "but I'm not getting any signals from you at all. Why is that Mel? Don't you care even a little about me?"

"I do care for you Pauline, but I've only known you for a short time. I don't jump in and out of love that fast." Quick thinking Mel, a splendid reply. "Let's just eat and try to be lighthearted just for tonight, okay?"

"I know you're ducking the issue, but you always say just enough to keep my interest and hopes pretty high. You're half-hearted, casual manner is almost evil I think. So, if this is so tough for you, let me make it easier: go screw yourself, okay? I'm out of here for good! I must be crazy to deceive myself into thinking you could love me, or anyone else for that matter."

At that moment, she began to cry big old tears, and I don't know about other guys, but that just drives me insane. I'm not up for this much drama, but I've go to suck it up and be a little kind even if I didn't give a shit about her. Tears are a woman's greatest emotional weapon, damn it!

"Look, will you just calm down for a second? Let's just finish our dinner and talk about anything you want---except where our relationship is headed, ok? I still want to be with you some of the time, just not all the time—not now. Hell, I'm just trying to survive medical school and come out on the other side relatively sane."

" Nice try fella, but not good enough. I think I'll call my girlfriend and have dinner with her. I don't want to see you anymore; not here or anywhere else. Besides, you're acting like a guy who has someone else on his mind. Good-bye Mel!"

And just like that, JBH was out of my life; hopefully for good. I sat there and pondered the whole situation that had just unfolded and thought what a break. After five or ten second of deep though, I dashed off to see if I could hook up with Suzanne. She was getting ready to go out by herself unless she heard from me. I was, happy as heel to see her---just a little out of breath from running all the way. I hugged her for a long time---I just couldn't let her go, not ever.

Chapter 20

Tonight my wife Debbie asked how I felt about being almost sixty, and not having a nice little nestegg to fall back on. After some thought, my initial response was, I thought, profound and, at the same time, diplomatic.

"You know honey, we all arrive here with nothing, and we leave with nothing. So, what's the big deal about having a king's ransom salted away? I'm still going to live my life the way I want – without certain material excesses perhaps, but I'll be just as happy so long as I remain enthusiastic about my career and true to the people that I feel give a damn about me. And as long as I can hold a guitar and play, badly perhaps, or hold a golf club in my hands with continued optimism and pleasure, or read a good book, or perhaps, even write a good book, what else is there? Death will greet us all, regardless of our means. No one gets out of this world alive, although I bet some rich fold think otherwise. Yep, they are going to take it with them, oil royalty checks and all."

"Mel, you take everything I say so seriously. I wasn't trying to hurt your feelings, or make you feel in any way inadequate. I love you, rich or poor or in between. Just forget what I said and let's go to bed—its getting pretty late."

I stayed up for a while trying to write, but her question kept nagging at me. Did she think I was just an old burnout—a middle-aged failure? See, here's the problem with marrying a much younger, beautiful woman: you're constantly scanning the landscape with your screwed up radar, ready to pounce on comments or questions that really are totally innocent. Man, I've been paranoid lately, and intensely more aware of our generational gap. Sometimes I feel like we're from different planets, not just different eras. So, from her perspective at age forty-one, she probably does see me, at age fifty nine, as a failure in many ways. In particular, I haven't accumulated the funds to deal with the present, and preserve the future. I plead guilty! After two divorces, and inevitable two bankruptcies that followed, and too numerous to mention back stabbings and anal probing (without lubricant) by too many assholes to mention, wealth accumulation has become nearly impossible. You don't earn millions and lose it without some serious help, damn it!

And what the hell does she mean when she adds stuff like, "you're a lot of work Mel." I could have sworn that I was doing all the work to keep her happy and maintain a certain lifestyle for both of us. Forty-one years old, and not earning one thin peso to help me build the retirement "nest egg." Yes, she does work part-time in a fancy dress salon, but all that income goes towards adding to her already extensive wardrobe. That's right, she works for discounted clothing! I'm torn between biting her head off and telling her to go out and make her financial mark in the world: or keeping her barefoot (and not pregnant) in the casa. I'm not too keen on the first option, after all, a woman of her physical assets and charm wouldn't find it too hard to attract a much younger, affluent stud. Am I fucked up or what?

I've never before questioned my intelligence, physical presentation, or money-making ability, so why now? I guess I've just entered that precarious age in life ---"the mid-life zone" --- and answers don't come to me with the speed and clarity that they once did. So, suddenly, I question everything about myself. Am I maker her the scapegoat for all my insecurities? Probably, but who the hell wants' to be that honest and five up any edge you might have in the male-female tug of war. The eternal conundrum between man and woman continues – at least for me.

Chapter 21

Great luck – Suzanne hadn't left the youth hostel yet. She was obviously surprised to see me there since we didn't have concrete plans to see each other that evening. But, unlike most people (including myself) she didn't question the situation, but rather, just accepted it as good fortune. To make a long story longer, we had unquestionably the most wonderful evening of both our young lives. We ate, we drank, we made love all night, and profess our love for one another. Of course, love at this age and in these unusual circumstances, is perceived as the equivalent to infatuation and sex, especially sin e you hardly know the other person. It's easy now to see what this was, with the perspective that the passing of time and the aquistion of a little maturity gives you. That having been said, it was an still is one of my dearest memories of that time in my life. And with respect to my so-called girlfriend Linda, seeing her had been a non-event for me. Maybe I would Feel differently at summer's end, but I wasn't really concerned about our relationship anymore. We did, however, promise to look each other up back in London in September before our flight home.

   Come morning, Suzanne and I, had to say good-bye, at least for a little while. We vowed to rendezvous in Florence in a month or so. She was headed to Germany, and I for Normandy and then on to wine country. After one last kiss and embrace, I pulled myself away and left for "home."

Chapter 22

November 5, 2005

Today I got a call from my best friend, Sam Pace. He informed me that he was in the emergency room at Northwest Hospital in Amarillo. He had been having severe chest pain that , in fact, had been occurring intermittently for a couple of days. Sam said that his ekg didn't look too good, and he was being transferred to another hospital for an angiogram (a procedure to visualize the arteries that supply the heart) and more lab tests. Needless to say I was deeply saddened to hear this news, but not terribly surprised. Sam has had a long history of cardiac disease, culminating in a bypass procedure some ten years ago. Since that time, he had had several close calls with angina chest pain, stent insertion, and carotid artery surgery to remove debris from the artery walls, thus restoring normal circulation to the brain. Both operations were a success, although I think Sam showed symptoms of mild brain dysfunction after that carotid surgery. Of course, in keeping with our mutually sick senses of humor, I told him that I thought the changes I noticed were for the better, since he was much more fucked up before the surgery , and I thought the things he was forgetting were events and people we wanted to forget anyway. Come to think of it, if selective memory could be developed in pill form, the inventor would make a fortune. His description of his symptoms reminded me of the time I first met Sam. Our mutual friend, Joe R., had arranged a golf game for the three of us at my home golf club, Tascosa Country Club. On the first tee, Sam prepared to hit his first drive. He placed his golf ball and tee in the ground, and when he straightened up, h was profoundly short of breath. I asked him if he was having chest pain or any other symptoms and he replied that it was just his "asthma." Judging from Sam's overall appearance and demeanor, I strongly advised him to see me in my office first thing Monday morning. He said he'd probably do just that especially since he hadn't had a check up in years. I have to add that Sam was severely overweight, and, during the course of the round, he remained mildly short of breath, with occasional episodes of sweating in spite of the cool, crisp fall day. I liked Sam, almost immediately. How could anyone dislike someone so affable, kindhearted and generous of spirit; someone without a mean bone in his body? By day's end, I had indeed made a great friend, and I hoped to hell that I'd see him on Monday in my office.

Well, Monday morning came, and Sam did in fact show up. He must have been very suspicious that it was much more than 'asthma'. And, as I suspected, it was serious. Sam was in congestive heart failure, and his electrocardiogram showed that he had already suffered a heart attack. He wasn't all that surprised when I told him my findings. Sam told me that all the males in his family had had heart problems, and there were many fatalities among them, including a younger brother and his father. I immediately called a cardiologist, another good friend of mine named Ron Fortner, and we agreed that Sam needed hospitalization and angiography asap. I sent Sam to the emergency room at St. Anthony Hospital where I officed. His angiogram revealed five coronary blood vessels that were almost completely occluded. Ron got a cardiac surgeon involved right away, and, that same evening, Sam had a quintuple bypass procedure. Sam made a good recovery, and complied with his rehabilitation program, losing weight and exercising aerobically for the first time in his life. Until today, he has done pretty well for a guy who should have died that day long ago on the golf course.

Sam's adventures in bad health, and subsequent trials and tribulations, causes me to ponder the course of my life----what is truly important and meaningful, and what is just nonsense. When I think back on my experiences that summer of '68, and how utterly carefree and happy I was, I am somewhat saddened when I contrast that time with many aspects of my life and career over the past thirty-five years that have not turned out as I would have hoped. And I think of the baggage that weighs me down even today-------all the worries and stresses that I allow into my deepest self, which cripple and depress me. Maybe I should go back to Paris, to that time and place where it seemed too perfect; breathe that air, see those sights, remember those people that touched my life. Maybe then I can recapture the feelings of my youth, especially the passion I had to live and, especially, to love. What is the ingredient that is missing from my life that will free me to feel that way again?

I have a lot of questions and few answers. But, I do know how Sam would respond to these mysteries of life. He would tell me to not forget beautiful things from the past, but also to not dwell on them-----live your life today and appreciate every precious second you have, because it is precious and it's over all too soon. If you don't enjoy your work, then do something else besides whine. If you don't love someone, then find the one you can love until you aren't here to love. Don't spurn those who love you simply because they may not share your adolescent remembrance of youthful passion, which, if you really thought about it, brought with it a hell of a lot of pain. And most of all, learn to love yourself, and forgive yourself for all the things that you think you should have accomplished. Let go for God's sake, and just live your life as I have------playing the cards I was dealt.

Sam has played those cards without regrets or complaints. And he is a happy man who appreciates all aspects of his life, even some of the unpleasantness of it. He loves his wife and family with passion! He loves his job, hard as it may be, and performs with passion! In short, he is love with life, and for that reason, he is a very lucky man. Were he to die today, he would not feel that he missed out on anything in this world because he took nothing or granted. I have criticized him in the past for working too hard, tolerating too much nonsense from his children, taking on the added burden of two grandchildren born out of wedlock to one of his daughters, and for not finding a way to a more leisurely lifestyle wherein he could enjoy those things that I thought gave him the greatest pleasure-----golf for example. But I was completely and utterly wrong-------he already had everything he needed to be happy.

Sam and I have seen each other through some of our most difficult times: job changes, financial disasters, including bankruptcy for both of us, and even marital mysteries no man can solve. We have joked together, philosophized, analyzed and dissected all the worlds' problems together, and, generally, had a great time with our verbal nonsense. But , these conversations kept us both going during the bad times, and I have always looked forward to our next chat. I believe without reservation, that we have saved each others' lives many times over, and I am eternally grateful to have such a friend-----a gift from above. I love Sam Pace, and, I very much envy his passion for life in the face of enormous adversity. He has no real heart problem-----his heart is too resilient to succumb to human disease. God, let me find the peace that lies within the kind and generous hear of my beloved friend.

Chapter 23

Thinking back on those wonderful, guiltless, mindless days of college, and my reminiscences of European adventures past, it seems ludicrous that I would become so hung up on the topic of sex. After all, this wasn't even remotely a problem worthy of contemplation----not when you're young and horny, hormones raging and erections that an overdose of Viagra could not achieve. And yet, here I sit, wondering why and when did it all change. Ironically, Viagra has become an important part of my life as much as I hate to admit it. Oh, sometimes I can 'perform' quite nicely if I'm completely at ease, and have no expectations that sex will occur at a particular time and place. But as one gets older, physical and mental stresses occur to every man that usually have a profound affect on his once intact virility. Thirty-seven years ago, I'm interacting physically with all sorts of young women at home and abroad, and now look at me; I'm reduced to a middle-aged cliché. I thought I was bulletproof, and sexual dysfunction only occurred to other men. I have heard my male patients talk at length about these issues, and I discovered two things: first and foremost, regardless of age, depression and anxiety are the commonest causes of e.d. (erectile dysfunction.) If a man was having serious marital problems, or going through some financial crisis, presto gizmo------all of a sudden, he cant sustain an erection, and in some more severe cases, cant even get the beginnings of one. Yes, even young and studdly males can suffer this humiliation. Secondly, and much less likely, physical problems and side affects of certain medications, could throw a guy off his game. At least there is a concrete problem medically that you can point the blame at, and perhaps, do something about. The psychological issues are far more difficult to deal with, and that is why God invented Viagra, Levitra, Cialis, et al.

It's really not too hard to imagine how things can deteriorate in a man over time. Let me use myself as a prime example, someone who was supremely confident in his sexual prowess for most of his adult life, that is, until about seven years ago. That was when I made the oh- so-brilliant decision to sell my practice in Amarillo. I wont elaborate on that horrific time right now; suffice to say, what ensued was pure misery and chaos. I can summarize the beginning of my sexual problems in one word: Oklahoma! Not the musical, the state. All the gruesome details of my experiences in this wretched place will be chronicled later on in the book; suffice it to say for now that what happened there annihilated my sanity; my dick's demise followed shortly thereafter. I was more surprised that anyone could imagine when I began to fail the as a spontaneous and energetic lover. My wife was pretty damned shocked too, and, of course, she immediately assumed that I must be having an affair. After all, isn't that a woman's best defense------a food offense? I was painfully honest with her and myself about the situation, but that just wasn't enough to cure it. In the end, the only solution was to see my friendly urologist for advice and a prescription for 'Big Blue.' My doctor reassured me that it wasn't my age, or any medication I was taking for high blood pressure and cholesterol. It was simply a case of too much stress to cope with at one time, and e.d. was just the natural consequence of said stress. I was relieved in a way to know that I was okay physically, but if it was all in my head, what was the answer to that besides the use of Viagra ad infinitum?

In the end, I had to leave Oklahoma City. Oklahoma----not OK. I was certain that I would also leave behind my physical issues, but I was wrong again. Oh, it was better certainly, but sex would never be the same again for me. To this day, I have to use 'Big Blue' on occasion, to fulfill my sexual urges, and please my wife. On a positive note, I have been able to perform more often without it lately, so I am cautiously optimistic. As much as I understand how irrational it is to feel stigmatized by having to use a 'supplement', I do have feelings of guilt and failure about it. Ah, but a ray of hope shone though just the other night, and a brilliant idea was born. My gal was very restless for some reason after going to bed, up and down repeatedly. I suggested that we have sex just to relax her, and her reply was classic: "I'm not in the mood for that."

"What's that got to do with anything?" I smartly replied. "Since when did being in the mood ever stop people from fucking?" Look, I have an idea that should appeal to your more rational side. I will take a month-long sabbatical from sex, including no masturbation. Just think about it, no pressure for either one of us to do it------especially for me. I think that at the end of this time, having felt no guilt or shame about inconsistent performance, I might just be permanently cured of this devilish plague I caught back in Oklahoma. Don't you see the beauty of this--- I man, its just what this doctor ordered." There was a dead silence for at least five minutes. And then she spoke:

"Have you completely lost your mind? I swear, you are the most frustratingly complicated man I've ever known-----and you're wearing me out! Look, as far as sex goes, what are you so uptight about? After all, its just me, your wife of ten years. God knows how I survived this long with a headcase like you. Stop dwelling on sex-----are you just obsessed about this twenty-four/seven, or does it just seem that way? Maybe if you give it a rest, your so-called problems will go away, and life can to normal. Until then however, don't bother me with your mind games; all it does is tire me out. Mel, you just exhaust me."

I knew she was right about me. She's has me pegged from day one, although she initially didn't grasp the extent of my mental health issues. Obviously, I abandoned the thirty day plan, and the second I did, I felt relieved to just forget and let go. I was so relieved in fact, that I could feel a hormonal rush which lasted all day and well into the evening. That night, I made love to my incredible, gorgeous wife and it was almost too perfect.

Chapter 24

When I finally arrived back at the walkup. Mike was up and about, getting ready fro the next leg of our journey. We were driving out to Normandy to check out the World War II beachheads and memorials – exciting stuff. If was a rustic but beautiful drive through the Brittany countryside. We pressed on towards the battlefields of Normandy – Omaha Beach specifically. The country folk in this part of France were completely different than the not so subtle snobbiest of Parisiennes – friendly, warm and hospitable. We knew just enough French to get by, and come off as friends instead of tourists. I must add however that it was important for us to distinguish ourselves as Canadians, not Americans. Yanks just weren't the French cup of tea, and genuinely disliked. Looking out over the beaches of Normandy, I couldn't help but wonder at the irony of the French attitude towards Americans, given the inestimable sacrifices made by those young men on the beachheads, for these very people. Lucky for them they showed up when they did, or they would be marching, goosestep fashion, to German military music. There is an old joke that asks in what position do French babies first present after birth? Why, with their hands over their heads of course. But, we had to keep in mind the European attitude, generally hostile, towards the increasing American involvement in Vietnam, especially ugly in France. Funny , I thought the French were there first, and got their butts kicked in by the North Vietnamese and Viet Cong. The French military is well practiced at the art of surrender, tails between legs, beating a hasty retreat to Frogland. What hypocrites!! And the sacrifices made by all the Allied forces them were staggering. I was humbled as I surveyed the battlefield remnants, my mind flashing back to those old black and white documentaries of D-Day. Could I have been one of those who bravely stormed those beaches? I doubt it, unless it was to save my own skin. But who really knows what heroes will emerge when everything is on the line? It was a day of quiet reflection and paying one's respect to those who did rise to the occasion – and bravely gave their lives for their fellow man. Years later, I would think back to this day in Normandy when I saw the movie "Saving Private Ryan," and I felt so lucky to have visited this place. And I felt incredibly proud to be an American citizen, and the one good thing that came out of my stay in Oklahoma in 1998.

Chapter 25

After staying overnight in a local Bed and Breakfast, we got our few belongings together and headed back to Paris. It was like seeing home when we returned to our quaint little walkup, and the old Madame was there to greet us with a big cup of hot chocolate. Every morning, this frail little gal climbed six flights of stairs with two, two liter mugs of hot chocolate and a loaf of French bread. Now this was a heavy load for an average sized person to carry, let alone Madame. I don't know where she got the strength to do this every day, but I'm glad she could—breakfast was delicious, simple though it may have been.

Next morning, Mike was keen to tour the Louvre, so, after our breakfast feast, we headed for the Right Bank, walking along the Champs Elysees, and though the Bios de Bologne. Seeing the Arc de Triomphe reminded me of our embarrassingly frantic drive into Paris. There are about twelve lanes of traffic circling the Arc, with streets running off this hub like spokes of a wheel. It was a great achievement indeed if you could negotiate your way from the inside lanes, to the extreme outside lane to exit at your desired street. If you missed it, you were screwed for at least another twenty or thirty minutes, since you somehow ended up back in the middle of the wheel. We almost ran out of gas before we finally found our way out of this maze onto our desired street exit.

This time, for obvious reasons we took the subway. After waling through and pas the Bios de Bologne, I became rather excited to see a huge sign reading "The Louvre" a couple of blocks down. What an enormous structure – three blocks long at least. Suddenly, I heard Mike burst into uncontrollable laughter.

"That's the Louvre department store you dumb shit, not the museum."

"Oh God, I'm so fucking sophisticated, eh Mike?"

I've never quite lived down that little moment of embarrassment, although, in looking back, I am far more forgiving of myself for my youthful innocence and stupidity. At any rate, the real Louvre was more than enormous in size – it was gargantuan. It overwhelmed my senses, so much to see in so little time. I quickly decided, after the anticlimactic viewing of the Mona Lisa that, in spite of its grandness and the scope of its collection of timeless treasures, in the final analysis it still was just a museum. I have to be honest and say that all museums, and most art galleries, bore me to tears, even the Louvre. Oh yes, as for Ms. Mona Lisa, those of you who have been there will probably agree that it is disappointing at best. It is very small, guarded closely, and sits behind a thick glass enclosure: bulletproof of course. You can't get a sense of it at all from an artistic standpoint, so why bother to try. I was glad to leave and get on down the road. But now, some thirty-seven years later, I know I would appreciate all the Louvre had to off and much more, and someday I will return, a mature man with a deeper sense of history, culture, and love of art.

Chapter 26

It was with great anticipation and relief that we loaded up the old Deux Cheveaux and headed south through the Loire Valley. I, for one, was glad to exchange the big city scene for this beautiful countryside. Magnificent chateaux, vineyards, and quaint villages greeted us on this part of the trip. I kept reminding myself to try and absorb everything and store it forever in the memory bank – appreciate all of this for you may never pass this way again. I know that sounds pretty corny, but that's how I felt at the time. I know that it's hard for young people to savor the moment, and I'm sure also that any such advice from me or anyone else would be given little weight, coming from an "old man," but I still feel compelled, futile though it may be, to give it a shot.

On our way to the next youth hostel stopover, I began to develop the most God-awful belly cramps. All that rich French food I ate in Paris was finally taking measure of my colon, and every passing mile was becoming more and more unbearable. And there were no roadside rest areas like back home -- in short, no where to deposit your load. With all the traffic on this particular route, I couldn't just get out of the vehicle and defecate out in the open. I suppose I could be arrested for such a lude public act, but since I had no clear alternative, that's what seemed likely to occur – and very soon! Behold, we made it to the youth hostel in the nick of time -- sort of. I bolted out of the car, and ran into the building, barely stopping to ask the gent at the desk where the toilette was. He motioned towards the back of the building, and I arrived at the outdoor facility, opened the door , and found nothing inside! What? No John? Nope, but there was a hole in the ground and some newspaper beside it to wipe your behind. Just as I was going to drop my trousers, all hell broke loose. Not to offend dear reader, but I had the singularly nastiest crap of my life, into my pats, down my legs, and generally everywhere but in that stupid little hole. I was one bloody mess! I yelled for Mike to come and bring me some clean clothes, and whatever he could find to clean myself off. Thank God he heard me, and, after what seemed like an eternity, I finished the nasty job of decontamination. I wrapped my ruined clothing in some sheets, and disposed of the bundle in the trash bin in at the rear of the property (no pun intended).

Following this embarrassment, I ate a light meal that evening, and retired early. Mike and I were up bright and early, staying on schedule as best we could. We were heading for Spain, and in particular, Pamplona, for the Running of the Bulls festival the first week of July. The festival was actually one mad, week-long drunk – outrageous behavior by just about everyone, natives and tourists alike. And, of course, we wanted to be a part of it all. Our little car struggled up the Pyrennes' mountainside, never quite stalling out, God bless its four little cylinders. After what seemed like an eternity of climbing, we finally began our descent into Pamplona in the hart of Basque Country. Again, words cannot describe how beautiful that drive was. In every direction you looked from the summit, there was another postcard picture. We must have taken thirty or more pictures before getting on down the road.

Small and quaint town this Pamplona we thought; no hint of madness at this point, but the festivities were not quite in full swing. It was hard to find a place to bed down with the influx of tourists and natives from surrounding villages and towns all here, but we managed to find a hole in the wall motel just outside the city limits. What a dive, but it was our only alternative. Definitely no nice old Madams to bring you breakfast as in Paris, but at least the beds were fairly comfortable. We had to share a bathroom – one per floor, but again, who was concerned with hygiene at this point.

Chapter 27

I have only two clear recollections of the next few days. The first was watching my brave companion Mike attempt to run with the bulls. All the participants, thousands it seemed, had a one minute head start before the young bulls were released. The distance to be traveled was about one thousand yards, ending at the bullfighting arena. Mike and I had walked the course the night before, looking for escape hatches in case one stumbled, or couldn't run fast enough. Happily, Mike didn't need to stop and take shelter since he was a decent runner, and was able to avoid all the drunken buffoons in his path. He easily made it into the arena without being trampled by man or beast. And what a relief for me since I really hate long farewell tributes interrupting a good story. Once inside the arena, .the bulls are-taunted by some of the inebriated crowd of young 'matadors', some of whom receive their appropriate reward a young bull's horn in the ass. Even a young animal can inflict severe damage with their smaller horns. Score: bulls ten-- drunken slobs zero.

Now you might ask why did I not participate in this thrilling event. Truth be told, I am a coward and a liar: yes, a Liar. In later years Ive 'distorted' the facts somewhat to depict myself as brave and macho, running the bulls fearlessly. It's made a great story, but still, its a pitiful lie, and I'm truly ashamed. Not!!! The words Jew and macho seldom appear in the same sentence unless you're talking about an Israeli commando.

I did remain in the arena to witness my first and last bullfight. Bloodsports such as this are just plain obscene. Id rather have seen two of those ridiculous, drunken fools have a duel to the death as watch a handsome animal be slowly slaughtered. My second vivid memory is one I won't treasure; an all-night puke fest thanks to cheap Spanish wine. I can't recall ever being that sick from booze, but-enough said about that. It was definitely time to leave Pamplona, so onward we journeyed towards the coastal city of Barcelona, part of the Spanish-Riviera (Costa Brava.) After an uneventful drive, we landed in the old part of the city----very much different than Paris, but with its own, more primitive beauty nonetheless. We easily found a local youth hostel (God bless 'em) and immediately thereafter headed into the commercial part of town in search of Mikes dream---a handmade classical guitar. We found the specific shop he was looking for, and he purchased a magnificent instrument for the grand sum of one-hundred and fifty dollars Canadian. Even by 1968 standards, this was highway robbery. And Mike could really play that thing, a talent I surely envied. I had dabbled at guitar, taking a few lessons back home; but I wasn1t even in the-same-ballpark as this fellow.

Visions of Latin beauties by the seaside vanished quickly as there were none. Did Spanish parents prohibit their daughters from going to the beach for fear that we dangerous foreigners would likely harass, them, or worse, get physical against their wishes? Hell, I don't know, but that sure was disappointing. The presence of quite a few gendarmes on the beach was interesting, perhaps verifying my previous suspicions. However, all was not lost since the food was spectacular, especially the fish dishes. I ate a lot of things that weren't recognizable, but I was reassured by other tourists that everything was quite safe. Paela was particularly intriguing, a saffron-flavored dish consisting of rice; meat, seafood and vegetables. Included in this brew was squid, which tastes and feels pretty much the way you would imagine it-----like eating pieces of garden hose but not as tasty. But hey, for two bucks it was a great treat. On our meager budget, two dollars 'was quite a splurge, but well worth it. That night, unfortunately, the meal played havoc with my gut, but, thank God, unlike my cheap Spanish wine experience, I didn1t puke. In the morning, we were heading for the French Riviera. Surely our luck would change for the better as far-as girl watching was concerned. I couldn't imagine-much inhibition on their part, especially since I knew in my extensive pre-trip research, that there were several nude beaches along the coast: Cannes, here we come!

Chapter 28

Even after Paris, I was still preoccupied with women, but after all, I was only twenty-three-----what else was worth obsessing about away from school? Mike didn't say much, but I knew he was of like mind on this subject, maybe with the exception of his devotion to his new guitar. So, Cannes, home of the oldest film festival on the planet and a favorite play ground of the rich and famous, should have been spectacular, right? Wrong! It was a quaint little town, but what they call a beach to me was just a gravel pit. People were actually lying on crushed stone mixed with a little sand; not a very comfortable way to sunbathe. Granted there were a few top less gals, quite advanced for 1968 I thought, but there was-no surplus of sexy young women. As a matter of fact, I quickly learned that most women should keep their tops on since their breasts weren't worthy of a public-viewing. Now, looking- back, I was quite correct: not too many women look good in the nude. I hasten to add that the same applies to most, if not all men.

Ever the optimists, we pushed on to Nice, and our optimism was not unfounded here. Nice was, in a word, magnificent, a beautiful pearl of a coastal city, full of beautiful sights and beautiful people (except the two of us of course). We were beginning to look rather travel-worn-and-weary. I had started growing a beard, which added to my increasingly grungy appearance, which was not cool in 1968; at least not in Southern France; Lord knows I desperately need new underwear, t-shirts and pants, all of which I couldn't afford. Financial perspectives are very different looking back from this twenty-first century. After years of backbreaking work for not insignificant compensation, accumulating along the way material things long seem meaningless, I can't relate to those wondrously meager days in the summer of 1968, when I couldn't afford a pair of jockey shorts.

I had nothing, but I was just so content with my place, and circumstances. No one can tell me that money can bring you all the happiness you want----no damned way I left all my worries and neuroses behind and was totally carefree, unburdened if you will, of the nasty little details of my life. In short, I was, for- one of the-few times in my life past and present, totally happy with myself------I loved who I was and that was all I needed to be whole.

Mike and I went down to the local American Express office to check for any mail or messages. We were both cheered to receive greetings from friends and family back home. Also, I received a thoughtfully-worded postcard from Linda. She was waxing sentimental about us and our future as a couple, and she proposed a rendezvous back in London in early September, just prior to our return home. Right now that seems a century away----so much to see and do lay ahead, but I suppose I will look forward to seeing her again. My expectations are still miniscule in this Linda situation. Her attitude towards me changes about as fast as I change my socks. I must always keep in mind her past lack of commitment and general equivocation on matters of the heart. So I'm keeping my guard up since I'm not that much of a masochist that I would wish more pain for myself.

After reading his mail, Mike was upbeat. Apparently his girlfriend was still his girlfriend which was good I suppose. I'm not used to that level of devotion and faithfulness. He was also encouraged that a letter he received from his mom was signed by both his parents, since they had been separated several times in the past. So we were both in good form as we walked the streets of Nice, a bastion of French impressionist art treasures. I'm no expert on class, but, to me this city was the definition of class; and lots and lots of beautiful people were on display. Once again, as in Denmark, acne was not allowed on any young face---probably against the law. Even older women had flawless complexions, and they carried themselves with a certain grace and composure seldom seen back home. We are such slobs compared to middle class Europeans, especially in France and, as I would soon discover, in Italy as well.

Unfortunately, Mike began to develop a rather nasty cold which was robbing him of some of that terrific stamina he usually possessed. He was toughing it out as best he could, he being the last to complain about anything. Mike had a quiet dignity about him that I really admired and even envied---but I've always sold myself short an the-character issue. I now know, in retrospect that I can give myself credit for fortitude and inner strength I never realized I possessed. Hell, I even learned, out of obvious necessity, how to drive that damned standard-shift vehicle with some degree of proficiency. Mike was getting too sick to drive for any length of time, so I took charge of most of the driving chores, and Mike assumed my role of navigator.

We were on the road again heading for Monte Carlo, and then on to Italy. Just a word in passing about Monte Carlo. I couldn't come close-to being able to relate to the opulence and excesses of that town. A harbor teaming with private yachts, one: bigger than the next; a hillside with one mansion grander than its neighbor; and more exotic cars than I could count. This was flat out the most obscene display of material wealth I had witnessed to date. Was I jealous of those who owned these riches? Hell no! It would be embarrassing for me to be such an exhibitionist---flaunting my wealth as it were. To me this was the ultimate display of hedonism and self-absorption. Fuck them!! You know, whether It's 1968, or 2005, in my life experience I have found most obscenely wealthy people to be the least generous in sharing even the tiniest fraction of their worth with the deserving needy of our society. My disdain for people of this ilk makes me want to contribute what I can, financially and otherwise, to charities of my choice. Like the famous song by 'Kansas' says, 'all your money won't another minute buy.' Might as well share eh? I find my self from time to time breaking into this rhetoric of righteous indignation, and maybe that's a tad self indulgent. But what the hell, this is my damned effort here, and if I feel the need to vent occasionally then I bloody well will! Glad to get that off my chest, but I digress----onward with Mel's great European travelogue.

Chapter 29

We made the obligatory stop in Pia and found that, indeed, the tower was still leaning. I climbed the stairs to the top of the tower, stopping for a few minutes to enjoy the view. I've been told that I had a rather slanted, off-center viewpoint, and now that had come to fruition. Ironically, soon after our visit, no one has been allowed to climb the tower for fear of further damage to the structure.

Soon after arriving in Florence, Mike's cough had reached pneumonic proportions, reminiscent of lung cancer patients I have known. They sound like they are expectorating their left lunch every morning, but Mike had never smoked a cigarette in his young life. He was pathetically sick, and I, a soon-to-be senior med student, couldn't think of one thing I could do to help him, save search for local apothecary for something over the counter that might give a little relief. Fortunately, we found a B&B rather quickly that was quite acceptable, and Mike hit the sheets asap. Funny, it never dawned on me that he might be sick enough to die, but knowing what I know now, as a physician, he certainly could have, it wasn't out of the question given his clinical presentation. But he didn't, thank God. Like I said, Mike was one tough nut.

The next morning, feeling fractionally better, mike desperately wanted to get out of bed and tour Florence with me, but in his present condition, even Mr. Tough guy wasn't going anywhere. Why one of us didn't have the common sense to consider dragging his sad ass to the nearest hospital, I haven't got a clue. Just young, stupid, and invincible, right?

As was my routine by now, my first stop was at the American Express office to check for any mail or messages. Wouldn't you know it, Linda had left me a note saying that hse had arrived in Florence the day before, and would I please contact her when I arrived. I was a little excited, abut had become quite cautious when it came to this gal and her peculiar brand of ambiguity. I'm actuely aware now of how easily she can fuck with my fragile ego, so I remain on the defensive. I left a message for her that I would meet her that afternoon in L'Academie, home to Michaelgelo's "David." Next, I headed dwon to the railroad station for lunch. Now that might sound like an unappetizing choice for a favorite eating spot, but damned if they didn't have the best pasta I'd ever eaten in Italy—or anywhere else for that matter. Most importantly, it was cheap—always mindful of the miniscule budget I was trying to survive on. Incidentally, Italian folks don't eat spaghetti like my so-called "cultured" friends back home. They don't carefully curl the noodles with a fork and spoon, concerned with neatness and civility. Nope, the natives just shovel it in as fast as possible. Remind me of Chinese folks eating rice with chopsticks out of large bowls. My method of choice was the "shovel and toss," occasionally missing the intended target completely, but I wasn't in the slightest embarrassed since I was eating like a true Italia no. Italian cuisine never tasted so good, but perhaps that was partially due to the fact that it was so inexpensive too. Peculiar psychology I suppose, the thought that something would taste better because it was cheap. Usually it's the reverse, especially among the yuppie wannabes and true upper crust.

After lunch I strolled along the streets of downtown Florence, past such art treasures as the Golden Doors of Ghiberti, and various versions of David and Piata – excellent fakes. The real David, as mentioned earlier, had been moved inside many years ago to protect it from the elements. It was housed in a building known was L'Academie. When you first enter it, there is nothing on earth that can prepare for the magnitude of the work -- both size and perfection. It is, in a word, gargantuan, enormous in scope from any angle. And, of course, the craftsmanship of its creator leaves you breathless. I did wonder if the artist suffered from some form of penis envy. After all, my God what enormous genital is (and hands), considerably out of proportion to the rest of his anatomy. But, from all accounts, Michelangelo was pretty light in the loafers (or sandals). Not surprising then with that information in mind.

I was so preoccupied with the sculpture that I didn't even notice Linda approaching. Only when she was within five feet did I realize she was there – my erstwhile "girlfriend." "You look great, " I blurted out unexpectedly, "a sight for sore eyes, to coin an old phrase" some degree of sincerity I thought. " Sometimes I just forget how attractive a guy you really are. I'm sorry if you think I take you for granted, but I don't really know." "Well

Linda you know what they say absence makes the heart grow founder, ha, ha!" She said, "aren't you the clever one now come here and give me a big hug and kiss, will you?"

So we hugged and kissed for several minutes I wasn't really timing it. This was an unusually long romantic interluede for us though, ad I was actually enjoying it. Amazingly, I felt that perhaps she was coming from a much deeper and more sincere placein her heart, and I could trust my instincts for this once. What I really wanted to say to her then was something like, "honey I beseech thee, please don't yank my chain this time, ok?" That's what I should have said but natuarally I didn't. I thougth it best to just go with it and relish the moment – no questions, doubts, or paranoia, all specialities of mine. We left the L'Academie walking hand in hand, chatting each other up about nothing really, just enjoying the day and each others' company. Somewhere during the small talk my mind flashed back to Denmark and Suzanne. How odd—I felt that I was cheating on her even though we had no real commitment. For that instant, I wished that I was holding hands with my beautiful Danish friend, and a wave of guilt overcame me. However, it quickly passed with unusual powers of concentration on my part, and an especially vigorous assgrab by Linda, who pressed me close to her, giving me along, deep, wet, chock full of tongue kiss. Interesting how daydreams can be quickly shattered by a sudden testosterone surge.

Linda and I walked back to my digs to check on Mike, bue he wasn't anywhere in sight. I should have known that even a little pneumonia couldn't slow the boy down. Now in West Texas, you call Mike's condition "walking pneumonia." Where the hell this term came from I have don't exactly know, but I suppose that if you indeed have pneumonia, and can still manage to walk, that what ya got, right? Another great Texasism, but as a doctor it still drives me nuts to hear this old slang baloney from my down home patients. A wheelchair patiens said those very words just the other day, and I was sorely tempted to say "hey buddy, if you can't walk how in the name of Hades can you have "walkin' pneumonia?" Of course I didn't say that – have to be politically correct about mose anything these days, especially wtiht he handicapped. Nope, you can't be yourself and use irreverent humour in the workplace. If you are misinterpreted, especially by a female, you could be in a shitload of trouble in a heartbeat, for sexual harassment in particular. I say we are all victims of legalized pettiness, propagated by the trail lawyers (of course), of which there are far too many making afr too little money as ambulance chasers. As Sahkespeare said, first, we must kill al the lawyers. A close second – IRS agents, but that's a while other story worthy of at the least a novella.

Let's see, where was I now? Oh yes, I remember now. Mike had gone "walkabout" so we were along in the apartment. This would seem like a perfect opportunity to make love, right? Wrong again! After considerable time and effort put into foreplay by yours truly, the wench declined. That is to say, she requested a cessation of "holstilities" ad assessed me with a ten yard penalty for unnecessary roughness. "Same old same old," as they say in Texas. Thrust and parry, attack and withdraw: I'm more convenced than ever that this will end very badly, but I am into deep to easily extract myself. It's like quicksand, the more you struggle to get out, the faster you sink. So, I guess I'll just go with the flow. Fine, no sex, so be it! Anway, sometimes I'd prefer to be alone and enjoy a good self-induced orgasm inspired by fantasy gals much more stimulating than Linda D. And, at the very least, I'm making love with someone I truly love and admire.

Linda left by herself, and went back to her residence. I begged off since I was profoundly tired, and secondly, profoundly frustrated, and very, very angry – angry with both of us. We both seem to enjoy masochism, but on her part, I believe there is also a touch of sadism. If she were kidn, she would break this off quick and clean; and if I'd had half a brain, I would have told her to take a proverbial hike. My thoguth for this day: no guts, no gratification. She said that we should meet one more time back in London just before the journey home. I agreed that his would be a fine idea, but in truth I was pissed off, trying my best to be magnanimous. Perhaps she can be cruel and inconsiderate, but I cannot and willnot sink to her level. I was beginning to realize that this relationship would be nothing more than a character builder, and I'll hope ofr just that because I really don't want to look back on it as being completely negative. That's not the way I want to live my life, nor how I want to view people in general. "Dear God, let me be a better person than that" -- so goes my prayer for then and now.

Chapter 30

Mike finally arrived back home, still a little sick but in good spirits nonetheless. He had made a valiant effort to see some of Florence but he just "pooped out" as he put it. "How did your day go?" he asked. " Oh, same old shit different day, I had lunch with Linda and then we shared a frustrating but mercifully brief physical interlude." "So you didn't get laid, right?" Mike asked, in his sly, facetious way. Good comeback I thought. "Gee Mike, how'd you become so fucking perceptive -- was it the pneumonia, or do you actually have a brain tumor? Of course I didn't get laid asshole! I've been dating the only twenty-three year old virgin on the continent for Christ's sake, or so she claims, ha ha."

"When are you going to wise up man; this check is playing you for a fool, and I think you know it. And isn't it painfully obvious to everyone but you that there's a third person in this equation?' Mike had hit the nail squarely on the head.

"I had dismissed that as a possibility after she came to the airport to see me off, but lately, as you have opined, I tend to agree with you, painful as it is to admit." I was more that a little irritated that my "benign" friend was being so damned clever, pointing out how unclever I had been for so long. "Actually, I think it is more painful for me to admit that you are right about this since this would be a first for you." "Thanks a lot friend" Mike replied with more than a little sarcasm.

"Okay, okay, I was just joshing you. I like to see you get riled up once in a while. I mean, doesn't anything ever get you charged up emotionally? You are so damned even keel, it is unsettling. Maybe you should get pissed off occasionally—I think ti would do you a world of good; you hold your cards more to close to the vest pal. And furthermore, as if you need more, I don't particularly trust people who are so calm, quiet and introspective."

"Mel, that's because you don't know the meaning of the word "quiet" or "calm." If you would shut up for a second, maybe you could really listen for a change. You might even learn something from others, a near improbability in your book I reckon. And while I have your attention, have you considered just how self absorbed and egotistical you are? It is not always about you you know. So get over yourself, would ya?"

"Mike you got me man, I am whipped; good for you. I need some shut eye now, so goodnight." I was thoroughly pissed off, but I wasn't going to let Mike know that. After all, it would just support all his opinions of me and my gigantic ego issues. Actually, I can't recall the last time I was that short with someone I really felt close to, but I just didn't have anything else to say, plus I was, indeed, bone tired. I don't think Mike was offended, he was smart enough o know that he had given me a lot of truth I had to digest, and he just left it at that.

Chapter 31

January 2, 2006

Another year come and gone, and another eventful New Year's long weekend. On Saturday,. I played gold with my regular playing partner Victor. You couldn't find a nicer person on this or any other planet. Funny how you click with someone without knowing anything about their past or present circumstances. Vic is even more of a golf enthusiast than I, and certainly is a better player; but I like that, it spurs me on to improve my game. Besides, the company is most agreeable. At any rate, we played on a very windy day, and it was challenging to maintain concentration with the gusts of up to forty miles an hour hitting us unexpectedly from every direction. On the eleventh hole, a long par three, Vic hit a shot thirty yards to the left of the green, allowing for the wind to bring it back to the right. He guesses perfectly, and, to make a long story short, the ball hit the green and rolled directly into the hold. A hole in one! I was almost as excited as Vic, who almost tore my shoulder off giving me the high five and a big bear hug. What great fun, seeing someone so full of joy. I was truly happy for him and felt lucky to even witness an ace, let alone make one myself. This was the highlight of the weekend. All that was needed to complete the New Year's Eve evening, was a long, romantic night with my wife, Debbie. I rented a very appropriate date movie for the occasion, "Must Love Dogs." We both enjoyed the flick, and began getting ready for bed. Here comes the bad part – we did not have sex; not even heavy petting as we used to call it back in the day. Just as I was getting amorous, she informed me that she was not feeling well at all, so there would be no physical activity this night. Are you fucking kidding me? I know we're old married people now, almost got eleven years under our belts in fact. But does that mean that passion must, as a matter of natural course, slowly wane to the point where not even New Years can bring out the animal in you. I'll bet most animals have sex even when they are not "feeling too well."

Beig the deeply disturbed individual that I am, I become quite upset – even agitated. But I tried not to show it to her. After eleven years, trying to hid my displeasure from my wife was futile; of course she knew I was pissed, which in turn, got her pretty darned pissed off herself.

"All you care about is the sex, not me as a person, right Mel? I'm getting sick, and all you can do is pout like a little school kid who doesn't get his way. Look, I can help you get relief which you obviously need; I just can't have intercourse, okay?"

"Ah, just forget it," I said. My sick brain was telling me to decline this kind offer since that was something I could do alone. I was becoming increasingly irrational, so, before I said something I would regret, I put my coat on and drove to the supermarket to pick up a few snacks. I left the house at ten minutes before the New Year arrived. As I walked the aisles at the sore, I was fluming, muttering all sorts of profanity to myself. I'm sure the handful of people in the sore thought I was nuts, and they would have been correct. When I arrived back at the casa, Debbie was in bed waiting up for me. I did get her one of her favorite snacks, sugar-free Jello. Debbie is compulsive about no sugar, which is to say, she is compulsive about her weight. And that is why, unlike almost everyone else in West Texas, she has a fantastic body, one that I would like to ravage more often.

"Why did you leave so abruptly? Are you that upset at me?" she asked. She was being quite sincere, no hint of anger at all.

"Deb, I guess after eleven years, the bloom is off the rose, right? I mean, as time has passed, so has the romantic, passionate feelings we once had for each other, and that saddens and disappoints me."

" You think of yourself as this great romantic figure Mel, but that is bullshit and you know it. I think you are more in love with the idea of being romantic than you actually show – at least to me." Now she was getting real hostile, not that I could blame her.

"I think its best if I just shut up now, and go to sleep. Maybe we can discuss this tomorrow when I can be more coherent. I guess I'm just too worked up right now to be able to express my thoughts on this subject of romance with the clarity that I want to. Besides, it is difficult topic for me to discuss this with you: you always get mad, and tell me to go find someone else if I'm so damned unhappy with you. That ends any further conversation, and we never get our real feelings out on the table.

"Well, isn't that really what you want, a girlfriend who is more exciting than me? Someone new to rekindle the passion – isn't that your true wish Mel?"

"I'm not going to say anymore tonight. Look, I'm sorry if you are feeling crummy, but that's not too uncommon for you lately wouldn't you say?"

"Are you implying that I'm faking being ill?"

"Well, you never seem to feel bad around your friends and workmates. And what's more, you are more joyful with others than with me. I don't know if you enjoy my company anymore; maybe that's more to heart of the matter. All I know is something we once had is now missing, and I want it back G—damn it! Now let's just go to sleep, okay Deb? We can continue this in the morning."

"There's nothing to continue. I think you've made yourself pretty clear: you're sick of me, and would prefer other female company. If that's what you want, then go for it Mel. I'm exhausted trying to keep up with your emotional roller coaster mind. Just do what you've gotta do, but don't tell me afterwards that is all I ask."

The next day, we had both settled down, although, in truth, I was still a bit angry and disappointed. Another great New Year's weekend, eh? But Debbie was right about my romantic nature. I do want passion – what's wrong with that? She says all that is being horny at the beginning of a relationship, but I beg to differ. Couples can rekindle the flame if they really want to; I just think that their preconceived notions about marriage and how folks should behave as the years go by, as regards to feelings of romance and being passionate, is an artificial barrier that they put up for themselves. That's when passion is stifled – when you've given up on the whole notion that it can still exist. I couldn't agree more with my lovely wife, and we obviously will have an ongoing problem here since I don't believe her to be a true romantic like me. How can she possibly understand where I'm coming from if she seldom has felt true passion for anyone? I feat that I may end up alone once again, but I'm determined to make this third marriage work, even if that means that I must forgo the real "juice" of life – the passion, the romance, the intensity of it all that I have always cherished as being the ideal way for a couple to feel towards each other. Unlike my peculiar relationships of the past, such as the doomed affair with Linds D Way back in 1968, I really love Deb, and desperately want this to be it – my one true love, and my final marriage. I know she loves me, so, there's no reason we can't co e to some sort of understanding about how we should treat one another. One positive thing has come out of this lousy weekend though: I may be sixty, but, damn it, I still have an abundance of circulating in my body!

Chapter 32

There isn't much else to report about my final year of med school, save that by some miracle I managed to slip through and graduate. Unfortunately, my less than stellar class ranking would never grant me access to my hospital of first choice for my internship. However, I did fool everyone, including my pessimistic parents, in achieving my dream of becoming a medical doctor. I think I was the least surprised that I made it, given how devoted I had been towards this goal. The incredibly long hours of study, along with chronic sleep deprivation and fatigue, had paid off, not that I was an exception in a class full of obsessive-compulsive, highly motivated and competitive young men and women. I now had a whole two weeks to savor this moment, and then begin the most taxing year of all-------internship.

Think of the hardest work you've ever done in your life and multiply that by a factor of infinity-----that is the definition of my internship year. Yes, the real fun was about to begin-------impossibly long hours, hard work, perpetual anxiety, sleeplessness, and all this for minimum wage. Sounds great, eh?

As expected, I didn't get into Toronto General Hospital, but I did get my second choice, New Mt. Sinai Hospital right across the street from T.G.H. Five of the top ten ranked students in my class were also interning at Sinai. I would assume, given their class standing, that Sinai was indeed their first choice of hospitals. This may turn out much better than I could have imagined: Sinai was good enough for these top-ranked students, therefore I have to surmise that I will have a very good educational experience her. I was damned lucky ---or was I?

Most of my colleagues at Sinai were decent citizens, although a tad overzealous. But here's always a couple of exceptions, isn't there? Take Jack

Dubinski for example: this guy could kiss more ass than a gaggle of gays at an Elton John concert. Tall, gangly and awkward, Jack was the ultimate 'dork'. But he was cunning in his own way, finding all sorts of inventive ways to make himself look better to the department heads, usually at the expense of others. He was a dork on a mission, a wolf in intern's clothing if you will. He's that rare person that makes you search desperately for your nausea medication when you are anywhere near him.

And guess who else I have run into here? My old 'friends' Mike and Mark, the M&M twins were also interning at Sinai. What fucking luck! Of all the nice, decent people in my graduating class that I could have been matched up with at Sinai, I get these two elitist snobs. You know, in my not so humble opinion, there are so few caring and capable docs in this country, and now I know why. It is because medical schools accept and churn out heartless bastards like these fine young men.

Luckily, it turned out that saw very little of M&M over the next twelve months. Frankly, we were all too busy and worn out most of the time to waste precious energy on old grudges. My first rotation was physically the most challenging of the year--obstetrics. Initially, I was terrified---I can't imagine any rookie feeling differently. I wasn't allowed to deliver babies on my own at first, thank God. The staff Obstetrical docs were just terrific, uniformly patient with us while slowly guiding us along the path towards competency. Not to brag, but I quickly learned that I had a fair amount of aptitude for delivering babies, and, in short order, I was in the delivery room flying solo. Of course you always had a life line with the residents and staff doc on call for emergencies. Fortunately, Ob. goes smoothly and uneventfully ninety-five percent of the time but that other five percent can be catastrophic, These are true emergencies and immediate action must be taken or you could lose the baby, or the mother, or both. There isn't much in-between in obstetrics, either smooth sailing or near disaster.

In routine deliveries, truth be told, you could easily replace the doctor with a mid-wife (or a chimpanzee.) It's not rocket science folks---a lot of these babies would deliver themselves if doctors didn't get in the damned way. I know that now, but back then, it was exciting, heroic stuff. Maybe I'm just so jaded by decades of repetitive work, including hundreds of deliveries, that most of the time, not much gets me worked up or even mildly enthusiastic in the wide, wide world of medicine. Perhaps new challenges beckon to extract me from the rut I currently find myself in. But that's another story, and probably, another book.

Chapter 33

Danish Redux.

I had just completed thirty-six sleep-deprived hours on call for obstetrics, and had gone back to my tiny bachelor apartment where I lapsed into a deep coma. I loved ob. but the hours were brutal. I was asleep just a few minutes when, sure enough, the phone rang. I fumbled around to find the damned thing, finally locating it on the floor beside the bed.

"Hello, Mel, is that you?" I detected, through my sleepy haze, a slightly familiar female voice on the other end.

"Yeah, this is he---who is this, or am I dreaming the phone rang?"

"I'm terribly sorry I woke you, but I had to call as soon as I arrived. It's me, Suzanne---I'm just letting you know that I've, here in Toronto to visit you."

I was not even remotely awake, nonetheless, I was still feeling shocked at this development. "My God Suzanne, why didn't you give me some advance notice that you were coming?"

I was still desperately struggling to regain consciousness.

"I really wanted to surprise you, and besides, my travel schedule was not precise-----so I didn't know exactly when I'd be here to see you."

"You mean you came all this way just to visit me?" I was still in semi-comatose shock.

"Of course: Mel, you know I love you don't you? I was missing you terribly, and so I made a decision of the moment to come to Canada." Her English was still far from perfect, but decidedly improved. "I've already been to New York City and Montreal, and this is my final stop."

"Well then, how much time do you have here before you must leave?" I asked.

"The way I planned it, I wanted to spend the most time with you, of course, in Toronto. I have five days before my train leaves. I'm going back to Quebec, it is so beautiful and interesting, and I will fly home from Montreal, but I don't really want to leave without knowing that you will be with me again soon.

I had to change the subject quickly. "Okay, so where exactly are you right now?"

"Not too far away from you I think. I told the cab driver to find me the cheapest hotel near your hospital. I think its called the Ford."

When I heard that name, I could feel my pupils dilate and my heart rate increase as I became acutely anxious about her safety. This was the seediest joint in Toronto, where punks, hoodlums, and prostitutes hung out. The week before, a man was stabbed to death in the elevator! In a city that has few violent crimes reported everywhere else, this downtown area was renowned for random acts of violence ..

"Suzanne, listen carefully-----don't move a muscle, I'm coming right over. You can't stay there, trust me!"

"Okay Mel, I'll stay in the room-----number 420. You sound worried about something---what's the matter?"

"I'll explain later, just promise me you won't move, okay?"

"I understand" she replied. "But I feel safe just talking to you and knowing you are close-by, so don't be so nervous for me Mel."

"I'll be right there, stay put!"

A defining moment in my life was unfolding----right now! This incredible girl has come all this way from Denmark, and its not just to sightsee-------it is specifically to see me and, I presume, discuss our future together. This should be a no-brainer, right? Wrong, wrong, wrong! Shit, I don't know what I want right now, and I'm too tired to even consider such weighty matters. But getting right down to the bare bones of it, I don't really know if I love her or not. Yes, she's gorgeous---as beautiful as any man could desire. Yes, she's highly intelligent, and sweet and considerate to boot. And finally, as if that weren't enough, she truly believes she loves me. Still, I don't know where I stand on this love issue. Maybe I'll get lucky and she won't even bring up the subject of long-term commitment. Sure! Right! She came all this way just to make small talk!

Chapter 34

I was off call for several days, so her timing in coming to Toronto wasn't a complete disaster. I sprung (limped is more like it) into action and drove over to the infamous Ford Hotel. What a dive, littered with unsavory characters everywhere you looked. After double-parking, I ran into the hotel, and took an elevator that reminded me of the proverbial slow boat to China. By the grace of God, I made it to the fourth floor, and knocked on the door of room 420. Suzanne cautiously opened it, and, just like the first time I saw her, I was taken aback by this vision of female splendor. How could I not love this girl? She was wearing a daring outfit for the Toronto of 1970 to say the least: low-cut blouse, tied at the waist, revealing a bare midriff without a trace of fat anywhere in sight; no makeup whatsoever----why would someone with a flawless complexion need that? She never wore jewelry---no need to accessorize and muck up the elegant simplicity she embodied. Her long, blonde hair lay perfectly on her shoulders and back, and, as if all that weren't enough, she had the body of a Venus de Milo. She was just a dish of a gal! I stopped staring and regained some composure, finally asking her if she had any idea what a dangerous place she was in. I recounted the tale of the gruesome murder that had occurred the previous week.

"How on earth did you find this dump" I asked.

"Well, I asked the driver to find me a very inexpensive hotel, and he took me here."

"We're getting out of here stat! I'll get your bag---is there anything else?"

"No, I'm afraid I brought very little----mainly, I brought myself. Isn't that enough for you Mel?"

"In your case, it's plenty my dear Suzanne." Maybe too much, I silently pondered. Since there was virtually no room in my bachelor covey hole, and certainly no privacy to speak of, I quickly concluded that the best course of action was to ask my parents if they would put her up for a few days. Suzanne was quite agreeable, and, in fact, expressed a strong desire to meet them. She was just so damned easygoing, something I had not run into with a girl I was attracted to, but it was also a bit unnerving.

I wasn't too apprehensive about this meeting because, back then, my folks were quite different then in later years----softer, with some compassion for a select few outside of just our little family. Also, I know they were more than a little curious to see if Suzanne even remotely resembled the girl I had described to them upon my return from Europe. So, when I called, they were hospitable and cooperative, with no hesitation in putting her up during her Toronto stay. I was floored by their new-found gracious spirit----and, I thought, perhaps this would be good for them as an object lesson in being kind to strangers. Probably wishful thinking, but one must remain optimistic even in the face of years of experience that would strongly suggest that any learning about being kind and giving, at this stage of their lives, was virtually impossible.

I drove Suzanne to my parents' home, and introduced her to them. Shockingly, they embraced her and were incredibly warm towards her. How extraordinary! They took to her instantly, something I had never witnessed before with any of my ex-girlfriends. My mother, in particular, despised every single one of them. After all, they represented a threat to her hold on her precious only child; at least, that was her perception. Mom had been disdainful of all these girls until this moment. Suzanne just had that affect on people, even those as distant and cold as the folks. I witnessed a meltdown of greater proportion than Three Mile Island.

Chapter 35

I was still apprehensive about this Suzanne situation. I'm feeling pressure to make a life-altering decision, although she hasn't asked the big questions yet; but it's coming, I can feel it. I had a busy night at the hospital, with complications arising in two postpartum patients, thus not getting as much sleep as I had hoped for. I needed to be fresh and clear-headed when next I spoke with Suzanne.

As planned, I picked her up at the folks' house. While I was waiting for her to get ready, I asked my dad what they had done the previous evening. A big smile came over his face, as he described his trip to the local mall with my gal. Apparently they strolled around there, arm in arm, having quite the conversation.

"I could feel everyone staring at us" he said, "or should I say, at her. I guess they thought I was her sugar-daddy or something."

"And how did that feel dad?" I asked.

"I have to admit that it felt pretty darned good, and I guess I forgot how old I was for a little while."

"Why you horny old fart" I said, "at least you can still feel excited by a pretty woman. That's a sign of youthful zest and vigor, which is a good thing, you know? But dad, tell me, what do you think of her in general, besides her looks."

"Well Melvyn, let me put it to you this way; even if she wasn't physically beautiful, which she most certainly is, she would still seem attractive to me because of her sweet nature. She was very kind and considerate of this old man, I must say, and a darned good sport about everything. Frankly, I think you're lucky as hell to have someone of her caliber interested in you, and, probably, in love with you. She couldn't stop asking questions and talking about 'Dr. Mel.' You know, I really didn't believe you when you described her in such glowing terms, but it turns out that you had actually been understated in your description of her".

I swear to God my father was blushing. He hadn't talked about another female, aside from mother, for forty years----not in those terms. I was getting quite a kick over his obvious pleasure in describing his mall adventure. From my current perspective at age fifty-six, I can more clearly understand how it felt for him to be with a young, gorgeous woman. It would be invigorating, an all-too-brief reminder of long-deceased feelings of lust, self-esteem, and, above all, manhood. I mean, this guy had been sans penis for thirty plus years, so what just transpired was a big deal! To me he was the archetypal castrated Jewish male, completely dominated by his spouse. Oh, and along with his dick, she made off with most of his frontal lobes; a sort of figurative lobotomization. I'm surprised the poor bastard can still walk and talk!

After leaving ground zero, I drove Suzanne to Edward's Gardens, a perfect setting for a heart to heart. This place rivals the best garden spots anywhere, an oasis of beauty in the middle of the city. Once we arrived, we walked for a while until we found a nice, shady spot with a view. We spread a blanket over the grass, and sat down. It was a typical hot, muggy, sunny August day in Toronto, and, to my horror, Suzanne began to take off what little clothing she had on. I guess she forgot that this wasn't Denmark, where girls often went topless in parks on unusually warm days. I vividly remember how stunned I was to observe some of the younger hospital nurses in Copenhagen, sunning themselves, topless, in the park across from the hospital. What an enlightened society. But here we were in prudish old Toronto, so I had to ask Suzanne to put her blouse back on, or risk arrest. After some polite chit chat, she finally asked me 'The Question'.

"Mel, what would you say if I told you I wanted to come to Toronto for my post-graduate training?"

I was dreading this moment, but here it was! The real question was, how was I going to respond? Divine intervention had not favored me with an answer in the past twenty-four hours leading up to this moment, so I would just have to speak my truth---what I was feeling right now. Sadly, that truth was based in uncertainty, and sheer terror. How I wished that I could make a one hundred percent commitment to her, begging her to come here to stay, and live with me happily ever after. In 1970, the translation of 'live with me' was 'marry me', so this was a monumental and profoundly difficult decision. I was having trouble getting the words out, but finally, I said:

"You know Suzanne, Toronto is a great place to intern, and after that you can't go wrong with any specialty residency. Certainly your English is reaching a level now that won't handicap you. And, as you can see, this is a beautiful, cultured city, alive with activity both day and night. I can see you coming here and fitting in quite well. You already know quite a few of the med students and interns who have been to Copenhagen, so you won't be short of friends. The only thing I want to emphasize to you is this: don't come here just because of me. Do you know what I mean?" I wasn't feeling too good at this point.

"I'm not quite sure of your meaning Mel; are you trying to tell me in a polite sort of way that I should go home--and remain there? Let me be more clear, I want to study here and the main reason is that I want to be here with you-------together, you know?"

"But what if you come here Suzanne and it doesn't work out between us? We really don't know each other all that well, and if you come to feel differently about me, you'll resent the fact that I encouraged you, and I'd feel guilty about that forever. That's more pressure and responsibility than I can handle right now. I mean, I can barely think anyway I'm so tired from my obstetrical rotation, so how could you expect me to make such a weighty decision at this time?"

"Because I thought you cared for me---even loved me, and wanted me to be with you always, that is why! How could I have been so wrong? We were perfect together in Denmark, and Paris. What has happened to that feeling you had for me, Mel?"

"Suzanne, that was a splendid fairy tale---the best of my life, and you were the all-time champion of princesses in this tale. But this is real life now, and the fairy tale is a beautiful memory, one I'll never forget. I just can't say I love you, and know with absolute certainty that I do. I will admit this though: I'm still as attracted to you as ever, and flattered as hell that you would even consider me for your partner. I'd probably b e the luckiest man alive if I just told you 'yes', come here, marry me, and let's live happily ever after. But, God help me, I can't, because I don't know what I really want right now."

In truth, I was wondering how I would feel once the infatuation wore off (if it ever did that is). Who was this girl really? Culturally, we're still worlds apart, and, more importantly, she had detectable traces of that Scandinavian coolness and flat affect that really bothered me. Could I live with someone so controlled? That's why her spontaneity in showing up as she did, when she did, was such a shock. It just went against type---- Danish type, that is. Spontaneity is not their strong suit; nor is displays of emotional highs and lows. I rather prefer that range of feelings----at least you can understand the other person, and know where you stand in this, the most important relationship of your life.

Suzanne left Toronto a couple of days later, and I never saw heard from her again. Given how my first two marriages turned out, I've certainly had some regret that we didn't give it a shot. Hell, it couldn't have been any worse than what eventually occurred in my married life. Oh yes, I was going to write about how I trashed my car attempting to drive Suzanne to the railroad station, but it's just too damned embarrassing. I do have a good excuse however in that my chronic fatigue from ob. rotation, had finally got to me, and I fell dead asleep at the wheel! Now, my Danish dreamboat's last thoughts of me would be that of a bumbling, immature, uncoordinated boy, not a mature confident, self-assured man. Guess it didn't really matter at this point, since I'd already pissed her off enough to hasten her departure from Toronto. Ironically, my father had to come to the rescue, since my car had to be towed. He drove her the final few miles to catch her train for Montreal, which she had arranged two days earlier than her original schedule called for.

In retrospect, with regards to my feelings for her, the real proof of the, pudding, so to speak, was that I didn't regret her departure, and I didn't miss her. It wasn't the real McCoy:----I did not love her, that's all. She does, however, retain a precious place in my memory bank, even to this day. Don't tell my wife!!!!

Chapter 37

The Rumor Mill or It Takes a Village to Make A Really Bad Doctor.

Gossip is the life blood of any hospital, big or small. The day to day stresses and routine demand some form of relief, and gossip, the juicier the better, usually fits the bill. A hospital is just like a small town, with a lot of the same stereotypes. First you have your older, matronly women, Group A, just overflowing with happiness and good cheer. Most of these ladies are just playing out the string until their retirement------just hanging on in other words. You'll see them in small groups going on about their grand kids or discussing mutual resentment of daughters-in-law. Sometimes the conversation gets really heavy and they'll discuss cooking or the weather, specifically the lack of rain. In West Texas that's important stuff since we're usually in the middle of a drought. Soap operas used to be avidly followed by these ladies but that seems to have faded. Malicious gossip or rumor mongering is not really their thing; no, that's more the province of the younger nurses and ancillary personnel. In West Texas these gals are generally short, obese, chubby-cheeked, and in possession of the famous Big Texas Hairdo. But, most importantly, they are harmless, which makes them endearing on a certain level.

The real instigators of verbal venom are the Group B younger women----the thirty to forty something's. A small percentage of 'B' types are pleasant and seemingly well intended, but the vast majority are just the opposite. This clan is made up of nurses, lab and radiology techs, and, occasionally, some administrative staff. The key word in describing these folks is mean-spirited. How this group' individually, became so embittered and mean I can't say for sure, but I have a number of thoughts. First, you have your divorced or separated gals; no need to elaborate on their motivation. They are a dangerous group because of their bitterness towards the opposite sex, and their jealousy of members of their own sex who happen to be in happy relationships with men. Of course, any woman who claims to be in a mutually satisfying partnership is probably exaggerating, or just plain lying. That sounds cynical, but my experience leads me to conclude that this is factual. Simply put, there is a paucity of truly successful heterosexual unions. I challenge anyone to be objective in assessing their relationship, or their friends', or their relatives', or their colleagues at work. How many couples are actually in a happy, unselfish, mutually satisfying relationship?

Then you have your ladies in this group who couldn't attract a man even if they subjected themselves to numerous plastic surgeries. In other words, they are dogs. I know that's chauvinistic, but the truth of ugliness is painful, so get a grip on reality and stop being so damned polite! They hate men because no man has ever been attracted to them, not because men are so awful. And this bunch is particularly dangerous to male doctors. Malicious gossip is their stock and trade. They are whistle blowers in every respect. If an indiscretion has been deemed to have occurred involving a doctor and a female on staff, look out below! The dirt is going to fly fast and hard. Everyone in the hospital will be briefed in record time on this juicy tidbit. The male doctor in question will have his previously good name dragged through the muck, and he will suffer a loss of respect from all employees: from the *c.e.o.* to the housekeeping staff. And if he's married, his wife will almost certainly get the message, usually in some clandestine fashion. There is no rule book in this game of treachery. Admittedly, there are some men who deserve everything they get because of their sad lack of judgment, but in general, most of these rumors are bullshit initiated by some bitter lady may have even liked and respected at one time.

I myself was a victim of just such an individual, a nurse in the Coronary Care unit. Let me describe for you the circumstances: I was visiting my good friend Sam who had just had a coronary artery bypass operation. His spirits were high, and as usual, we were cutting up in spite of his being only two days post-op. I saw him every morning when I was making my rounds on my other patients, and again in the evening after office hours. On one particular night, I was kidding Sam about his current physical state, which included his lack of libido, when his nurse for the evening shift, a young woman I shall call Kathy, came into his cubicle with his p.m. medications. In keeping with the light-hearted mood of the moment, I asked Kathy if she would favor Sam with a sponge bath, something that might cure Sam's impotent state. We all had a chuckle over that comment, Kathy included. I still believe to this day that my remarks were completely inoffensive and unthreatening, and when I left the C.C.U. I gave it no thought whatsoever. Well, as you might expect in these times of increasingly intrusive political correctness, Kathy lodged a complaint against me with the director of nurses. Yours truly was called on the carpet by said D.O.N., and, in so many words, and in the strongest terms, she advised me to apologize to the nurse in question. Kathy, as I was told, have told her boss that she had been humiliated and belittled by me in front of her patient. Nowadays, of course, we call this sexual harassment, a term that has become all encompassing of even the remotest reference to sexuality. Being the hard-ass I can be, I flatly refused to apologize for something I deemed to be benign.

Accordingly, I was then reported by the nursing director to the chief of the medical staff, who, although sympathetic to my position, urged me to swallow my pride and apologize. The alternative was to have the matter brought up to the executive committee, where I would have to defend my ill-advised remarks in front of my colleagues and hospital administrator. Discretion being the better part of valor, I backed off, and submitted a written letter of apology to the nurse and her director. Having to do that pissed me off, and it still agitates me to this day. We have become a profession that has one eye on the patient, and the other on everyone else who can sue us for any bullshit reason imaginable. What a sorry state of affairs we have arrived at, eh?

The third subgroup in category B, is your lesbian clan. They'll bust your balls just to prove that they have them too. These gals are usually supportive of group B ladies in all subgroups. The flip side of this subgroup is the gay male employee population, usually nurses, although there is an occasional doc hidden in the closet in most hospitals. When there were orderlies in big institutions, they were almost uniformly gay. When I worked as one at Toronto General Hospital back in the mid sixties, virtually all my colleagues were light in the loafers, except of course for me (okay, so I'm a tad homophobic.) As opposed to the lesbians, the gay men were usually full of good humor, but professional to a fault. There is a popular television show today called "Queer Eye for the Straight Guy." I would say that these fellows would fit right into the mold of the male homosexual personalities in the hospital. They were okay with me. After all, there is so little humor to break up the monotony of the work day in a hospital, that any source of amusement and good cheer is most welcome, regardless of from where, and from whom it comes from. Even in my youthful orderly days in Toronto, I never once felt threatened sexually by any gay individual in the hospital. I was treated with nothing but respect and kindness, which is more than I can say for my treatment as an intern, at the hands of my clinical superiors, be they residents or staff physicians. Too bad that my arrogant 'bosses' weren't gay, which would have ensured that this horrid year of internship would have been a far more enjoyable experience. Why, there may have actually been some moments of light heartedness and laughter, God forbid.

My colleagues in arms when I was an intern were the same folks I knew in med school, so they really don't fit into any particular group in the hospital community. They hadn't changed much since early school days, so, needless to say, I had as little to do with them as possible. Unfortunately, none of my mates in my clinic group were interning at my hospital, and I didn't particularly relate to anyone else in my medical class. So I was stuck with the same elitist assholes that I despised in med school. Just my luck that the real jerks decided to intern at good old Mt. Sinai Hospital. The irony of this situation was that Sinai had been my fourth or fifth choice for internship in the matching system, whereas-my associates there had selected it as their number one pick. These were some of the higher ranking students in my graduating class. Truth is stranger than fiction, isn't that so? I, a decidedly mediocre student, was now co-mingling with the more elite academia's, most of whom, in my opinion, turned out to be crappy doctors in the real world; that is to say, the world outside the protective umbrella of academia.

Finally, you have the last subgroup, the physicians, of whom I have referred to as targets of most the of really nasty gossip. All I can add here is a platitude like "He who is without sin cast the first stone." Everyone fucks up sooner or later; it doesn't matter what group you belong to. Marital discord, hospital affairs, and rumors of sexual preference and or deviance-----this is the norm in a hospital in my experience. Let's face it, people love to talk disparagingly of doctors for all sorts of reasons, some of which I have discussed. A doctor's only defense is to develop a skin as thick as a coat of armor, and always be aware of the fact that no matter how exemplary a life you think you lead you can still be a target of rumor, innuendo, slander, and most of all jealousy. I have learned the hard way, so have many who have gone before me. Perhaps by reading this, I will spare some young doctor from an embarrassment such as the one I suffered. My advice is simple: just shut the hell up, do your job, and go home as quickly as possible to those that love and understand you, and forget your work the second you leave the premises.

Chapter 38

Adventures in Surgery

I was assisting Dr. Posner with a thyroid tumor excision. As usual, he was complimenting himself as he went along since he was his biggest fan.

"Look at this closure technique Dr. Mel, it leaves little if any scar when I do it-----right nurse Jones?" (Ms. Jones was the scrub nurse.)

I remained silent as was my habit while assisting at surgeries, the main reason being that I hated surgery with a passion. Even more than surgery, I couldn't stand arrogant little blowhards like Dr. P. What a complete asshole! He was always onto me, like a buzzard on a shitwagon. He knew, or at leased sensed my dislike for his precious specialty, and also, more importantly, how much I loathed him. I think he talked even more incessantly when I assisted him just to annoy me, perhaps goading me into a dialogue about what I know not. Probably it concerned how clean his asshole was after he defecated; or perhaps it concerned how anyone could possibly have a tinier penis than he.

And so went my 'sentence' in surgery, counting the days until this damned rotation was over. Then it happened; he finally got to me, the little prick. It was just another routine surgery, or so I thought. Dr. P. was in his usual brilliant form, and he'd always be the first to tell anyone within earshot just that. Just a routine thyroidectomy, but to hear him tell it this procedure was tougher than brain surgery. He tried to engage me, as per usual, in some trivial conversation about his stellar technique. Suddenly, he looked up from the operating table, and eyeballed me for several seconds. Finally he said:

"Doctor Mel, you don't much care for surgery, do you?" My kneejerk, no thought involved response went as follows:

"Nope, truth be told sir, I can't stand it, and I'm counting the days, hours, minutes and seconds until this damned rotation is over."

As soon as the words left my big mouth, I knew he finally had me right where he wanted me.

With a supremely sarcastic tone, he replied: That's too bad doctor, I was hoping that I might have inspired you to apply for a surgical residency here at Sinai; or at least instilled in you some inkling of respect for the work I love. Perhaps another couple of weeks on my service would help your attitude. What do you think?"

I was thinking that this man of diminutive stature, literally and figuratively, had a Napoleonic complex together with an unusually small penis. Now that's a dangerous combination in one man.

"I don't mean any disrespect towards surgery per se sir, I just know that it's not for me, that's all. Please don't misconstrue my feelings about surgery to be a personal affront to your character or ability. I was simply expressing my honest opinion, nothing more. And, your question seemed to me to call for an honest, non-evasive response" .

With more than a little anger, Dr. P. snapped: "You know Mel, sometimes it's better to keep one's honest feelings and opinions to oneself, especially in the presence of a superior. That piece of advice may just serve you well in years to come, who knows' Now, let me express my honest feeling. I think you're an arrogant little shit who has no respect for the medical profession or the people who serve in it. Your remarks are selfish, self-serving, and offensive, and I do take them personally. You don't like surgery---fine, but you especially don't like me, do you wise guy? Do you have the guts to admit that I wonder Mr. 'I'm bored with surgery, what a waste of my time'?

A full frontal assault had unexpectedly been hurled at me by this little fart, catching me quite by surprise. This was quite a dialogue, if that's the right word for it, we were having considering that we were in the middle of a delicate neck operation on a real person, in a real operating room, with real nursing staff all around us. Shit!!! I don't believe this is happening--- right here and right now! More importantly, how was I going to extricate myself from this untenable position this jerk had put me in? The demise of my future career was flashing before my eyes. I simply had to stand down (as they say in the military); after all, he had all the power, and thus, all the cards were in his hand. All I had was a bigger dick than him: I knew that without a formal measurement. Small consolation since I had to 'suck it up' and be a pussy.

"Sir, may I suggest another idea here." I was being quite contrite which was difficult for me in any circumstance. "Why not allow me to exchange my last two weeks with you for two additional weeks of obstetrics. I really need more time there since I'll be doing ob. when I go into practice. What do you think of that sir?"

"I think you're way too sure that you'll get through your internship and ever enter private practice, that's what I think hotshot! However, since you're such a royal pain in the ass, "I grant your request for a transfer. Okay?"

"That's most generous of you Dr. Posner. You don't know how appreciative I am." Pass my nausea medication, please.

"You know Genraich, someday I think you'll wish you had spent more time in surgery. Believe it or not, you will need some technical skills out there in the real world, but I know that you don't really believe that. At any rate, good luck to you; with your attitude, you'll need it."

Dr. P. was dead wrong. I didn't miss the last two weeks in surgery rotation one little bit, but, out in 'the real world' as he put it, I became quite proficient at minor procedures, thanks to some great mentors in various specialties. Not to mention, the extra two weeks on obstetrics was very helpful. I will admit that Dr. P. surpassed my minimal expectations of him in that he did grant me an early exit from his service. Maybe, underneath his veneer of arrogance, there really was a decent person lurking------nahhhh!

Chapter 39

Misadventures in Marriage

The routine had set in: work, sleep, work, no sleep, etc. I somehow survived until reaching my internal medicine rotation, physically the least demanding of the year. The residents and staff physicians were fairly decent folks, a pleasant change indeed. Why is it that in surgery the order of the day is 'abuse and humiliate students and interns to the best of your ability?' I have no idea, but I think it has a lot to do with machismo, which surgeons must possess in abundance if they are to succeed----or so they believe. In fact, the opposite is true in my experience. Kindness and consideration, along with technical skill, are what earns the respect and admiration of most colleagues and patients, including me. But we must always remember that the surgeon is a special breed, superior in every way.

Just ask one----he'll tell you.

It was during my medicine rotation that I came to know Milly(Mirjam), my first wife-to-be. I like to use Mirjam because she hated that name. A former classmate of mine, Howard S., was visiting Toronto, taking a break from his internship in Vancouver. He was universally liked, and knew almost everyone interning at Sinai. I ran into him at the interns' residence and we chatted for a little while. Somewhere during this conversation, he mentioned a girl's name, one Milly B. He classified her as a good friend, and said that he thought that she and I would get along famously. According to Howie, she was pretty in a petite sort of way, very intelligent, and funny -- in short, a treat to be with.

What did I have to lose; after all, I wasn't dating anyone at this point. I could barely muster the enthusiasm or energy to even give myself an occasional tug. Now there's one definition of depression, boredom, or whatever: you can't even masturbate because its too much effort to conjure up appropriate fantasy images that might elicit an ejaculatory response. Oh hell, I guess I'll give her a call. It's not like my social calendar is crammed and I can't possibly squeeze, another engagement in. So I called, and unwittingly set off a chain of events that would affect the rest of my life, adversely for the most part.

Milly was cute; one might even say she was mildly pretty in a Jewish sort of way. She had long blonde (dyed) hair, blue eyes, a perfect complexion, and, sadly, very tiny breasts. Who's perfect anyway, except of course for my Suzanne. The package, as a whole, wasn't bad at all, and the lack of breast tissue could be easily amended with implants. After all, why did God create plastic surgeons? Call me a male chauvinist, but to me a woman isn't really a woman without breasts that can be easily visualized from a minimum of twenty yards away.

Along with my breast fetish, I appreciate long, shapely legs. Unfortunately, this girl had neither of these two features, but for some reason it wasn't as important in her case. Perhaps it was her zest for life, or her sunny personality, seemingly free of the usual hang-ups young ladies usually have. She wasn't exciting to be with, but lots of fun. Hormonal urges were present, just not in the usual amounts; in retrospect, a bad omen. It should be unbearably painful, in a good way, to want to be with someone all the time, not to mention, being desirous of sexual gratification with that person, a substantial percentage of the time. That's the benchmark standard of a fulfilling, long-term relationship that will certainly follow. I wasn't paying enough respect to my lack of sex drive with respect to this girl, a mistake I was fated to make in another marriage to come.

So I called Milly up and, unfortunately, we began to date. She could really carry the conversation, which took a lot of pressure off me to be witty and clever, not that I was feeling very witty or clever in recent weeks. Since I was so damned fatigued, I needed something, or someone, to help get me through this hellish year. I was already consuming enough coffee and nicotine to double my target heart rate, and even then wasn't sustaining any reasonable energy level. I knew that some folks were using different combinations of 'chemicals', but that just didn't seem like a viable (or healthy) alternative to me. Chemistry never was one of my favorite subjects anyway. Besides, I wasn't much of a daredevil when it came to illicit drugs or excessive amounts of alcohol, having observed how these things affected people in a decidedly negative way. Even at the worst times of my life, I valued being alive, which precluded any adventurous behavior with street drugs.

Milly filled a huge gap in my life, especially after Suzanne's abrupt departure, which I was beginning to regret. However, I now had some semblance of a personal love life, albeit, without great passion----at least on my part. But she seemed quite keen on me and went out of her way to be kind and considerate. Some nights she would cook me a meal at my apartment, and she was a darned good cook. Other times she would get takeout for both of us, and we'd just chill out on the couch and watch television, or just talk. She was really more of a good pal than a love interest, but she pursued the romantic angle of this relationship with a passion I couldn't muster. I was growing fond of her and appreciative of her taking care of me in the fashion I have described, but was that enough to sustain a relationship that she obviously wants to elevate to the next level? As usual, there was no clear-cut answer to that question, so I decided not to decide anything, and just see what developed on my part. Psychologically, I was unfit to make any major commitment decision to anyone; I just wanted to finish my internship in one piece, that's all. I know it sounds selfish, but I needed Milly to help me get through this difficult year. Maybe love would gradually sneak up on me, without me stressing about it.

Just let it happen if that's what's meant to be, that's my motto.

Let me hasten to add that Milly was not without her own devious, self-serving agenda. There was, in fact, a method to her kindness and availability. I think I can summarize Milly with two words: fake orgasm. Or, here's another two: fake virginity. That last one requires a little explanation, so let me describe the scenario that led to this conclusion. I was working at the nursing home, part of my rotation on internal medicine, and there was a particularly nice intern quarters in one wing of the center, where there was actually some privacy. The apartment actually had a kitchenette, along with other useful amenities. One evening, just as I was about to turn in, and behold, Milly paid me a surprise visit. And she had brought sustenance, which was very welcome indeed since I hadn't had time to eat dinner earlier. She made supper for us, and we engaged in casual conversation. Shockingly, she asked if she could spend the night with me, something we hadn't done up to this point. We had done some 'heavy petting' as we used to call it back in the Stone Age. I think they call it oral sex these days. This was serious. I had to make a quick decision, but was unnecessary once my penis reached its full potential (at warp speed.) When you're a twenty-five year old male, just the hint of possible sexual activity was adequate for instant arousal. So I was raring to go, no negative thoughts in sight.

And so it was, we made love for the first time. But just prior to intercourse, she informed me that she was a virgin and it might be difficult at first for her. The only problem with that statement was that it turned out to be pure bullshit. There was absolutely no physical difficulty having coitus for either one of us, although she feigned some pain-----not convincing at all. Afterwards, she apologized for the fuss she had made, not to mention the blood all over the sheets. It didn't take a rocket scientist to figure out that she was on her 'monthly,' especially since rupturing the hymen doesn't precipitate profuse bleeding as in this case. Yes our Milly was quite the schemer; she would lie through her teeth to get what she wanted; very goal oriented indeed. And what she wanted was a doctor; more specifically, a Jewish doctor, and I was just that fellow to fit the bill----unless of course a better looking, richer Jew doc came along during our courtship. Jewish was paramount, but money was a close second priority to this gal. Also, I suspected, and quite rightly as I later learned, that she was very much in love with Howie, but the feeling wasn't mutual. Of necessity, she settled for a good friendship with him. He was too savvy to fall for her routine, but I was a babe in the woods.

Milly was different from anyone I had ever dated: aggression disguised in a seemingly benign package. In point of fact, she was lethal. If you were to ask me today why I continued this relationship which ended in marriage, I couldn't give you a clear-cut answer. I will say that I was lonely, and feeling quite vulnerable since I was toting a mighty heavy load of low self-esteem and feelings of inadequacy engendered by a job that fostered that emotion in just about everyone. I needed the companionship and the sex, and for the most part, she was great company. The sex was so-so, but occasionally she would let herself go and have an honest to God orgasm; but usually she faked it. She was persistent and relentless, and I succumbed without much of a struggle. Before I knew it, we were engaged. I can't even remember who asked who, it just sort of evolved. Like death and taxes, it was inevitable, but much worse as it turned out.

Chapter 40

Meanwhile, Back at Mt. Sinal Hospital

The remainder of my medicine rotation was relatively uneventful except for one never-to-be-forgotten incident. Unfortunately, what I am about to describe happens every day in every major hospital in this country. It was true in 1969 and its true to this day. Human error should be avoidable, especially given the reams of documentation required from nurses and doctors alike. We are buried in paper, but shit still happens.

I was called to the CCU (coronary care unit) one evening by a distraught young R.N. She had been taking care of an old woman who had been admitted for an acute coronary event (heart attack,) her third. Her hospital course had been rocky, with changing heart rhythms occurring with increasing frequency. I ordered electrolytes to be checked especially since she was on powerful diuretics (to eliminate excess fluid that accumulates with, in this case, heart failure.) Sure enough, she was very low on potassium, which can cause heart irregularity and even death from a fatal arrhythmia. I ordered potassium to be given in her IV bottle over the next few hours, since potassium must be given slowly to avoid disaster as described above (too much or too little potassium can have the same dire consequences.) However, the inexperienced R.N. did not read the order correctly, and, instead of following my verbal and written instructions, she injected all the potassium directly into her IV line; that is to say, she gave a bolus of medicine instead of a slow infusion from the bottle. In just a few seconds, the overdose of potassium threw the poor woman into an irreversible ventricular arrhythmia, and her heart stopped. She could not be resuscitated.

Only that nurse in charge of that patient, and me, knew what had just transpired. The patient was, in fact, terminally ill, so what was I to do: report the nurse and get her fired? It was probably her first job for God's sake, which made it even more perplexing. Since she had called a code blue, the cardiac arrest team was on its way, and I had to make a quick decision. To make a long story short, I did not report this nurse. The patient was elderly and terminal; therefore I just couldn't rationalize jeopardizing this young woman's career when it had barely just begun. Also, the patient's outcome, almost certainly, would have been the same without this unfortunate incident. A tough lesson to learn, to be sure, for anyone, and the young nurse was trembling and teary in the aftermath. She will never forget this event and its disastrous finale, but, in my opinion, she will go on to get a great nurse because she obviously cares deeply about her patients and her profession. To this day, I would staunchly defend my decision as sensible and the right thing to do. I'm sure though, that today's extreme religious right would have a ball with something like this. However, I don't have much respect for a lot of their distorted opinions and value judgments anyway, so what the hell! Besides, they're too busy bombing abortion clinics, and killing their doctors and nurses.

Chapter 41

Beginning a Career

My first year in practice was spent working for a group of Jewish doctors in downtown Toronto. I made a pittance, the tradeoff being that I gained a world of experience in a hurry. That seemed fair to me, I made them a lot of money, in return for which I received their pearls of wisdom and knowledge as veterans of the medical wars.

Collectively, they were quite humorous, each doctor having his own style. One doc by the name of Marty, had a sly, sardonic wit, putting my sarcastic barbs to shame. I wasn't in the same league as this fellow. Also, he really enjoyed teaching, never quite losing his sense of humor except when confronted by the tragic, sad cases. Morrie was the elder statesman and founder of the group. He bore a striking resemblance to the late actor Richard Farnsworth. He fancied himself quite the dermatologist, and I must give him his due there as he was quite astute in this area of medicine.

As luck would have it, one night both Morrie and I were working the late shift at the clinic----just the two of us. Unbeknownst to me because I was attending to a patient in another exam room, my nurse had brought a young woman into my second exam room. I should point out that at night we only had one nurse on duty for both docs, so I had no idea what awaited me in the other room. When I finished with the first patient, I finally made it to room two, just in time to see a drop-dead, instant erection, Playboy Bunny-type young gal, who was chewing away at her was of gum, patiently awaiting my arrival. My initial reaction was to silently give thanks to almighty God for this moment; however, I was able to quickly regain my professional demeanor, asking her what problem had brought her to the clinic. She replied that she had been suffering from a rash that was spreading to all parts of her body. I handed her a hospital-type gown, and excused myself.

I went back to my office to finish charting on patient number one, and then returned to Miss Goodbody. I was startled, to say the least, to see this young woman clad only in bra and panties, not an unpleasant sight at all. This gal had absolutely no excess fat in all the places women dread having it. Maintaining my composure, I proceeded to check her skin for any signs of disease. Except for a few interesting tattoos, there was no rash to be found, not even with a magnifying glass. I had a fleeting notion to call Morrie in for a consultation, but decided against that. Hell, given what a cheap, crusty old bastard he was, why should I give him that bit of pleasure? At any rate, I asked her to get dressed and quickly left the room.

When she had finished dressing, I met with her in my office. I told her that there were no positive findings, but if something should come up, return to the clinic and I would recheck her. She had other ideas .

"To tell you the truth" she said, "I really came here just to meet you. I've seen you come and go, and you always look so sad. I thought maybe you'd like to have a little company tonight, so here I am. How would you like to have coffee with me at my place?"

I'll be damned! She's a hooker, the first one I've talked to since Amsterdam a few years ago. I actually considered her offer for a second, given that things weren't going too well on the home front.

"Thanks much for the invitation, but I just can't do that. After all, technically you are my patient, and I have to obey strict ethical guidelines, not to mention that I am married. Now, if you have any further medical issues, don't hesitate to use the clinic again. Have a pleasant evening, what's left of it."

What discipline, what self-control. Not really, I just valued my medical license too much to risk my career on a one-nighter, with a hooker no less. That was one unique experience which, thank God, hasn't repeated itself. But, for sheer entertainment value, it was the one highlight of my work at 'Down and Out Medical Clinic,' Toronto.

Chapter 41

The Big Sleep

The only other event that really sticks out in my mind concerning my time with that bunch was a little party that Marty and his wife Ellen hosted at their home. The main course for the evening was some 'incredible shit' as Marty described his marijuana stash. This was going to blow our collective minds, or so he said; and soon, all worries and woes would vanish, at least for one night. That night, we thought we were just about the coolest bunch of grown-ups on the planet. Too bad no one really knew how to roll a joint, but, eventually, we sort of figured it out and we were on our way to bliss.

You know that old saw about how grass makes you somnolent, and voraciously hungry? Well, sadly to say, its quite true. As it turned out, the weed really was potent, and, shortly after a few inhalations, everyone fell into a deep sleep. It was like a scene out of "Coma." I did wake up before the others, and my God, was I starving! I got up and stumbled to the kitchen, still pretty groggy. What a beautiful sight awaited me when I opened the fridge door------a huge, wonderfully prepared roast chicken, just sitting there waiting for me to devour. And devour it I did, the whole damned bird gone in a heartbeat. After polishing off the fowl, I meandered back into the living room, feeling quite satisfied after my meal. I soon rejoined the others in peaceful slumber. About an hour later I managed to rouse the wife, and somehow, navigated my way back home.

The next day I awoke with the worst hangover you could imagine. Thank God it was Sunday. My wife told me she had received a very strange phone call from a distraught Ellen, Marty's wife. Apparently, she was having a big dinner party that night, and the main course had been eaten. Milly asked me if I had any idea what might have happened to the bird.

Coward that I was, I flatly denied any knowledge of events surrounding the birds disappearance. Actually, it was a *fuzzy* memory, but I knew that I had committed the foul deed.

My remaining time at the clinic was uneventful, but quite instructional for my future diverse career in family practice. I was, however, growing increasingly restless and resentful of my miserable salary pitted against my substantial workload. Like I said, these guys were cheap, but, as I have come to discover over the last thirty plus years, who isn't? In the big business of medicine these days, what chief executive of a large health organization gives a shit about anything except the bottom line? Why hadn't I become a plumber or electrician, some trade with a real financial future? Thus, I packed my stethoscope, and shuffled off to an uncertain fate in the wilds of suburban Toronto.

Chapter 42

Solo Practice

After an educational, albeit decidedly unprofitable year in inner city Toronto, I bravely embarked upon a solo career in the eastern suburban wilderness known as Scarborough. The most rewarding aspect of this experience, was my participation as an active medical staff member in the finest hospital in the area, Scarborough General. S.G.H. was a wonderful institution owned and managed by the Sisters of Misericorde, God bless them. In many ways, from a career standpoint, this was the happiest time of my life. There was a certain esprit de corps amongst all the staff, and I could feel it the second I first entered the hospital. I hadn't experienced anything like it before, and, since then, haven't encountered that feeling anywhere else I've worked. There was always someone willing to help you out in a difficult situation, be it a nurse or a fellow doctor. You just felt so secure, and my confidence grew in that environment of friendship, co-operation, and camaraderie.

In short order, I was doing a fair amount of obstetrics, plus I began to moonlight evening and graveyard shifts in the emergency department. My office practice, too, was quickly growing, and I had every reason to be optimistic about the indefinite future. My office was in a little strip shopping center on the second floor. My next door neighbor was the (aforementioned) Henry Aranoff, dentist extraordinaire, one of the most affable chaps one could wish to meet. My tiny office was 'staffed', if that's the right word, by two people: yours truly and an incredible lady named Margaret, who wore many hats. She was the de facto nurse (but didn't have a degree,) receptionist, filing and billing clerk, and one-gal collection agency. Oh yes, and she was also my surrogate mother: kind, loving, professional in everything she said and did, and also was generous to a fault--------just a sweetheart. Margaret was universally loved, and people quickly sensed her kindness and concern that she genuinely felt for them. In those days, with no particular worries about legal technicalities or political correctness that plague us today, the two of us made a great team, able to see a large volume of patients in an eight hour day. Today's docs, myself included, are incredibly spoiled, requiring many more employees to function as well as I did with one. In any business, I have come to learn that bigger is not necessarily better and oftentimes it's much worse and decidedly less profitable. These were, indeed, the good old days.

Chapter 43

The Lunch Club in the Burbs

I quickly became fast friends with my new office neighbor, a dentist by the name of Henry Aronoff. We had much in common, being Jewish for starters, thus understanding and empathizing with the core beliefs and values of our heritage. Secondly, and more importantly, we shared the same sick sense of humor, and therefore we got it------no further explanation needed for jokes or commentary laced with sarcasm and double entendre. We had darned good fun, but never at the expense of another friend. For example, Henry had a partner named Steve Moskowitz, who was hilarious in his own right. But, more often than not, he was on the butt end of many a sarcastic assault, which he handled quite well, I must say, and he usually managed to return in kind that which he had received.

Almost every afternoon we three lunched at a local greasy spoon, the infamous Watts Restaurant. Our discussions ranged from descriptions of 'our more colorful, quirky patients, to regurgitating the latest and greatest jokes, and on to political and economic issues of the day (not that we were consumed with current events and political ideology.) As soon as someone made a serious comment about, for example, the conflict in the Middle East, there was a rapid response------a zingy one-liner, or caustic remark, that would restore the lighthearted mood. No one took offense because friends can get away with this sort of grand nonsense.

On a subconscious level, we were collectively easing our work generated stress and mental fatigue. In spite of the high cholesterol diet, this was a very healthy way to spend the lunch hour, as we returned to work rejuvenated and re-energized by our 'noon nonsense.' I would characterize this time as a poor man's version of a Friar Club Roast, each of us in turn being the roastee.

Henry had a younger sister named Gloria. She was a living doll, and smart as a whip. She was quite young, barely finishing up undergrad school. She too was headed for dental school, and her future seemed full of great promise. Occasionally I reflected on how unfortunate it was that I was already married, especially considering how my marriage was already showing signs of strain. If I had had any balls at all I'd have ended it before children came along. I could have saved both of us a boatload of misery, not to mention the financial devastation I incurred which dogged me for many years following our inevitable divorce.

I mention Gloria because I obviously had a huge crush on her, and were I a single man would have pursued her vigorously. But alas, I remained faithful to my wife, and Henry's sister became just another missed opportunity at a passionate relationship that might have ended in a great marriage.

As expected, Gloria went on to get her degree in dentistry. A few years later, I learned from Henry that she had married a well-to-do Jewish financier, and settled into family life, and all that goes with that boring, contented lifestyle.

Chapter 59

Adventures in Chemistry

As time went on, I found it increasingly difficult to maintain the workload in all areas of my practice: the office, the delivery room (obstetrics,) assisting at surgery, and even house calls. However, I found a couple of good friends and allies to help me in my varied and exhausting duties. Their names were Percodan and Valium, with additional assistance from my close acquaintances, caffeine and nicotine. This was a potent combination: Valium for the anxieties brought on by the nature of the work plus the impossible hours; Percodan for extra energy and heightened awareness; along with gallons of coffee and cartons of cigarettes. Of course, all that caffeine and nicotine made it necessary to consume more Valium to steady my nerves and allow me to catch a few winks. As your tolerance to these substances builds, its amazing how much one can consume without being either asleep all the time, or just plain *crazy* most of the time.

Like most drug dependants, and that includes a 'healthy' percentage of health care professionals, I felt that my 'friends' enabled me to function at a higher level for longer periods of time. They also helped me forget how much I increasingly despised my personal life, resenting my wife Milly more and more for a multitude of reasons, some of which, I'm sure, were elevated in importance by my over-stimulated brain. And how clever, infinitely wise and witty you think you are when under the influence of a codeine product. You're just the smartest, funniest damned person anyone could meet. But if that were really true, we should prescribe codeine for every depressed, unfulfilled wretch we encounter in practice. In truth, the objective picture you present to the world is exactly the opposite of what you believe you are projecting. You are, in fact, obnoxious, at times cruel, not in the least bit humorous, and, most importantly, you are definitely not omnipotent.

How I functioned in this state is still a mystery to me. To the best of my knowledge, I didn't kill anybody with incorrect medication dosages, or inappropriate therapies. I somehow managed to deliver upwards of seven hundred babies without incident. Of course, I don't remember most of what transpired when there was a delivery, especially in the wee small hours of the am. Just as scary, I don't even remember the drive to the hospital. By all rights, I should have had a fatal car crash while speeding on the highway on my way to a delivery. I can only conclude that someone was watching over me, and I was supposed to survive for some reason: after all, how else could I have come out on the other side of all this physical abuse unscathed.

I never knew just how many of my colleagues had gone through the same difficulties with various substances; that is, until I began practice in Texas. In this state, and I'm sure the other forty-nine as well, the State Board of Medical Examiners publishes a quarterly report, naming I numerous physicians and mid-levels as regards their substance abuse problems. Licenses to practice are either suspended or revoked, and seeing this in black is chilling to say the least .. By this time however, I was no longer dependant on prescription drugs, and had even quit smoking. I remain, to this day, free of addiction to everything except my beloved caffeine.

Chapter 45

After seven years of busting my butt in Toronto it was not a difficult decision to leave Canada. If I had remained on the treadmill I was on, I firmly believe that I would have died before my allotted time on planet earth had expired.

One of my last vivid recollections of wintertime in Toronto was standing in line to see a movie, the bitter-cold sleet going right through my four layers of clothing. I turned to my friend Mark, and said "you know what Mark, this is actually a momentous occasion, because it's the last time I will ever stand outside in weather like this to see anything, even if it were an act of God. I'm sick of this place and its endless winter. This is my solemn vow----I am out of here for good!"

"Right Mel" replied my friend and colleague. "Listen, I know you you're fickle and a tad reckless with words, and I say you will be back here in less than three years."

Coincidently, the last movie we saw on that miserable night was 'Network', very appropriate considering the state of mind I was in. Peter Finch's famous line "I'm mad as hell and I'm not going to take it anymore" resonated loudly with me that night. Toronto had beaten me down and I too was mad as hell. Mark was wrong as rain: I, in fact, never returned to Toronto in the dead of winter----not for any reason. Thirty-one years of Canadian winters plus the increasingly socialized Canadian health system, was quite enough for moi!

Chapter 46

A Word About Malpractice

I am now in my thirty-sixth year of medical practice, during which time I have been named in only one malpractice action. This occurred in, of all places, Levelland, Texas, a dot on the West Texas landscape. I was there briefly in 1986-87, as a locum tenens (temporary help) for an ailing physician, a Dr. Cuesta. This was to be a short stop-over on my way to a permanent position awaiting me in Amarillo. Part of my duties in Levelland, aside from seeing Dr. C's office patients, involved covering the emergency room once a week. It was while working in the hospital's ER. that my one and only legal incident took place-the only blemish on my record as a physician, both in Canada and the U.S.A. As a matter of course, I realize that everyone proclaims them self innocent of wrong doing in any potential litigious action, but in this case, it is fair to say that I should have been held harmless. let me outline the events of that night and the subsequent fallout.

I was on duty one fateful evening in the emergency room, when an attractive young woman and her mother showed up, the daughter having been involved in a motor vehicle accident. Also present was the daughter's girlfriend, who had also been in the vehicle, but had gone unharmed probably because she was restrained. The daughter had been the driver, and her car head been rear-ended by a lighter and smaller vehicle. Unfortunately, she hadn't fastened her seat belt, and thus was propelled forward by the blow, her face hitting the steering wheel.

On examination, she had moderate swelling and tenderness of her nose, and the facial bones below her eyes. There was a small abrasion on the bridge of her nose, but no deep laceration. She was complaining bitterly of pain, way out of proportion to the rather minor injuries I observed. The X-Rays I ordered, which included several additional views of the nasal bones, in my judgment, revealed only a possible fracture of the tip of the nose, but nothing that would seem compatible to the degree of pain she was exhibiting. I informed the patient and her mother that the films were essentially negative for serious injury, save for a possible flake of bone avulsed from the tip of the nose. I added that the films would be read again in the morning by our radiologist, and if there was a difference of opinion, I would notify them right away. The reaction, by mom in particular, to my report was hostile to say the least. She was indignant that I had not found the real cause of her child's 'intolerable pain and suffering.' I was so naive in those days that I didn't see this little passion play for what it was: a prelude to a lawsuit.

I shrugged off her 'attitude', and finished my treatment of her offspring. Since she still had some nasal bleeding, I packed one side of her nose, and, because she didn't have a regular family doc, asked her to return in the morning to the ER, when I could remove the packing and recheck her injuries, as well as reporting to her on our radiologist's findings. Naturally, she did not return, and I never saw or heard from the patient or her mother again. But, several years later, when I was working in my own private practice in Amarillo, I most definitely heard from their attorney. It was a certified letter from the court in Hockley County. I opened the letter, and could hardly believe a word I was reading. I had been named in a lawsuit along with several other physicians and hospitals, the accusation being 'failure to diagnose' the young lady's 'extensive' injuries. According to the court document, she had suffered grievous trauma to her face, including a severely fractured nose, and terrible facial fractures requiring three surgeries to correct this horrific mess.

'Mommy Dearest' had taken her child to a high-priced plastic surgeon, a well known shyster I'll call 'Dr. Moneymaker.' When I had an opportunity to read his notes, I couldn't believe that I was reading about the same patient that I had seen four years prior. He described 'devastating' injuries to her face and nose that would require several surgeries to restore the anatomy to its pre-accident state. By this time, THREE Board Certified Radiologists had read her films, and she had had two more sets of X-Rays taken. Two of the three radiologists stated that they could detect no injuries whatsoever, while the third found only a minor flake fracture at the tip of the nasal septum, which is exactly what I had seen. So three capable, experienced radiologists could find no serious injuries in this young gal's face, which was in complete contradiction to the surgeon's documented findings. And yet, before me was this court document outlining the terrible mistakes that I and my colleagues had made, which begs the question: where in the hell did all of these 'devastating' injuries come from'?

The easy answer to that question would simply be that our friendly plastic surgeon had exaggerated the magnitude of the girl's injuries in order to line his own pocket by performing needless surgeries on her. I find that hard to believe in light of the discrepancies that existed between his notes and the actual X-Ray findings. And yet I hadn't seen any preoperative radiology reports to confirm his diagnoses, so there still remains that possibility.

The second, and most plausible theory that I could easily embrace as the truth, was that she probably had been involved in another 'accident', not necessarily of the motor vehicle variety. My guess is that some person or persons had popped her a few good licks in the face with their fists; but, just to be legally and politically correct, she may have accidentally walked into said fists.

After discussing the situation with the attorney assigned to my case by my malpractice insurance carrier, I felt confident that I could get my name removed from this action. Wrong again! The judge would have none of that, even after he had reviewed our brief, conclusively proving my innocence as regards this charge of 'failure to diagnose.' Against my wishes, my lawyer had entered into a settlement of the matter with the plaintiff's counselor. She explained that her first duty was to her employer the insurance company, and this would be the least expensive path to follow for them. Accordingly we settled the matter for a whopping fifteen hundred dollars! All that angst for a few measly bucks, right? Dead wrong as it turned out, because my name would now be forever ensconced in the National Data Bank. I didn't realize all the implications of that until a few years later. Now, whenever I apply for a new position or hospital privileges where I had previously not worked, I would have to give a detailed explanation of the circumstances surrounding this case. In other words, this would follow me everywhere forever since there is no statute of limitations when it comes to the Data Bank. What a pain in the ass!

As for our wonderful legal system, my innocence had nothing whatsoever to do with the outcome. Now I finally understood why so many of my colleagues practice defensive medicine, after all it's just the instinct for self-preservation. And furthermore, there is no need to wonder why the cost of medical care keeps rising when practitioners are ordering far too many expensive tests and medications for our patients to ensure that we have met our legal burden. The costs will continue to rise in concert with the size of malpractice awards, until our government officials finally have guts to do the right thing by first clapping awards at a reasonable level, and secondly, encouraging judges to throw out frivolous lawsuits. Fat chance that will ever happen, right? You'd have to search for that kind of political courage with a microscope.

Chapter 47

Back on the Road

If Florence was the 'City of Enlightenment' and culture, Venice was, well------not. Dirty water, dirty buildings, and pigeon shit everywhere, thus I'll label it 'City of Bird Shit.' Another charming sight was that of Italian sailors, who were always present in large numbers, chasing down foreign female tourists. I saw women literally running to get away from these louts. I thought I was actually going to witness a gang rape, but I did not. However, this was sexual harassment so I extreme, that, in America, there would be arrests and well deserved jail time. When your most vivid memories of a place are bird poop, and scumbag sailors running down women in open view of cops, I " think it time to love on. I think I'd rather frequent the fake Venice that exists today In Las Vegas----great atmosphere, great food, and good manners shown towards all guests by the employees. Also, there are beautiful people in abundance, and casino gambling, with no sign of bird crap anywhere. There's nothing wrong with opulence and good manners, but tell that to those Italian sailors.

So, leave Venice we did, thank God. Once again, we jumped into our trusty French vehicle, looking forward, not back. Better days lay ahead, of that we were sure. Even Mike, the eternal optimist, was less than thrilled with Venice, not to mention his near-death experience in Florence. Needless to say, he'd pretty much had it with Italy, so, instead of proceeding south to Rome, where we had been told it was a hundred degrees in the shade, we pointed the car north towards the Swiss border. As we approached Cortina, the views became increasingly spectacular. No picture can prepare you for the majesticbeauty of the Alps. After a brief overnight stay in Cortina, we made our way to Grindewald, not too far from the Matterhorn. We quickly located a youth hostel, and were more than satisfied with the view from our dorm window, the famous North Wall of the Eiger. Suddenly, I felt like writing a song or poem, but the end product would have been far too corny. Mike later got out his wonderful new guitar, and played some classic Gordon Lightfoot. "Song For a Winter's Night' was particularly appropriate for the setting. I, of course, couldn't play a lick, but when I was going through my second divorce in my midforties, I did fulfill my lifelong dream and learned to play guitar, although not with the proficiency of Michael Adams. I should add here that Mike had purchased this hand- made classical guitar in Barcelona for the incredibly low price of one hundred dollars Canadian. Today, that same instrument would set you back close to two thousand dollars were it purchased anywhere in North America.

I'll tell you how naive I was back then: I had no idea what a girl magnet the guitar was. That evening I found out! After our evening meal, Mike and I walked up the hill behind the hostel, and camped out at the top. Mike, as I said earlier, had his guitar, which he was seldom without on any given night, and was finger-picking Lightfoot, and other folk heroes of that era. I did my best to add some vocal harmony, which I think sounded almost decent. In short order, we were joined by a couple of gals from the hostel, who added a nice vocal chorus. Within ten minutes max, virtually all of the residents below had made their way up the hillside, and became a quite appreciative audience. Mike was suddenly thrust into the role of 'Swiss Stud Guitar Guy', surrounded by a bevy of really cute girls. They were lapping this shit up, and, quite unintentionally, I became the other happy recipient of this female attention. After all, we were a team, right? Share and share alike, that's my motto. It didn't occur to me right at that moment, but I soon realized just what a prick I had been. I mean, here I had been juggling three gals in Paris and elsewhere, and I hadn't had the presence of mind, the sheer decency, to share my 'good fortune' (dilemma) with my friend and traveling companion. I've been a selfish ass hole, and, as I said from the beginning, an egocentric, self-interested sack of shit. Shame on me!

Justice was served, and Mike got his just rewards that night. A beautiful German girl had latched onto him, and they really hit it off, so much so that they bedded down together back at H.Q. I felt so good for Mike and so ashamed of my previous behavior, that I couldn't have slept with any looker from anywhere. Instead, I slept with an ugly girl from anywhere. Now that's what I call sacrifice in the name of guilt.

Chapter 48

Germany damn this is a huge country, and it took what seemed forever just to get the hell out of it. Some places are hard to leave, try as you may. Finally, after two days of driving, we crossed the border into Holland. All the tension in my body suddenly disappeared, and I once again felt happy to be alive. Mike didn't feel quite as negatively about Germany as I did, but, still, he didn't seem altogether unhappy to be elsewhere. We trudged onwards toward Amsterdam, one tough city to navigate. By now, I fancied myself quite the trail guide, but I never quite figured out this layout. Consequently, we ended up going in circles quite a bit. We did, however, find the youth hostel recommended in our travel guide, 'Europe on Five Dollars a Day', the bible for us starving foreign students. As promised in the guide, it was clean, centrally located, and quite hospitable. As expected, it was another mini-United Nations of fellow student voyagers. Yes, I had met some interesting and diverse folks in hostels, and here, one person stood out from the rest. He was an Aussie named Stuart, and, like most of his compatriots that I had met on the road, he was charming and full of fun. All the gals at the hostel were obviously attracted to him: with his combination of charm and good looks, how could he miss? I confess that I was a tad envious of the tall, blonde-headed, elegant Aussie, but he was such a decent sort that petty jealousy was inappropriate. In fact, we became quite good friends over the next few, adventurous days.

It was Saturday night and a few of us headed for----where else in Amsterdam-----the Red Light District. I'd read and heard about Holland's legal prostitution, and I was anxious to see it for myself, having no realistic thoughts about an actual sexual adventure for a fee, especially given my current state of 'fee-less-ness.' The atmosphere was an illusion of gaiety and light-heartedness, for, in fact, this was dead serious business. Imposing looking pimps were everywhere in sight, protecting their 'investments.' Most of the hookers posed in picture-frame windows, or stood in their doorways, posing seductively in minimalist lingerie. It was a Victoria's Secret catalogue- come to life, with girls who were, for the most part, young and gorgeous---not the drugged-out, tired old hags one sees on the streets of most North American cities.

Mike was still feeling a little puny from his bout of pneumonia in Italy, so he stayed behind at the hostel, while I ventured out with my new Aussie friend, Stuart. We strolled through the streets of the District, checking out the fare on this menu, stopping dead in our tracks in front of a little brownstone house. It wasn't the charm of the house that made us stop, but, rather, it was what stood in the doorway of the house. She was a stunning creature, appearing to have a delightful mixture of Asian, Anglo, and, perhaps, a dash of African-American. There may have been several other components in this racial mix, but what did it matter when the end product was one of God's divine creations. Her name was Mika, although I suspect she had another, less exotic, handle. Stuart was obviously taken with her, and, with ridiculous ease, struck up a conversation with her. You'd think he had known her all his life, just old pals and all that. Damn those Aussies, they make it look so easy. And, to no one's surprise, she seemed to be eating this nonsense up, not like a hooker, but rather, like a teenage schoolgirl swooning over the campus stud. Sooner or later, this had to end in some type of business proposal, and, direct and honest to a fault, Stuart simply asked her "How much for a little romp?" Her mood shifted seamlessly into professional gear, as she replied that a 'normal service' would cost ten kroners. She did offer him a slight discount, given that he was one charming devil, and it would cost him a mere seven k. His casual and straightforward reply was classic Stuart.

"Well" he said, "you are very lovely and most desirable indeed, but I'm afraid that my budget won't allow for your infinite charms. However, I've thoroughly enjoyed meeting you and have a very pleasant evening. Cheerio for now then."

I never heard anyone talk like that to a woman in my entire life, and certainly not in a sexually charged environment. It was bloody unnerving, his total lack of self-consciousness and sheer cool. He was suave and sophisticated and I most decidedly, was not. I could barely muster the courage to utter a single word to this girl, let alone actually converse. I did manage a rather feeble introduction, which went something like: " Mika, my name is Mel" desperately trying to come off as confident. "Perhaps I'll see you again soon." How bold! I'm sure she'll remember me now. Right! I did, however, have a plan: I decided that I would indeed return-----on Monday night instead of a Saturday, which turned out to be a madhouse, with throngs of people of both sexes, and a few individuals of questionable gender. And the girls, along with their pimps, were especially eager to do volume business on the weekend. With fewer folks there Monday, I would be more relaxed, and able to pursue my goal with more ease-----to get laid for money. My first hooker---an exciting prospect to be sure. Quite a civilized way for a man to get rid of sexual frustrations I believe. After all, this is merely a business arrangement, with no potential for personal entanglements. Many marriages could be saved if a guy could summon, legally that is, a prostitute, instead of having the dreaded 'affair'. I can just hear the discussion between a married couple, nerves frayed, tempers about to flare:

He: "Sheila, we just aren't having much fun anymore, and certainly, not a hell of a lot of sex."

She: "Look Arnold, I work too you know, and I'm pretty damned tired at the end of the day. In spite of that, I have to cook for you and the kids and clean up around here, a concept foreign to you."

He: "I think you're just looking for excuses to avoid having sex"

She: "Hey buster, I'll have you know that I love sex, even with you, jerk-off, but I don't have as much energy at night as I used to. In other words, no way Jose, at least not tonight."

He: "With all I have to do and worry about----pay the bills, fix the plumbing, maintain the cars, chief landscaper and bottle washer, hell-I'm plenty tired too. But mostly, I'm stressed out, and sex is better than a god-damned Valium to relax me."

She: "Tell you what honey, why don't you call "Handy Hookers" and make your usual appointment. I'll concede that you do need a good lay, and I'm just too damned tired to service you right now. Okay?"

He: "Great idea babe, I'll call right now and set it up. Do you need me home at any particular time?"

She: "Eleven would be good; that way/I'll still be up and you won't wake me."

He: "Okay, great; I'll set it up."

She: "That's fine honey. I'll get supper ready now so you'll be on time.

Now, isn't that infinitely better than what could have happened here? A civilized solution to a common marital problem, that's all I'm saying. Envision this television commercial:

"Ladies, having a little down cycle in your marriage because of unreasonable sexual demands made upon you by your significant other? No problem----just have him call us at 1-800-GET LAID. We here at 'Handy Hooker Service are professionals, and, as always, confidentiality is unsurpassed. Let us perform the sexual acrobatics for him that you aren't available for right now. We guarantee his satisfaction, or your money cheerfully refunded. Oh and we must add that we are definitely not into pain; but all other options are available."

I surprised myself and returned to the red light district Monday night as planned. For once, I conquered and my lifelong inhibitions and cowardice, and took a lesson in courage from my friend Stuart. The scene was a marked contrast from Saturday night: hardly any tourists, but also, very few girls were on display. So I guessed right. I wasted no time, heading straight for the little brownstone house off the main drag, looking for that incredible creature I had met the other night. As luck would have it, she was one of the few gals doing business this lovely evening. What was even more shocking was the fact that she remembered me.

"Good evening Mel, how are you tonight?" she said. Trying my best to mimic Stuart, I replied "I'm doing just fine Mika, and might I say that you are looking particularly lovely. Have you been very busy?"

"Oh, it's very slow on Mondays Mel, so I have a considerable amount of time if you want it. What do you say?" I quickly lost my 'Stuart Cool' and answered: "Does the pope wear a funny hat? Sure, you bet, absolutely, terrific!"

What remarkable composure, eh? I'm sure that just impressed the hell out of her. Nonetheless, we went inside, and she fixed us some tea, a very nice gesture I thought. After some pleasant small talk, something I was never very good at, she took me by the hand and led me to her bedroom. Slowly, seductively, she undressed both of us. My manhood was in full bloom just watching her make the tea, so you can imagine where I was at this point. And then we got into bed and made love. I haven't used the 'f' word here because I really liked this girl, prostitute or not. To me, it felt as though we were, indeed, making love, not just fucking. When we were done, I got up and began to get dressed, but she made me an offer neither I, nor any male on this planet, could reject. She said that because it had been so slow, I could stay as long as I wished-----in fact, until daybreak.

What dumb fucking luck! St following my gut instincts and showing up on a slow Monday night, I had lucked into an all-nighter with the prettiest professional in the red light district of Amsterdam. Obviously, I need to trust my gut much more. I'm usually much too cerebral, which gives me the propensity to think myself out of some interesting possibilities. But not this time!!

I'm never cynical about sex and love when they occur simultaneously, but, separately, there can be room for humor and sarcasm. A good example of this was my relationship with my first wife. When she did feel love for me, it was never during sex; and there was always a hidden agenda when sex did occur, rare as that was. As for me, the only time I did feel any hint of love for her was during sex. Confusing hormones with love can be a very tricky business, and, in retrospect, occasionally quite amusing. I've loved many females for several minutes at a time, but, outside of sex, my feelings were' usually neutral: not negative, just blah. However, in this instance in Amsterdam, my lovemaking had no attachments or hidden agendas for either party; just total, guiltless pleasure. For that reason, I felt love as well as physical satisfaction. I loved this girl, but I wasn't in love with her, if that makes any sense. I could just be myself with her, no game-playing, no mental gymnastics. She made me forget completely that, after all, this was a business arrangement. Some businesses are more blessed than others I reckon.

The next morning, after the greatest night of my young life, Mika got up and made us breakfast. I was starving, and just devoured my meal with almost as much passion as my evening's sexual efforts. I can't remember being this happy and hungry at the same time. After eating, Mika excused herself, stating that she had many errands to run before work that night. Work!? Stark, ugly reality came crashing down all over me. Hey fool, this is merely a job to her, remember? But she continued to say that she would love to see me again the next time I was in town. Furthermore, I wasn't charged a penny for the past twelve hours!! Damn, maybe she actually enjoyed being with me!

Wait fool! This girl after all, is still a hooker! Stop these foolish ramble motions in spite of how kindly you were treated. Just take a deep breath and say goodbye like a man.

I did give her a big hug, said my farewell, and left knowing I would never forget this historic moment in my young life.

Chapter 49

1968

After leaving the Amex office, I made my way back to the hostel, where I immediately encountered my long-lost traveling companion, Mike. It seemed like a month since I'd last seen him I guess because so much had occurred in the past couple of days. .

"Slumming around again, eh Genraich" Mike good-naturedly queried. "I hear you've turned into quite the stud now, haven't you? I . suppose you're convinced that you're God's gift to women, right?"

"Okay, okay, you've had your fun with me Michael; and given that one of us didn't get laid last night, that's quite alright----I can take it."

"Rub it in asshole! Look, if you and you're tiny member have had enough pussy for awhile, maybe we can get on with this trip. We seriously need to plan our next few destinations. I need to get back on the road a.s.a.p. This place is boring as hell."

"Hey Mike, buddy, I wish you could have had some good times here, you know that don't you? I wouldn't want to upset you for anything. You're my partner in crime here, and, besides, I can hardly drive this damned standard shift vehicle. I need you buddy."

"Mel, shut the hell up already, would you? You've had your moments on this little journey, so maybe now it's my turn to make some, decisions, okay 'buddy'?

"Michael, mon ami, from now on you are 'The Man.' Let's move out."

I realized at that moment, that Mike was the last person on earth that I wanted to piss off because he is one stand-up guy. In Jewish, we call someone like him a 'mensch'. Roughly translated, that means a genuine human being---- a person of integrity and honor.

Chapter 50

Toronto 1977----THE VISIT!

I have two grown children from my first marriage, Blake and Ina. My first wife, Milly (Mirjam), has done a crackerjack job on these kids, convincing them that I'm the Antichrist, or, in this case, the Antimoses. This indoctrination occurred over many years, requiring persistent training by this woman, who I affectionately refer to as 'The Terminator'. Her methodology was not too dissimilar from the techniques depicted in the movie "The Manchurian Candidate", although I know that she is capable of infinitely more cruelty than that of the film.

I made the cardinal sin of leaving her, and no one dares defy her, let alone reject her. Such behavior is simply not acceptable nor tolerated, and, aside from myself, no one has dared to challenge her absolute authority: not her parents, not her sister, not her friends, not her children, and, finally, for fourteen rotten years, not even me. But that all changed as of July tenth, 1977. You see, that was the day I told her that I didn't love her, and, in fact, probably never had.

We were back in Toronto for a visit, our first trip back home since moving to Houston in January. I had reached the point that, in my heart of hearts, I knew this marriage was over; I just didn't have the guts and common decency to end it. Hey, they shoot horses don't they? Not until I got back to Toronto and ran into an old friend of Milly's, did the light go on. Her name was Lucille, but everyone called her Luci, and I considered her my friend as well, but I had to admit to myself that I always had had a little crush on her. She could make me laugh quite spontaneously with her quirky sense of humor, and she was sort of good-looking in her own Jewish way. She was a redhead, and a bit on the chubby side, but carried herself quite well. Most importantly, she was kind. What a stark contrast she was to Milly, who was many light years removed from kind. Our second evening back in Toronto, we drove over to Luci's apartment. I was rather looking forward to seeing her again, but also, I felt a tinge of excitement from where I know not.

Luci was from Connecticut, and worked, wouldn't you guess, as a social worker. She had a thick Brooklyn/Jewish accent with no hint of New England in there at all. Conversely, her sister and room-mate Elaine, had a pronounced Bostonian speech pattern, which I believed was exaggerated to make herself sound more sophisticated. Okay, so Luci was not your classic beauty, but the total package of physical and personality attributes, was appealing. And, as always, I was a sucker for redheads. She didn't have the' perfect' (read anorectic) figure to be sure, but I rather liked the way' her weight was distributed, everything in its rightful place. Now, would most guys say that Marilyn Monroe, definitely a full figured gal, was unattractive? I think not! Of course today's fashion mavens would probably consider her obese, but would you rather be seen with a cocaine-addicted, anorectic super model as depicted in all the famous ladies' magazines these days? Pretty darned appealing----so much so that it gives me erectile dysfunction just thinking about these wretched creatures. But I digress: so Luci was well put together, okay? And she was bright, witty, charming, kind, and considerate of others; in short, all the things my dear wife was not. I was really fond of this girl, but never before in a lustful way; at least not until I saw her on this particular night. Milly, who liked to take charge of everything including the vehicle', parked the car while I went up to Luci's apartment. I got off the elevator, and was about to knock on the door, but Luci beat me to it, and opened it first. An acute chemical reaction occurred when we saw each other, not unlike nuclear fission. It was intense and bewildering for me, and, I suspect, her as well. I gave her a big hug, and, seemingly from out of nowhere, planted a big, wet kiss firmly on her luscious lips.

I don't remember much more of the details of that night, except for a lot of furtive glances cast in both directions by Luci and I, while Milly, as usual, took command of the conversation. Since she was always anxious to seize control of any social interaction with others, I'm quite certain she had no idea of the silent communication that was taking place. After beaucoups of girl small talk, it was finally time to leave. Naturally, my bride left first to ensure her continued vehicular control, leaving me alone for a moment with Luci. Again, without a word spoken between us, we hugged and kissed with considerable passion. Such a sweet moment in my miserable life! It was delicious, and I was energized and reinvigorated for the first time in years. A strangely familiar sensation came over me, but at first I didn't recognize what was happening. Suddenly it dawned on me-----I was getting sexually aroused. I hadn't had an erection like this in years! It was better than an overdose of Viagra. In other words, the polar opposite of my marital sex life. Painful to contemplate, but there it was, summed up in this one brief moment of bliss.

I failed to mention earlier that Luci had been in one miserable, abusive marriage, and several unpleasant relationships had followed, including one that involved, once again, physical abuse. To me, it was unimaginable that some ass hole could lay a glove on this lovely human being. Sure, I'll admit to my profound naivety on this subject, but I'll put forth this rhetorical question anyway: why do men get so fucked up that they feel compelled to take out their misery and failures in life, on the weaker sex? Sometimes I feel ashamed to be a male when I hear of atrocities committed by such sick men.

Nowadays, these acts seem to occur so frequently, it makes me wonder why all women haven't become lesbians. Thank God Luci hadn't yet converted.

Standing in the hallway outside her apartment, I blurted out something like "I'm not sure what just happened, but I'm sure grateful for whatever this is. I need to call you tomorrow and talk this out. Please humor me, okay?"

"I want you to call me Mel" she replied. "I'm just as bewildered as you. I had no idea my feelings for you were anything but platonic. After all, you are my girlfriend's husband, for God's sake! Let me rephrase that------I'm actually a big liar. Truth be told, I've always felt drawn to you in some way, and now I know what way that is. Let's not say anymore tonight, alright? I need to sleep on it, and maybe some clarity will arrive by tomorrow morning. I'll be home between two and five; I'll expect your call, alright? Goodnight Mel, my dear friend. By the way, has anyone told you lately just how sexy you look? Bye for now."

"No to your question, and yes, I will call you tomorrow. I just hope I can get some sleep tonight after this."

And just like that, I was downstairs and in the car with Milly, "The Terminator." I suppose she was yapping at me about this and that, but I was lost in my own little warm, fuzzy world, replaying m

precious few moments with Lucy over and over again in my mind.

Tonight, Melvyn H. Genraich MD. returned to the land of the living. I had become invisible to my friends and family, and more importantly, to myself. I had been a lost and lifeless soul in need of resuscitation. My life had become passionless, and therefore had little meaning.

One must have some passion for life's precious gifts, but I had lost the thread connecting me to that principal. Instead, I had embraced monotony, drudgery, and, sexually, a hollow shell of a marriage with a soulless robot----a Chatty Kathy doll in the place of a human being.

That night, as expected, I didn't sleep a wink. I counted the hours until daylight, which seemed like an eternity away. When it finally arrived, I goofed around doing nothing in particular, while trying to look cool and nonchalant. Milly had gone shopping with her sister Florence, someone I actually had once thought of as a darned nice person. Unfortunately, she had spent far too much time with big sister, causing the inevitable deterioration of character, common decency, and kindness that one would have expected to occur. In short, by this point in time, she was pretty much fucked up!

The good new was that I was alone, and I could talk freely on the phone to arrange my meeting with Lucy. Three p.m. finally arrived, and, since I thought I'd try to seem cool, I called her at approximately one second past three. To cut to the chase, we arranged to meet at four at the Prince Hotel, not far from her apartment. I was nervous as hell, but at the same time, filled with adolescent anticipation. I couldn't wait to see her again, and kiss her, and hug her, and share all my sad, lonely stories with her. On second thought, I decided to skip the sad, lonely stories, and not taint the mood with downer rhetoric.

Chapter 51

The Rendezvous

She was sitting at the patio bar, and was looking just gorgeous. As the kids say today, she was 'styling.' And so, I might add, was I. I was feeling quite sexy, which surely must have deceived me into believing that I also looked damned sexy and even handsome. I certainly had my ego-inflated self pumped up for this historic rendezvous. I first gave her a big hug, but not too big so as not to put her on the defensive. I sat down beside her and ordered my usual Coke on the rocks. I like to live dangerously, on the edge so to speak, so I consume massive quantities of caffeine laced with Real Sugar. Risky stuff for yuppies, eh?

She leaned over and, still a little shocked by this whole situation, she kissed me. Instinctively, I kissed her back. After that moment, whatever cool I thought I had brought with me, vanished without a trace.

"This may seem like a spur of the moment thing" I said, "but I think I'm in love with you, and probably always have been. I've felt drawn to you, and I now can appreciate what I was feeling when I knew I'd be seeing you. I finally understand."

"Somehow Mel, I think that you're in love with the idea of being in love, especially since you seem so obviously miserable with Milly" she replied.

"Okay, I'll concede that there may be a little truth in that, but I can see and feel your apprehension which may be clouding your judgment. I know you feel strongly about me too, or else why would you be here? Here's what I really think. I think that we've had a strong mutual attraction for years, but never acted on it for obvious reasons. Let me just lay it out for you-----I don't love my wife, and, come to find out, I never have. I'm not saying that because I'm infatuated with you, or simply horny. After moving away from here and gaining some perspective, I can now see quite clearly the person I'm married to, and believe me, it's not a pretty picture. It's just plain over between us. I feel nothing for her, and all I want is to be rid of this -miserable bitch."

"Mel, I would appreciate it if you would avoid the derogatory remarks about my friend and your wife, okay? Having said that, let me try to be completely honest with you. Yes, I care for you deeply, and I am strongly attracted to you. But you're not exactly available now, are you?" Of course she was right on the mark.

"That can be fixed quickly" I replied. "I'm filing for divorce the second I get back to Houston. This charade of a marriage is over, finito, kaput! Conversely, I think you and I have a real shot at something special here, and I don't think we should blow it off. These opportunities come rarely in a lifetime, and I say, Lucy, you've got to embrace and accept them for what they are-----uncovered treasure.

All I'm asking you is to be patient and wait for me to do what I have to do. Hell, its taken us seven years to get to this place, where we recognize that we love each other. What's another few months, for God's sake?" After a few minutes of silence, Lucy finally spoke:

"Okay Mel, you do have me there. We have waited a long time for honesty to surface about our feelings. Although I can't believe I'm saying this, and never thought I would or could, I do love you with all my heart. Milly's a fool who doesn't remotely appreciate you for the great person you are. Now that is something I've observed for quite a while on her part. You obviously have so much to give that I would consider myself lucky as hell if I were the one you wanted to give your love to. 50, to answer your original question in this roundabout way, yes Mel, I'll wait for you and do my best to be patient. Just one more thing though----I'm scared as hell!!!!!"

"And you think I'm not? Like this situation with my wife is easy for me?" I said.

"No, I know this must be very traumatic for you. I understand what you're going through. I guess we've all been there in our lives at some point" she said .

And with that, we finished our drinks, kissed one last delicious time, and said good-bye, for now at least. I said that I would call her as soon as I got back to Houston. I watched her walk to her car and drive off. I hadn't been this happy since I learned how to masturbate. Seriously, it had been a hellish long time between passions, and I was savoring every second. The flip side of the coin was the dread I felt contemplating the inevitable confrontation with 'The Terminator.' I'd rather have a root canal without local.

Chapter 52

January 3, 2006

Last night my wife Debbie informed me that, after who was a particularly satisfying sexual interlude for both parties, did not actually know where her clitoris was. Now that's a j thirty-five plus years as a medical doctor, and thousands of, exams, how on earth could I have forgotten where that little sucker was? Not to mention, I have been with a few women in my almost sixty years, and not once had I heard a disparaging word about my knowledge of female anatomy. Instead of getting angry, I made a brilliant recovery by suggesting to her that she allow me to continue searching for the next few nights, and then, maybe, I'd get lucky and find it.

Chapter 53

Paris Redux

Holland was swell, but Paris once again beckoned. Now that has a nice poetic ring to it, doesn't it? Actually Suzanne beckoned, and hopefully she would be in Paris when I arrived back there. Mike was getting antsy to move on anyway, so we packed up the ever dependable Deux, Cheveaux, and got back on the road, heading towards France. As best as I could tell, Mike had been having a good experience in Europe, aside from his near fatal bout of pneumonia in Italy. However, Mike was a tough one to read: his highs weren't very high, and his lows weren't too low. Mr. 'Even Keel,' that's him, but he's been really good for me since he is the antitheses of manic-depressive personality, my special gift. Just by being the steady, faithful, and dependable person he was, he's brought some sanity to all the peculiar goings-on in my life during this trip. When I have needed an uncommon degree of friendship and good-will, he's been there-----my rock, so to speak.

As I said earlier, I didn't really know what to expect from Mike since we weren't close friends back at school. I found him to be friendly, in a superficial, passing sort of way, but now, what a pleasant surprise. I promised myself that when I looked back on this adventure in years to come, I would always remember, what a great person Michael Adams was. I can only hope that someday he has a chance to read this, and come to know what high esteem I held him in. If I go on much longer about Mike, you'll think I'm gay, so I'll stop here and just say 'Mike, I hope you're alive and well, and happy as hell!' (No offense intended EEOC, ACLU, and gay activists everywhere.)

Onward we plodded, south through Holland, and down into Belgium, bypassing Brussels since we simply didn't have enough time to do justice to another major city. After what seemed like an eternity, we found ourselves back in Paris, travel weary as hell. Frankly, I remember very little of the countryside we'd driven through from Amsterdam, because my mind was focused on two goals: first, to see Suzanne again, and second, to simply get some rest.

We easily found our quaint little walk-up apartment on the Left Bank, complete with grouch old madame. It felt like we had arrived home. God, I loved Paris, and, someday, I know that I must return, to show 'my city' to my darling wife Debbie. After getting my few belongings put away, Even though I had to urinate badly, I immediately grabbed the phone to give Suzanne a ring. You know how it is when you are so excited to see someone that you overlook any discomfort, right? Besides, there was always the bidet in the center of the 'living room' for emergencies. Enough basic physiology, and on to my calling my Danish friend. I must confess that after Amsterdam I was feeling a little guilty, even though I had made no specific commitment to Suzanne. Somehow though, I feel that I let down. Don't you hate it when guilt is such an annoyance?

So, I rang her hotel, but she wasn't in. I then decided to get out and just walk the streets to clear my road-weary head, and hopefully, to exorcise all traces of guilt about Amsterdam. Mike went straight off to the Louvre to continue his tour of that majestic museum. I have to admit that I never was big on museums, especially those that occupy several city blocks, thus we went our separate ways as was our established custom.

That brings to mind, unfortunately, an embarrassment I'll never live down. The first time in Paris, Mike and I headed from our hotel over to the Champs Elysee, the Louvre being our destination fa the day. That was one damned long walk! I had naively thought that Paris was rather small and quaint: wrong bucko! It's a major city, fool, and you should have driven. Oh well, nothing about this walk was boring or unpleasant to look at. Finally, I spotted a huge building with an equally huge sign that read 'The Louvre' on the top floor.

"Hey Mike, look---we finally made it" I said with some relief.

"I'm not so sure Mel, that doesn't look like much of a cultural icon to me."

To make a long story short, Mike was right: this was not 'The Louvre,' but rather, this was, in fact, the Louvre Department Store. How terribly clever of me, eh what? I felt like the biggest hick on the planet for a few minutes. To be honest, since that incident remains with me to this day, I still feel a bit like a hick, albeit an educated one. Oh well, at least I don't spit n' chew.

On the second go-round, I did know where the Louvre was, but that was not my destination. I was bound and determined to hook up with Suzanne, although I didn't know at that moment exactly where she was. As I approached her hotel, I suddenly felt a sense of apprehension and even fear, that this beautiful creature would ultimately reject me. My old friends, self-doubt and insecurity, were creeping back into my sick, neurotic mind. How could she be remotely attracted to me? After all, I was kind of geeky all through high-school. Med school was some improvement, but I still hadn't really connected with the better looking gals. Oh sure, there always was a supply of young ladies who were seeking something other than studs-----they wanted to marry a doctor, or future doctor. That is not a cliche friends; I've seen unfortunate looking male med students hanging out with some of the real lookers on campus. I guess they were just more conniving and manipulative than I could ever be, so they got to home plate while I was still stranded on second base.

Of course, there was always the lovely Linda, but I think she's been playing me for some time now, just biding her time until her real lover-boy materialized. Intuitively I've know this, but damn it, I was still drawn to her for some reason. Who am I to try to explain chemistry, given that countless writers of exquisite literature have failed miserably at defining that special something that attracts one person to another.

The most important lesson I'm learning now is to trust my instincts; they're usually right on target. The Linda situation will sort itself out, one way or another, when I get back home. Until then however, I'm concentrating on one special young lady------Suzanne Holke from Copenhagen, Denmark. Screw doubts and insecurities and just go for it for once in your miserable life------that's what I was repeating to myself as I strolled through Paris on that beautiful mid-August morning. I must admit though, that in Suzanne's case, it was quite difficult to sort out the real person inside from the timeless physical beauty on the outside. Was I just conning myself into believing that she was all things wonderful, or was I just so hormonally challenged, that rational thought didn't enter into it at all? Ah, the eternal question of what constitutes love continues to plague me. Ironically, for me, that had never posed much of a dilemma because I hadn't known that many truly beautiful women in my young life; at least not in an intimate way.

Sadly, I never caught up with Suzanne again that summer; not in Paris, nor anywhere else in Europe. However, I did see her one more time a little over one year later---in my home town of Toronto no less, and with no advance notice. Suffice it to say, I was more than surprised to see her after all the time that had passed since last we were together.

Chapter 54

Back to London

I was deeply disappointed (and depressed) not to have seen Suzanne one last time before heading home. I couldn't imagine what had happened. Was this the proverbial brush-off, or just an innocent misunderstanding? Oh well, I can't dwell on this or, almost certainly, my insecure, paranoid tendencies will override my normally rational thought process. Besides, we had to move on and get back to London. The summer was almost over, and our return to Canada was imminent.

Mike and I dropped our trusty Citroen off at the designated site, and took the train to Calais, where we would catch the ferry to Dover. Unbeknownst to me, the English Channel was and is one of the roughest bodies of water on earth. That crossing. ranks as the worst short trip of my life, before or since. Talk about nausea, this was akin to chemotherapy sickness. However, I remain proud to this day of the accomplishment of not tossing my cookies on that nightmarish Channel crossing. Most everyone else on board was hanging their heads over the side, losing all stomach contents and then some. Funny thing though, there's always a handful of folks who have a gastrointestinal tract lined with steel. They can drink large quantities of alcoholic beverage, smoke, and eat anything with no serious consequences; all the while, laughing their collective asses off at the rest of us poor, sick souls. I hated those damned jerks.

The singularly most beautiful sight I could imagine presented itself at daybreak----the white cliffs of Dover. I would soon be back on terra firma, thank God. It seemed like an eternity until we finally docked and departed the boat. I was shaky and vertiginous at first, but soon regained my balance, and lost the nausea. Mike, damn him, was one of the 'steel stomachs,' and I wasn't about to talk to him until he apologized for teasing me unmercifully during and after our passage. We actually had a good laugh about it some time later, and he did express some sympathy for my "pathetic lack of sea legs."

When we got into London proper, Mike and I went our separate ways-------no fanfare, no tearful goodbyes, just "see ya back home buddy." Mutually, there was no sentimentality, just a feeling that we each had shared a great experience with a pleasant companion. I thought to myself 'there goes that cool, cautious person again, retreating back into himself a unique and, at the same time, strange individual. But, as I've said before, he was one hell of a travel mate no whining, bitching, or temperamental nonsense: a straight arrow indeed. He was just what I needed as a counterbalance to my intermittently unstable, over-reactive personality. I was definitely not a straight arrow, just a slightly crooked one.

I didn't see Mike again until we got back to Toronto. Strange as it may sound, we never again had a close relationship, not even reminiscences over a cup of coffee about our strange and wonderful journey. That was Mike, nothing personal on his part at all? Just a different breed of person.. I'd summarize Mike by simply saying that he was a very decent but strange guy.

Chapter 55

Back to London. (ctd.)

It was the first week of September in London, England, and the weather was magnificent. I could almost forget that in six days I would be flying home: home to my final year of medical school, and all the work and responsibilities that that entailed, home to my overbearing parents, and last, but not least home to my screwed up girlfriend. No more' Mr. Carefree, European Student-Tourist. No more go where the wind blows you. No more stay or leave on a whim.

My first time in London consisted of landing at Heathrow, and making a mad dash to Gatwick to catch the commuter plane to Copenhagen. This time around, I really was in London proper, and I could take my time seeing the sights. I had been quite frugal in my travels, and thus had a little extra change to see a London play, and even eat a few decent meals. I soon found out that finding decent food in London wasn't that easy to locate, but the theater district was just fine. Of course, going to a big-time Broadway play was more of a couples' thing to me, and I wasn't sure if I wanted to do that alone. Not to mention that, after a big night on the town, one might expect the pleasure of your gal's company for the balance of the evening. So the thought of flying solo for such an evening was, a tad depressing, given that the evening would conclude without any female companionship to provide a happy ending.

Having decided to ignore as best I could, my hormonal urges, I strolled over to the Strand, or, The Theater District. As I proceeded slowly down the street, I suddenly became aware of a familiar figure walking towards me on the opposite side of the street. I'll be damned--- it was Linda! My first knee-jerk instinct was to run over to her, sweep her up in my arms, and kiss her flush on the lips, something I hadn't thought of doing for some time. But I needed to play it far more cautiously this time around; stop the needy, clingy bullshit. Besides, these romantic feelings may simply be a manifestation of being alone for the first time all summer.

Guess what happened next? She lost her cool, ran across the street, and gave me a big hug and kiss, all of which was totally unsolicited! And then she spoke, a little shaky and weepy of all things.

"I'm overwhelmed to see you Mel, I've missed you terribly; I didn't realize how much until I saw you a minute ago." She was half sobbing and half laughing, a state I've never seen her in the three or so years I've known her. This was an enormous amount of emotion for this girl, and it caught me completely off-guard. In fact, I was speechless from shock, but still savoring the moment.

We hugged and kissed for some time, creating obvious irritation amongst her band of groupie friends. One gal even had the nerve to say "see you back at the hotel Linda, if you can ever break that death lock with your boyfriend."

Intellectually, I knew this was never, ever going to work out, and a tragic denouement was inevitable. On the other hand, I was still emotionally involved far too much------don't ask me why. I guess the heart sometimes wants what the brain knows is impossible. We walked back to my hotel, and she elected to spend the night with me. I desperately wanted to make love to her, but she was not having any part of total physical commitment, not now and not in the past. I wasn't that naïve about this. Obviously, any girl of her age and background had already had plenty of sex, so virginity was long gone. She just didn't want that degree of intimacy with me, which said it all. But I still wanted her to be close to me, and I didn't mind all that much that sex wasn't on the menu on this particular evening. I needed a warm body beside me for the night, and, by God, that's what I had and I was content with that. But in the morning, I was torn between telling her to get the hell out, and getting down on my hands and knees to thank her for spending the night. How fucked up was that?

Linda and I had breakfast downstairs in the hotel, and afterwards, bid each other adieu. We vowed to see each other the second I got back to Toronto (she was preceding me home by three days.) As a matter of fact, she insisted that I call from the airport to let her know I'd made it home safely. That sounded loving and considerate, didn't it? I promised her that I would call right away, as she, not I, insisted I do.

You know how some things, for whatever irrational reasons, just feel right? Well, this wasn't feeling that way at all. One way or another, things will sort themselves out back home, but this vague discomfort I was experiencing concerning Linda was haunting me.

Chapter 56

Homeward Bound

The remainder of my time in London is just a blur to me now---I just wanted to get the hell home. I finally had had it, first, with the 'Accidental Tourist' bit, and, a close second, was the crummy English food. The capper to all my angst was the insanely steamy hot weather in London. Great luck, eh what? The best moment I had that last time in London, was just getting to the airport and parking my ass in my seat on the plane. Looking around inside the cabin, I saw many familiar faces of weary fellow students. They all appeared to be as ready as I was to say good-bye to Europe. We collectively knew that the time had come to get home after a long, eventful summer. I spotted my faithful travel buddy Mike, and we reminisced about the many gifts that summer had presented to us, especially the gift of camaraderie. We realized how much we had appreciated each other during this great adventure that we had been fortunate enough to experience.

Once I took my seat, and, before I had time to think about it, we were aloft. Within minutes, I fell into a deep sleep. Sleep deprivation had finally taken its toll on me. When I awoke, the mainland of Canada was just coming into view------what a beautiful sight. It's always good to come home regardless of where home is-that much I have learned in my travels over the past thirty plus years.

My parents picked me up at the airport, by which time I was wide awake. As a matter of fact, I couldn't shut-up for the entire trip home. There was so much to talk about, but some details were best left unsaid. Considering, after all, that these were still my parents, I had to censor certain stories of the road. One subject that I couldn't help but talk about at some length, was my Danish beauty queen 'girlfriend', Suzanne. The folks were surprisingly curious about her; I guess I made her sound too good to be true, which was saying a lot since my parents, like most typical Jewish moms and dads, didn't think any girl was good enough for their precious Jewish son; certainly not a non-Jew.

I hasten to add that they also were not too crazy about Linda, which, in retrospect, was quite perceptive of them. They instinctively knew that she wasn't right for me, and was probably just playing me.

After arriving home, I melted into bed. Mother woke me to eat supper, which I devoured like a starving animal. Immediately thereafter, I rang Linda as per her request. To be completely honest, I wasn't dying to talk to her, or see her for that matter, Oh, and did I mention that I completely forgot to call her from the airport? She had obviously become much less of a priority, something I hadn't realized until now. The phone rang, and she answered it, sounding genuinely happy to hear from me.

"Mel" she said, "why didn't you call me from the airport like you said you would?"

"Gee Linda, it was such a madhouse there, and I was so terminally exhausted that all I wanted to do was get home and hit the sack. Sorry, I know I promised. Tell you what, why don't I come over right now and see you?"

"Uh, listen Mel, now would be a really bad time, alright? How about in a couple of days; I've got company from out of town. I'm sure you can understand, right?"

"Are you shitting me? What's the problem, don't you think I'm good enough to meet your out-of-town company?" I was steamed! This was obvious baloney, and I knew it. This had gone on far too long, and I had to confront it stat! Besides, she was the one insisting on my calling her asap, not me.

"Linda, I'm coming over right bloody now, comprenez? No more conversation is necessary until I get there, so just stay put and I'll be there in a minute." Actually, it was more like fifteen minutes by car, but details are irrelevant when your blood is boiling. I didn't give her a chance to reply; what was the point? This relationship had finally come to an ugly end; all that was missing was the funeral.

Wait a minute: why was I so damned angry? I always knew that this day would come, so what's the commotion? Rejection isn't easy for anyone to take, especially me. And her pathological lying was hurtful and an insult to my intelligence. Of course she had a boyfriend on the side, and was just diddling me along for male companionship. So the question has to be/is ego and pride the real issues here, and not whether or not I actually loved this person? Vision, through the retrospect a scope is always twenty/twenty, and thus from my current vantage point some thirty years later, naturally it was a deflated ego and rejection that were my real issues, not love.

Chapter 57

The Confrontation-At Last

When I arrived at Linda's house she was waiting outside on the front porch, fearing, I'm sure, an embarrassing confrontation in front of her family and 'guests', God forbid. I asked her to take a walk with me in her neighborhood which she did, obviously relieved that this would remain a private matter. The next thirty minutes consisted of a continuous rant on my part, whereby I finally relieved myself of three years of pent up frustrations. Her response to this tirade was complete silence, which confirmed my worst fears. Everything I suspected was true indeed. Our relationship had, at least for her, merely been a convenience: I was Mr. Reliable---a date for all occasions, when her true love interest was unavailable. When I had finished my verbal assault, she asked if I was alright, and you know what? For the first time in three long years, I was really feeling great. An enormous sense of relief had come over me as this tremendous weight was lifted off my shoulders.

In the end, all I could do was wish her well in her life, and, as for my life, I would carryon unburdened by a doomed relationship. This was the classic anti-climactic conclusion----no hostility in sight. And I drove off, I knew with absolute certainty that our paths would never cross again. The learning curve continues, and, hopefully, one day, I will be better prepared to deal with such ambiguous, deceptive, and thoroughly unethical folks, while at the same time, remaining optimistic that there is someone out there who is perfect for me, and hopefully, I won't need E-Harmony.com to find her.

At least the evening wasn't a complete loss. I gave my friends John and Shalom a call, and we all met down at the local pool hall. I felt so incredibly lighthearted that I even laughed at John's bad jokes. John was in engineering and Shalom was just your basic dorky genius. I don't use the word 'genius' frivolously, because, without question, it applied to this fellow. He was at the top of his class in MP&C (math, physics and chemistry.) This was the most grueling test of academic skills in any top tier university, but didn't pose much of a challenge for Shalom. I could only imagine what the future held in store for him----probably a Nobel prize for one. Aside from his academic prowess, Shalom also possessed a keen sense of sarcastic humor, which I thoroughly appreciated since that was my specialty as well. His friendship was something I valued highly in my life. I didn't have the same trust in John, who was more frivolous in his relationships with both sexes, and I didn't feel that I could confide in him and still maintain confidentiality in all things personal.

After shooting pool, and sharing some good conversation over coffee at a local diner, I finally left them and went home. I slept as peacefully as I had in a very long while. Free at last!

Chapter 58

A Word About Depression.

I am fifty-six years old-----bearing down hard on sixty. Now that, in and of itself, is not depressing. What is depressing, however, is that I still haven't found my permanent 'home', the one place I can spend the rest of my life and be perfectly content. My personal life, ironically, is as good as it has ever been-----I'm deeply in love with my third wife, Debbie, and I know, without question, we will endure. This is not about marital woes, as it was in the past.

We are about to leave Monahans, Texas and head for Levelland, a town about twice the size. Levelland even has a well-attended community college, South Plains College, and, with this younger population aboard, things there seem to be a lot livelier. I've lined up a job with, I believe, great potential, and have signed a five year contract to serve as medical director for a community health center.

The salary and benefits are quite good, and one would expect this situation to bring with it a sense of stability and financial security. So then, what's the problem? Change, that is the issue! Once more into the breach of change I go, and it's bloody nerve-wracking, not to mention expensive and depressing as hell!

At the end-of-year Christmas party at Carolyn's house, she made quite a show of handing out bonus checks to herself and her two partners. Debbie didn't even get a simple 'thank you,' let alone a bonus. But we understood what that all was about: jealousy,insecurity, and a healthy dose of greed. But Carolyn had one major flaw superseding all others-----she coveted what others had that she did not, and I'm not referring to anything material. You see, Debbie has a faithful, devoted husband------namely me; whereas

Carolyn does not. Maybe that's why she's been a tad crazy -- her husband screwed around on her a few years ago, almost terminating the marriage. I rather liked Carl, her hubby, and, sadly for him I think, he returned to the fold. I say sadly because rumor has it that he really loved the 'other woman' in question, Of course, he did an about-turn primarily to continue living the good life thanks to Carolyn's share of the family fortune. He made his decision based on a practical assessment of his material needs, something I would never do. But Carl was a bright guy, and I'm sure that he thought this through quite analytically, opting for the economically expedient path in life, while discarding the notion that true love might be infinitely more satisfying. He seemed content with his decision, while his wife remained an insecure mess over his dalliance, exacerbating her already fractured ego. I believe tha,7even had this not occurred, Carolyn would still never be without a few loose screws upstairs.

I didn't mean to get off on this Carolyn tangent, but it does illustrate a point. Who can you really count on and trust in this world? Your supposed old friends? I think not! Acquaintances about town? Your spouse? In some cases, as I have illustrated, nope! So, who and what is there to miss when I leave? Well, no one really, except for those nice folks I work with at the clinic. They may live in a trailer park or a run-down house on the wrong side of town, but they are not trashy. Class is determined by character, not bank accounts or fancy homes, and these folks are indeed classy, salt of the earth types. Leaving, them will be difficult, and getting used to yet another group of clinical personnel difficult, just tedious and I dread it. Now that is the part of my depression that I can fully understand. Anytime you move out of your comfort zone, whether it's a job change, or a difference in geographic location, it is a major upheaval. Well, this too shall pass.

Chapter 60

Present Time

My wife Debbie, sleeps the sleep of angels--- no doubts, no fears, no cares or worries, just delicious sleep. I, on the other hand, remain awake with all my usual neuroses. Maybe that's the major difference between Jews and Christians-------we worry while they sleep. Of course we have every right to be paranoid. After numerous attempts to wipe us out by Arabs, Russians, Germans and Jewish mothers, we're still here, but we worry that someday we wont be. Gentiles worry not about their ability to continue to exist in a position of dominance. The sun will never set for them; or so they think. But maybe the Chinese, Hispanics, Africans, Muslims and Hindus, will have something to say about that. White, Anglo-Saxon Christians are rapidly becoming a minority group in most countries of the world. SO why are they so damned smug, confident of perpetual superiority? While they have their two point two children per family, the so-called minority groups are multiplying at the speed of light. Birth control----what's that white man? Maybe none of us, Jew and Gentile alike, should sleep so peacefully.

But I digress: I meant to talk about neuroses that plague me and keep me awake not about world order. If I didn't have A.D.D. I could stick to the subject at hand.

Chapter 61

Serving My Time----2001

While in Levelland, I part-time job at the West Texas State School, in reality a juvenile detention center (prison) in the middle of Nowhere West Texas (Pyote.) There I will do my best to look after my young' hoodlums, as I affectionately call them. These kids are the definition of lost losers, not that I feel particularly sorry for any of them. They have committed some pretty heinous crimes to be the guest of the state, and, whenever you are with them, you must never. for a second/lose sight of that fact. At a tender age, most have become con artists, liars, thieves, and, in some cases, murderers. So what the hell am I doing here you might ask? Making a Gd-----ed living of course, that's what! For a hundred and twenty-five dollars an hour, I'd look after Osama Bin Laden. Well, perhaps that's a stretch, but but you get the general idea here that I am being very well compensated, and God knows, I need the money. Or, should I say my good old Uncle Sam needs his back taxes paid asap.

Institutional medicine institutionalizes everyone in and around it---- nurses, doctors, custodians, clerical staff, and administrators, everyone! Eventually we all become desensitized to our surroundings, and develop a great denial system which allows us to rationalize our being there in the first place.

What medical problems I see there essentially add, up to much ado about nothing; which is to say that ninety-five percent of all the complaints are bullshit. These kids just want the following: 1) to break up their mundane routine for just a little while; 2) get out of any physical activity besides eating; and 3) obtain any kind of medicine or medical supply that they can use to barter or bribe their fellow inmates. It took me a

153

couple of weeks to catch on to the 'game,' but I think that I now have the proper cynical attitude and perspective required for this job. Despite my financial needs, I've come to despise these miserable few hours a week, and I anxiously await the miracle that will commute my sentence. This will occur, of course, only when I win the lottery.

So, after two divorces, two bankruptcies, a disaster of a job in Oklahoma, I've become much more open-minded as to where I'll work' to make a decent living. Next thing you know I'll be attempting rehabilitation for drug lords in a crack house for a lousy couple of bucks.

The best part of this half-day's labor is leaving the facility! It feels more like two days work then just four or five hours. As for my cynicism, most of these kids will never get their life back on track; in fact, almost all the occupants are repeat offenders, with little to no desire to alter the course of their futures. Not being terribly Liberal, my attitude boils down to just two words: fuck 'em!

Chapter 62

Suddenly Single

My divorce from wife number one was, in a word, brutal. In essence, it punished me financially for initiating a long overdue parting of the ways. Truth be told, I was so relieved, and at the same time, euphoric, that I gave her and her 'butch' attorney, almost everything they had demanded. For me, this was a seminal event, foreshadowing a painfully slow, downward financial spiral that would haunt me for the next ten years, culminating in bankruptcy court. Yes Virginia, doctors can and do go bankrupt too, and there is no Santa Claus to bail you out. As painful as the financial consequences were, it couldn't compare to the loss of my children. Before the ink dried on the divorce decree, my ex fled the country, children in tow, heading for the sanctuary of Toronto, Canada. That marked the end of my life as a parent. My children would detest me for the rest of my life, thanks to 'the evil one;' and I'm not referring to Osama Bin Laden. The C.I.A. could take lessons from my first wife on the art of brainwashing.

Single life at forty-should have been a blast, but that was not my reality. The euphoria of finally extricating myself from a lousy marriage ,wore off quickly, and I realized that being utterly alone was not for me. I found myself sinking deeper and deeper into a state of depression, even, though I knew that the only rational thing to do was to be alone and learn how to be happy with just me. I guess I never was very good by myself. I knew that achieving contentment and self assurance had to come from within, not from external factors. After all, isn't that what all the self-help books say? But I just couldn't embrace the concept of being happy all alone. Enter wife number two!

Chapter 63

Two Strikes and Counting----Wife #2

At the tail end of my stay in Houston (no pun Intended,) I was 'The Lonely Guy,' single and utterly alone. My work was satisfying, and my clinic prospered, but something was missing like a life for example. My office was in a renovated house owned by the dentist across the street from me, one Jim N. He was a tall, lanky fellow, seriously laid back in the fashion of one who did a lot of grass. We became quite friendly, but not bosom buddies by any means. It's hard to be friends with an alien, albeit a pleasant one.

Jim was sort of married, he being quite the ladies' man. He could make anyone feel at ease, and was one of the all-time great bullshitters. He could have been a hell of a snake charmer, but his forte was attracting gorgeous women. What a bevy of beauties he had working for him at his dental office; and it was obvious to me that they all adored him. I found it interesting that his wife worked part-time at the office, and was no slouch in the looks department as well. I always felt that they had a certain arrangement between them concerning the concept of open marriage. Her manner seemed as promiscuous as his, but I could never sense any animosity between them.

One day, over lunch, Jim told me he had a girl 'friend' he thought I might like. Her name was Bevin, and he described her in glowing terms. She was, according to Jim, tall, with long, dark hair, great legs, and brains to match. I told him that she sounded like someone he'd like to have an affair with, or had already had an affair with, but he just scoffed at that insinuation saying that they had just been good friends. Baloney, I thought, but what the hey, it wasn't exactly hard to clear my upcoming social calendar and make room for a date with 'Beautiful Bevin.' Jim gave me her number and encouraged me to give her a ring.

That evening, after several hours of guitar therapy, I finally worked up the enthusiasm to call her. She did sound very nice indeed, and, in particular, she had a great laugh. I love people with good laughs, even though, ironically, I hardly ever laugh spontaneously. Perhaps I've been joyless most of my life, or just plain depressed. What a terrible thought. At any rate, we had a very good first chat, and, with Jim's picture of her firmly planted in my brain, I asked her out for dinner the following evening. She accepted the invitation without any hesitation. This just might turn out quite well I thought. Finally I had something to look forward to, a most welcome change. Up to this point, the only love affair I'd had was with my always faithful acoustic guitar. Funny, I had always wanted to play guitar, and when my first marriage turned sour, I bought a cheap guitar and took a few lessons. I was hooked immediately, and have remained so to this day.

Work went well the next day, especially since I knew I had a date that night. When I got home, I called Bevin, and we discussed dinner plans. I knew that the Grammy Awards were on the tube that night, so I suggested we come back to my apartment after dinner to watch the show. She was more than agreeable to that plan, and even said she would drive over to my place and we could go from there. I thought that was most considerate, especially given that this was after all, our first date. How accommodating.

She certainly was punctual, as the doorbell rang at precisely seven-thirty. When I opened the door was surprised to find that Jim's description of her was spot on. She was, in fact, drop-dead gorgeous, with the greatest smile I had seen in a very long time. And as if that weren't enough, she was most amicable-----a sweet, good-natured sort. She put me at ease immediately. After some get-to-know-you chit-chat, we headed out to the Chinese restaurant we had agreed upon. The conversation over dinner went very well, an- with this gal, my normal first date jitters were all but absent.

After dinner, as planned, we came back to my apartment, and settled in to watch television. A few minutes into the Grammy show, I spontaneously leaned over and kissed her flush on the lips. For once in my life, I didn't think or debate with myself about doing something I really wanted to----I just did it. She didn't flinch, almost as if she was expecting it. We soon found ourselves naked and in bed, making love. Now this is my idea of one great first date------no doubts, no fears, no hesitation, just good clean fun between two very horny adults. Since it was Friday night, she stayed over and we alternated between sleep and sex all night long. In the morning she got up and made breakfast. What a gal! I really needed a night like this, and the right person to spend it with. Suddenly I wasn't painfully lonely and depressed. Was it her specifically, or just a great fuck? I didn't know right then, or care: just roll with it and enjoy the ride, that's the ticket.

It was a whirlwind courtship of three months, culminating in a November wedding. My parents flew down from Toronto to attend the nuptials. Ironically, it would be the last time either one would travel anywhere. Bevin and I had settled into a thoroughly comfortable, laid back relationship. In retrospect, I suppose that what we had was a lesser form of love, but without the same kind of passion that we shared on our first night together. A lot of what appealed to me about Bevin consisted of her sense of inner peace and calm; the total antithesis of Mrs. G. #1. No hysterics, no yelling or other forms of verbal abuse----ah, how pleasant. There was a genuine absence of that insatiable desire to dominate people and dictate the course of events that #1 possessed (or perhaps it possessed her.) These were very attractive character traits to me, and there was more of a sense of equality in this marriage, with mutual respect for each other's point of view. Hopefully, we would go forward carrying on the theme of equality, and the marriage would endure. Wrong!! This would not be enough to sustain our marriage, or, for that matter, anyone's marriage. Without passion on the daily menu, it would be ridiculous to think we could survive as a couple. It should always be lurking in the background, and at any given time, be ready to take center stage.

Yes, married life can be mundane, filled with daily tasks that are boring in their repetitiveness. But even the knowledge that passion does, in fact, still exist, can keep a marriage going. I personally don't know how one can separate love, passion, and companionship, but if I just want companionship, I'll buy a dog. Bevin and I had passion early on, along with a mutual sense of security, but the passion diminished faster than my bank account after a divorce. After a couple of years, this union was d.o.a., and it couldn't withstand the profound stress that was to come.

Chapter 64

Houston to Lubbock·One-Way Ticket

I sold my practice in Houston because a) the economic boom was showing definite signs of busting, and b) I had grown intolerant of the stifling heat and traffic. Also, occupational health was becoming a big, corporate affair, and I knew I'd be squeezed out in short order. This was just a harbinger of things to come in the world of medicine, as big business and merger-mania were about to take over. I dragged my new bride, Bevin, kicking and screaming, to Lubbock. She loved Houston, but if I couldn't make a decent living there, how could we stay and enjoy a decent lifestyle.

I had received an offer to work at Highland Hospital's new Family Practice Clinic. The honcho of this project was one Gerald Shill, or shill the Pill.' My initial impression of him was that he was a quiet, pleasant, polite fellow in short, a decent person. He even was an elder in the Church of Christ, which I now know should have been a clue as to his real character. What he was, in actuality, was the devil incarnate: mean, vindictive, hypocritical, and paranoid as hell. I won't elaborate on his general amorality, but let's just say that he enjoyed the company of certain women other than his wife, and, even worse, was a pathological liar.

Needless to say, this arrangement didn't last very long, and after a year of wasted time and energy in Lubbock, I was once again looking for work. I got wind of a temp. position (locum tenens) in Levelland, a small town twenty-five miles west of Lubbock. I was to assist a physician there who was .quite ill with cancer, and was quite weakened by his chemotherapy. He needed someone to run his large office practice for a few months, and I thought it would be a perfect place to hide out until something better turned up. It wasn't much of a commute from my home in Lubbock, but I would still have to rent an apartment for those nights and weekends that I would be on call for the hospital emergency room. Bevin and I had already purchased a home in Lubbock, and she had secured a job as a school counselor, a job she rather enjoyed. Also, she had made several friends through work. Funny, I could swear most of these new friends were of the lesbian persuasion; probably just my imagination running amok again.

Bevin and I were pretty much spent from our daily toil. Her evening routine consisted of changing immediately into an unattractive housecoat, opening a bottle of cheap wine, and, after preparing dinner, continuing a slow but steady consumption of said wine until bedtime. Once in bed, she curled up with a book and another glass or two of vi no, which ensured her of a good night's sleep. It also ensured me of no company for the rest of the evening, and definitely no semblance of a sex life. Most men in my situation would grow increasingly frustrated as their prostates gradually enlarged and their urinary stream grew weaker. But I, having no hang-ups about masturbation, had no physical issues. As a bonus, I was not prone to carpal tunnel syndrome because I was and am ambidextrous.

This marriage was doomed, but still, for reasons unknown to me to this day, we persevered a few more years. As for my job, good old Gerald fired me, and I ended up in Levelland (as I have already detailed). Momentous things happened to me there, such as Annie, and my one and only malpractice case, but then it was on to a new opportunity in Amarillo.

Chapter 65

Deja vu All Over Again -2002

Well, here I am again, back in loverly West Texas (Levelland), a place I briefly worked in back in 1986-87 as previously mentioned. Back then Levelland didn't seem like much of a town; just one big cotton field in the middle of nowhere. Actually, as I soon discovered, the town was only thirty miles from Lubbock, a city of two-hundred thousand. Lubbock had sufficient amenities for even a big city boy like me, and was the home of Texas Tech University, home to some of the prettiest co-eds I'd ever seen in my life. And I was on my own, having recently been separated from wife number two. Shortly after my arrival, I found a one bedroom apartment which was quite adequate for my simple needs, and was--conveniently located close to the hospital. My duties entailed working in Dr. Cuesta's clinic, covering the emergency room in rotation with the other docs, and occasionally, assisting Dr. C. in surgery. Even though he was ill and tired easily at times, he still did some general surgery, at which he was a master technician. He had been trained in Cuba and in America, and had been held in high esteem for his surgical skills and sound judgment by his colleagues and patients alike. And, above all, he was a gentleman in every sense of the word. He set the highest of standards for his ethics, kindness, generosity, love of his fellow human being, and for his abundant medical skills. I had no idea who this man was at first, but soon came to know him well. Looking back, I realize how fortunate I was to have worked for him, and to have just known him.

The only people I came to know fairly well were the hospital staff, as I rarely ventured far from the office or hospital. I was usually so tired at day's end that I was happy to retreat to my little apartment sanctuary.

But that routine was soon to be replaced with something a little more exciting, that something being a woman named Annie. I met her a few days into the job, when I went to check on some X-Rays I had ordered the day before. I was discussing the results with our quirky radiologist, Bob Wilcox, when into his office walked a gal so beautiful, I almost aspirated my coffee. Her name was Annie, and she was the head technician for the X-ray department. I knew immediately that I was in deep trouble, given my difficulty breathing, and obvious clumsiness. She was A Hispanic American, but I suspected she had to have some Anglo blood as well, given her exquisitely fine features. She was stunning, and everyone knew it except her. She wasn't falsely modest, just unassuming and less self aware then most of us. I tried to strike up some sort of conversation with her, but I failed miserably, so I backed off and let Bob have the floor. I was quite content to just stare and pretend I was listening to them. But I didn't hear a word, thoughts of how to romance this gorgeous gal racing through my head. She finally left without me saying another word to her. Rarely have I been so tongue-tied and awkward with any gal, but she just floored me. Okay, I know what you must be thinking. I am prone to exaggeration when it comes to beautiful women. Witness my Danish friend, Suzanne; didn't I drone on and on about her physical assets? Indeed I did, but we're comparing apples and oranges here. Suzanne was a classical Scandinavian beauty, while Annie was Miss Hispanic America. I realized immediately that I preferred the dark, striking Latino features of this woman over the blonde, blue-eyed Dane.

After a considerable period of time, I gradually worked up the nerve to have lengthier conversations with Annie, and the more I got to know her, the more I found myself falling for her. She was as kind and generous a person as I had ever met, and modest to a fault: no pretensions what-so-ever. As luck would have it, She and I were on call at the hospital most evenings, and we would frequently hook up for coffee breaks and, occasionally, dinner. We were slowly becoming confidants, and intimacy was also developing. It got to the point where we could tell each other just about anything, and have no worries about confidentiality. I learned that she too was in a miserable marriage, largely neglected by her husband. I couldn't imagine anyone being indifferent to this person, but, apparently he was quite the jerk. She had two children, both boys, and she adored them. She related that her boys were the only reason that her sham of a marriage still existed.

Over the next few weeks, our friendship gradually evolved into feelings of intimacy and romance, but we hadn't even kissed at this point, although I was dying to hug and kiss her, and never let her go. One night we were on call, there was a horrific snow storm, which dumped a few feet of the white stuff on our little town. It was actually quite wonderful since I hadn't seen snow since leaving Canada some ten years prior. Annie agreed to brave the elements with me and try to grab something to eat at K-Bobs just a half mile or so down the main drag. We made a run for it, getting soaking wet in the process. Great luck, K-Bobs was open, so we brushed off the snow, and settled in for a good meal. Bt this time we were both laughing hysterically at just how ridiculous we must have looked, cavorting in the snow like a couple of kids. We ordered steaks, and proceeded to talk our heads off. It seemed we both had a lot to unload, and we finally found someone to trust with our personal stories of life, love, and failed marriages. Occasionally I lost focus, just staring into those beautiful eyes. And she had the greatest smile, so warm and genuine. Hearing her laugh was like the sweetest music I could imagine--------so wonderfully distracting. As I said earlier, I was in deep, perhaps too deep. Was I in over my head here? I couldn't have cared less, and for once I let my instincts take over, leaving my brain out of the equation. After a great meal, I asked her back to my place for drinks and a movie I had rented. To my surprise and delight she accepted, and away we went, back into and through the elements. We arrived at the apartment none the worse for wear. I think our mutual adrenaline was flowing by this time because I don't remember either one of us complaining that it was too cold outside. I helped her off with her coat, and we settled in for a glass of wine and more chit chat before I played the movie. I had been perfectly relaxed and comfortable until this moment. I looked at her and suddenly I had nothing to say; I just wanted to grab her and kiss her. And that's exactly what I did. Thank God the feelings were mutual. She later related that she was hoping for the same thing to happen, but she was waiting for me to make the first move.

Needless to say, omitting some of the more boring details, we. slept together part of that night. Unfortunately, she had to leave at a 'respectable' hour to get home to her family. It was tough to see her go, but I knew this was just the beginning, not the end. To cut to the chase, we had a memorable affair, lasting several months. We thought we had been quite discreet, but, in later years upon my return to Levelland, I discovered that it was far from secret. In a town this small, I must have been dreaming to think our relationship had gone unnoticed. Not to be overly dramatic, but

I did want to describe our last night together. Now I know what the word 'bittersweet' really means. For the first and last time, as we lay together in bed, Annie told me that she loved me. And I told her that I also was in love with her, but what were we to do? She would not leave her husband even if he was a jerk who paid little attention to her. She would never break up because of her children whom she adored. I didn't argue with her, but I wanted to tell her how wrong that was for the children, staying in a miserable marriage. I did that for far too long the first time around, and all that accomplished was creating even more bitterness and heartache for them which would carryon into their adult lives. Rationally, I knew this was true, but I also knew that I could never convince her of that, so I just let it be. We parted as friends and lovers, never to see or talk to each other again. But I was lucky to have known someone like Annie at that time when I desperately needed someone to believe in. It was perfect timing for both of us, and I will always be grateful for what she gave me------a new sense of confidence, and an end to self-loathing.

Chapter 66

Amarillo By Morning

I was more than happy to leave Lubbock (and Levelland) behind, as I pointed my car northward to Amarillo, and my new job. I had accepted a position with two older docs, Dr. street, and Dr. Chambers. As always, it sounded very promising, and as always, it wasn't. Dr. street's idea of a thorough checkup was asking perhaps one question, and then ordering an injection or two, usually B 12 and a steroid. He almost never made physical contact with a patient, or, to put it more succinctly, he never fucking examined them! What a disgrace to the profession! And he is but one of many assholes I've encountered over the years that couldn't care less about their patients. I'm not disillusioned at this stage of the game, but I am still a little shocked at the sheer audacity of some docs, who make a lot of money by doing the bare minimum for their patients. Aside from these clinical issues, I had the strong sense of something going on financially that wasn't Kosher------in other words, creative bookkeeping. Obviously, I didn't last long at this pop stand. I felt that I was putting myself in legal jeopardy just being associated with these two characters. After my bitter experience with my peripheral involvement in a bogus malpractice case in Levelland, I wasn't about to run the gauntlet again by being part of a practice I considered substandard.

My next move was to get in touch with the chief executive officer of St. Anthony's Hospital, one Michael Callahan. The word was out that they were looking to get their family practice program back on line. At one time, perhaps twenty years previously, Saints was known as The primary care hospital, where most of the family docs were on active staff, admitting and treating their patients there. But over the next few years, the focus shifted to more of a specialist oriented facility, and the family doctors drifted away to the other side of town, where the two more modern facilities, High Plains Baptist and Northwest Texas Hospitals, were located. Saint Anthony's was getting long in the tooth----older and run down looking; not to mention it was on the wrong side of the tracks for the more middle and upper class affluent customers.

My timing was perfect for once. I became the only full time practicing f.p. at Saints, an enviable position to be sure since I had a lot of influence with the administrator, and also because I could grow my practice quickly with little or no competition. And so it was that I prospered for over nine years at Saint Anthony's Hospital, a time that I consider to be the best nine years of my career. My colleagues in the various specialties were generally very helpful and skilled, thus giving me a feeling of being insulated, confident in treating complicated cases. If I did run into a problem, help was readily available.

St. Anthony's didn't give me the sense of elitism and competitiveness (read greed) that the other hospitals did, especially High Plains Baptist. Power was wielded with an iron fist by everyone from chief executive officer to head nurse. Needless to say, I didn't find the atmosphere there warm or congenial at all, and I always felt a sense of relief when I left the premises. The third hospital in town, Northwest Texas, left me cold, with its wide, sterile hallways and generally unfriendly colleagues. It was the county hospital, and most people there had that government employee attitude, which, in short, was "Why should I give a shit?" As well, the quality of care was questionable, given the plethora of pending law suits at the time of my arrival in Amarillo.

A good example of cronyism (and despotism) in the medical world, occurred at Northwest Texas during my time there. This incident involved a good friend of mine, Joe R.,who was one hell of a trauma surgeon and intensivist. If you were in a desperate situation involving intensive care treatment, Joe was the doc you wanted. His skills and smarts were legendary, which really pissed off his so-called colleagues at Northwest. Accordingly, a plot was hatched to railroad the poor guy with phony charges of incompetence, and furthermore, accusing him of inappropriate behavior with staff and patients. This was a lunch mob for sure. These efforts to disgrace and banish Joe were self-serving at best, given that he was their chief competition, and was making them look like amateurs in comparison. I would also assume that administration was complicit in this action, although Tm not sure what their motivation would be, other than to placate the other physicians involved, who were the power brokers in that hospital.

The upshot of all this was that Joe, in effect, was put on trial. First, his privileges at the hospital were suspended, and second, even worse, his 'actions and inappropriate behavior' were reported to the licensing board and the Texas medical Association. He would have to defend himself to retain his medical license, which involved hiring a high dollar attorney in Austin, an expert in alleged medical malfeasance issues. Ironically, this catastrophic set of circumstances forced Joe to obtain privileges at St. Anthony, which is how we met each other. He would soon become one of my closest friends, a trusted colleague who was always there when I needed a surgical consult, or help in a dire emergency. Adding to my good fortune to meet Joe, he introduced me to his pal Sam Pace, who, ironically, has turned out to be my dearest friend over the past twelve turbulent years; a period of time when I have desperately needed a confidant.

As for Joe, he went through a painful exile to Lubbock, losing his position as chief of surgery for Texas Tech in Amarillo. Ultimately, Joe and his wife divorced, exacerbating his personal and financial miseries. Now you would think someone going through all this turmoil would cling to the few things in his life that provided some stability, such as his family and close friends, Sam and I. But no, that's exactly what he did nordo. In effect he abandoned everyone and everything associated with his past, cutting off all communication with those that truly cared about him. Even his own brother did not know about his emergency coronary by-pass surgery! How's that for strange? All I can surmise, in the final analysis, is that Joe just lost it after all that had befallen him. I can't assign rationality to any of his actions after leaving Amarillo, but that doesn't lessen my admiration for the man I knew.

Chapter 67

Bye-Bye Mrs.G. #2

The lifestyle that my wife and I had fallen into was becoming intolerable. All I could think about was how to extricate myself from this rotten marriage. And so it happened that one night I went out to hear my guitar teacher, Jerry, and his band at a local coffee house. I asked Bevin to come, but as usual, she feigned excessive fatigue (read depression.) So I went alone, which was fine with me.

When I got there, the joint was jumping---packed with all manner of folks from neo-hippies to yuppies, to aging college professor types, to wannabe musicians of all ages. I fit right in with the aging, wannabe musicians. I thought someone in the throng surely would get up and read some boring, narcissistic, new-age poetry crap, but mercifully, no one did.

In one corner of the room, I spotted a patient of mine----a 'sort of friend'. Her name was Liz, and I admit that I had a crush on her that I had never acted on. We had both been quite flirtatious over the few years I had known her as a patient, and I knew far too much about her personal life than was prudent for maintaining a professional relationship. We had spoken at length about our mutual spousal issues, acknowledging that we both were miserable, but we never quite reached the next level----a very dangerous threshold that I, as a doctor, could not cross. We did, however, acknowledge that there was a spark between us. The only obstacle was our mutual spousal issues, thus we had to refrain from keeping company outside the office.

Given my attraction to Liz, I finally gave in to my feelings for her, and suggested to her that I go ahead and formally discharge her from my practice. She agreed to this without hesitation. I found another family doc to assume her medical care, and the stage was set for a brief, passionate, and very tumultuous relationship. This was a storm I created for myself with no outside help at all. I've become very accomplished at getting myself into untenable, rocky relationships, and this was no exception.

Meanwhile, back at the club, Liz and I got into a long, convoluted conversation about all things personal. She reaffirmed her attraction to me and her increasing resentment towards her husband. He was a radio Disc Jockey and advertising guru who was a workaholic to the nth degree. Even though Liz was his business partner, he largely ignored her. She already knew the details of my home life, namely that I had none.

It was a very good night. Jerry and the band were killing, and Liz and I were getting closer by the second. The food and coffee were great. And the crowd was in high spirits. I hated for the evening to end. As Liz and I departed the club, I suggested a future rendezvous. "Another time, another place" she said, as she slowly walked towards her car. That statement would be prophetic. There would be many more times and places in the next few months, but in the deep recesses of my subconscious, I knew that this relationship had nowhere to go---no future, just a hedonistic present for both of us.

You know the story: hot sex for a while, gradually fading as you get to know the person and her irritating habits and quirks that just drive you crazy. But to be honest, we were both too disturbed to keep company for long. She was pathologically paranoid and neurotic, and I was manic or depressed depending on what hour of the day it was. It was during this period, however, that two very good things happened: first, my separation and subsequent divorce, and the second, a surprise call and letter from my long-lost daughter, Ina. She said that she had been reconsidering her opinion of me. After living with her momma for the past ten years, I could understand her switching gears. Maybe I wasn't devil incarnate after all. Maybe everything momma said wasn't the gospel truth, and just maybe, she still loved me.

I was euphoric over this development. Oh, and the capper was her saying that it might be a good idea for her to come down to Texas and live with me for a year----an experiment in better living so to speak. Wow!! It finally happened. The kids (at least Ina) were opening their eyes and seeing their mother for the first time-not a pretty sight.

So Bevin and I went our separate ways, she to Austin, and I remained in Amarillo, with a half-built house at Tascosa Golf Club. This was supposed to be our dream house, but the dream turned out to be a financial nightmare. I suppose a partially built home was a pretty good metaphor for our marriage----only a shell of a relationship. I had to end the suffering for both of us.

The strange thing was that I thought she would be relieved and unemotional, as I already was. But wait, she's a woman, remember, and hell hath no fury, etc., etc. She was furious! Someone I thought couldn't care less about me blew her stack when I proposed that we separate. Here's how I put it: "Let's face it Bev, we don't love each other anymore, so let's just put a merciful end to this marriage and give it a decent funeral. Wouldn't you agree?"

"I think you should get the hell out of here right now, that's what I think! How could you do this to me Mel, and why now?" She was livid.

Mel: "Because I have slowly arrived at the conclusion that there is virtually nothing happening between us that brings any joy to either of us. I thought you'd be relieved that one of us finally had the guts to spell out, the truth of our relationship: namely, that there is no relationship anymore. Vik, we live entirely separate lives, and we're both miserable. So what the hell are you so agitated about?" I shouldn't have used the 'H' word. B. "Just get out, and I mean right damned now Jew boy who's going straight to hell!"

Ah, the prejudice finally surfaces. I've suspected that, underlying a lot of her problem with me, was the Jewish factor, but *now* I'm certain of it. This brings to mind a telling incident that occurred the previous summer. We were all out at her parents' lake house at Possum Kingdom. Her folks were pleasant enough, and always treated me with respect and consideration. I, in return, tried to be helpful in advising them on certain medical problems, and answering general questions that all lay people have about doctors and medical treatment. So there was a measure of mutual respect there, and I always enjoyed being out on the lake-----so peaceful and quiet. You could really hear nature in between the revving of jet –ski engines up and down the lake.

My wife, father-in-law, and I were in Mineral Wells one day, just piddling around really. When we arrived back at the house later that afternoon, the back porch screen, which had been blown down by strong winds and rain a few weeks before, was completely restored. That was quite, in one day, a feat. My father-in-law asked his wife, Barbra, (we called her Bar-you know, like George Bush Sr.'s wife) who had done such excellent and speedy work.

"Well" she said, "just after you left this morning, the repair crew arrived. There were four of them, three men and a 'Messican'." We laughed long and hard at the matter-of-factness of her statement. Years later, it's easy to assess the depth of prejudice that was inbred in those folks. Good church-going people, pillars of the community and all that shit. I'm ashamed of myself now, recalling my jocularity at her remark. I was turning into a racist buffoon my own self, and it was sobering to contemplate that fact.

Here's what I wished I had said to Miss Bevin: "what kind of self righteous bitch are you to tell anyone, Jew, Muslim, Buddhist, or even atheist, who's going to hell? Are you judge and jury, or just God's true representative on earth? Screw the Pope, eh? I finally see who you are and where you've come from. It sickens me to think of how much time I've wasted being with you. I'm fucking out of here. I'll grab my guitar, and you'll be rid of me, okay?"

After picking up the guitar, she actually said "you don't have to take your guitar and amp right now; I won't destroy it you know." "Yes, I think you will. I can't trust you now after tonight's awakening. I'll be back for the rest of my stuff. Good-bye Bev. By the way, I'll take responsibility for my part in this debacle of a marriage, and I apologize for all my shit."

The divorce was anti-climactic, just a great relief. I was unburdened and light-hearted for the first time in eight years.

Chapter 68

Single (Again.)

I found a decent house to rent, thanks to my officer manager, Fran. It was quiet, convenient, and, at first, painfully lonesome. With age and experience, however, some wisdom had crept in, and I learned to appreciate my solitude. I needed to be alone with myself for a while, and. not be dependant on anyone. Most people never get this opportunity, what with all the hubbub of children and other family buzzing around them most of their adult lives. I finally began to welcome the quiet time instead of fearing it. Most nights I spent reading or playing my faithful old guitar— not very well I might add.

Work was going much better since my separation, and both my parents and office staff noticed a much improved mood. Laughter came easily once again, as the cloud of depression lifted. Happiness is an elusive little devil, and not even a wife can help you find it. You'd better get happy with yourself before inflicting yourself on another. Furthermore, ditch the expectation another person can conjure up that magic potion that renders you fulfilled and content. Dream on: that's just not the reality I have come to learn the hard way.

That's not to say however, that I completely lost interest in the opposite sex. I've always like women. In general, they're so much easier to be with then men. No macho bullshit with women, just fragile egos and a mess of insecurity. Hidden agendas aren't as hidden (when they're with me anyway.) And they always seem eager to be themselves. Eventually, I emerged from my cocoon, and re-entered the world of singles, especially divorced re-treads like myself. It dawned on me that everyone I met since my separation had had at least one miserable marriage. But never having been in love with a spouse, I didn't think the term 'retread' applied to me. Dating again, given my new lease on life and attitude adjustment, wasn't unpleasant at all.

One fine day, a doctor friend of mine asked me if I had a date for the Symphony Ball coming up in a month or so. Understand that this was the highlight of the social season for the rich and infamous of Amarillo, most of whom were intolerable snobs. I had never been, or even dreamed of it, but, out of morbid curiosity I suppose, I agreed to be fixed up with a lady named Crystal, who was in need of an escort to the ball. As it turned out, she was a Heathcliff, (not her real name) just about the wealthiest person alive in the Texas Panhandle! This could be really interesting I thought. I've never hobnobbed with the wealthy crowd, and here's a once in a lifetime opportunity to check out life on the other side of the tracks.

I had an informal introduction to Miss Crystal at Rick's house. She was there to order some expensive clothing from his wife, who ran an upscale boutique from her home. Of course she didn't need to work at all, given that Rick was a wealthy surgeon, but the rich must get richer, right? Okay, I'll admit to just a smidgeon of jealousy. I rather Iiked Crystal. She was attractive in a slightly overweight way, with striking facial (and chest) features. She could be amusing and strange at the same time, and I was interested in learning more about her. We agreed to a formal date, a preamble so to speak, before our grand entrance at the Symphony Ball. A brief but memorable chapter in my life was about to unfold.

Chapter 69

The Play

One fine afternoon, at the end of my office hours, a patient of mine by the name of Janie, told me that she was going to read for a part in the upcoming production "The Boys Next Door,' at the Amarillo Little Theater. She and her friend Nancy were quite keen on acting, and had been in several productions over the years. Janie suggested that I read for a part in this play. I told her she was crazy to even think that I would do that. In College, I had been in a medical school comedy review, but that was the sum total of my stage experience. Granted, I was know as quite the humorist with my friends and colleagues, but never in front of five-hundred folks in a theater.

And then she did it! She dared me! Well hell, I won't ever shrink from a dare, just so long as bodily harm isn't a possibility. So that evening, I sauntered down to the Little Theater to read for a part in this play. I was mortified to see how many people of both sexes, were there to audition for a handful of parts. There weren't but six male leads, and a couple of supporting roles for women. Everyone has a little ham in them, including me I reckon. Before I could say Cary Grant, my name was called by the director, one Allen Shameless.

I was asked to read dialogue by a character named Arnold, who was a neurotic wreck. That wasn't hard to do since I was also a nervous mess. I felt that I had done quite well for a 'newbie', but had no false hopes of getting a part given the volume of good actors to follow. But after everyone had had their shot, the selection process began, and to my amazement, Allen asked me to stick around. There were eight of us left out of about a hundred 'actors'. We took turns reading different parts, after which Allen decided that I would play Barry. This character was a schizophrenic, and retained the delusion that he, in fact, was a professional golfer. Perfect! That's always been my delusion too!

Allen was right: I fit the part perfectly. Now all I had to do was become an actor in six weeks.

The rehearsal schedule would turn out to be one hell of a grind: work in the office all day, rehearse until midnight, go home, hit the sack, get up in the am and start all over again. Being an 'actor' wasn't too glamorous. In fact, it was damned hard work and for no pay in this case. Amidst all the fatigue and drudgery however, I did have a lot of fun. Our little troop became a very tight knit circle----all for one, one for all, and all that sort of shit. We were sharing a special experience, and the best part of that was that no one else could appreciate it but us.

During these six weeks, I was also trying to squeeze in a few dates with Crystal, but even that was becoming impossible with my schedule. The symphony ball was fast approaching, and she was getting a tad pissed off with me. As luck would have it, that night would be our first Saturday night performance, ending at about ten p.m. Great timing, eh? I would have to forego the customary post performance audience greeting by the cast, then run over to Crystal's (literally,) shave and shower, get into a tuxedo, and then drive over to the Amarillo Country Club, the site of the big bash. No sweat, right? P.S. it's damned hard to tie a bowtie even if you're not in a rush, but when you are, it's impossible. Crystal had to take over that job or we never would have left her house.

Somehow I made it through those six weeks of rehearsal, and opening night was suddenly upon us. I was nervous of course, but not as much as I had thought I would be. I've always been up for new experiences, and this was very new indeed. I was eager and prepared. It was Friday night, and it was a sellout----five-hundred pairs of eyes to scan your every move onstage. The crowd sounded boisterous, ready to be entertained. We could hear them even from backstage in our dressing rooms. It was the end of the work week, and they were ready to party. We had to be great or we'd be fucked three days to the ~ weekend.

I got to the theater one hour before show time, and felt surprisingly calm. Hopefully I would stay that way throughout the show. I must remember my lines! I had one of the five major parts, and had found it a challenge to memorize it all. I even had a soliloquy, whereby I would be seated center stage, all alone, with a spotlight on me and the rest of the theater blacked out. Furthermore, somewhere in the middle of this speech,

I had to cry!! Shit, that's hard enough for me to do in real life, 'let alone on stage in front of all these damned people. My respect for good actors had increased immeasurably since I began this process, especially the crying thing.

To accomplish this feat, I had to figure out what to focus on that would bring on tears. During rehearsals, it was hit and miss: I couldn't consistently cry at the scripted moment. Finally it dawned on me: there was one thing that could always evoke enough emotion to make me cry------my bankruptcy! And, by God, it worked every time! Once I had that image of being in bankruptcy court, feeling the profound humiliation and hopelessness of that situation, I could cry on queue without any problem.

The play began, and I waited in the wings for my first scene, which, thank the lord, was with Jerry. I say thank God, because.1erry, an older gentleman, had over thirty years of experience in the theater, and had been a lead actor in the famous outdoor production, 'Texas'. People came from all over the country to Palo Duro Canyon. In the Texas Panhandle, that was as big as it got. This would be a drop-dead cinch with and old pro by my side. The scene involved Barry, my character, trying to teach a Mr. hedges (Jerry) the art of the golf swing. It was really a funny bit of business, and in rehearsal, it always got a great laugh from my colleagues.

Suddenly, we were out there, Jerry and I. We worked our way into the scene quite well thought, and the enthusiastic laughter coming from the audience was like a shot of adrenalin. Then it happened. After saying my next line, there was dead silence------no response from Jerry. Looking over at him, I saw sheer terror in his eyes; he had *frozen* up on me! Hey,wait a darned minute here; he's supposed to be the veteran actor, not me. Shit!! The next few seconds felt like the proverbial eternity, but then, thank God, I was able to improvise something that was remotely on topic. This went on for about thirty seconds, until Jerry finally snapped out of his stage-fright stupor. As if woken from a coma, he jumped right into his next line, and we finished the scene to a rousing round of applause. Unbelievable: his misfortune had gone undetected judging from the crowd's response.

We got away with it, and I felt an incredible rush knowing that I could come through in a pinch. Jerry patted me heartily on the back, and thanked me repeatedly for "saving my ass." It felt like I had scored the winning touchdown, and all your teammates were high-fiving you. I was so proud, but, sadly, that was short-lived. My very next scene, I stepped on 'Arnold's' lines, and was completely out of sync for a few painful moments.

The rest of the performance went flawlessly, even my big soliloquy scene. I actually was able to cry onstage in front of all those people.

At the conclusion of the play, to say that I was drained both physically and emotionally, was an understatement. But it was also an exhilarating, fulfilling experience. Only six more shows to go. How was I going to survive?

Chapter 70

Saturday, the night of the symphony ball, was as frenetic as I expected it would be. First, I had to make rounds at the hospital and discharge three patients. I almost forgot that I was still practicing medicine as a hobby. My new jobs were acting, and male escort service. After the hospital, I had to go and pick up my tuxedo from the fancy, shmansy men's store. I had purchased this expensive monkey suit a week prior, under the watchful eye of Crystal, who always exhibited impeccable taste. Naturally, she picked the most expensive Italian tux and shoes in the store. You'd think she might have helped me with this purchase given her extreme wealth, and my relative poverty after divorce #2, but no-o-o-o. She may have had great taste, but she was also cheap as hell. he was, after all, dragging my tired ass to this damned ball, and I felt that the least she could do was foot some of the bill.

Wait a minute: that sort of reasoning made me feel like a male prostitute, and I had to stop it. let's stop this perverse train of thought, and try to be rational for a change, okay? She wasn't obliged to pay my way, and I was, much as I hated to admit it, looking forward to my first 'Ball.' I had never hob-knobbed with the rich and famous of Amarillo. Social climbing has never been part of my agenda. You've heard of 'lifestyles of the Rich and Famous?' Well, I dated girls whose lifestyles were more of the 'Poor and Infamous' variety. I was suddenly traveling in rarified company.

The play went quite well that night----another sell-out. Word of mouth was good. And anytime I could evoke tears in my big scene, I felt vindicated as an actor, and more importantly, the rest of my scenes went that much better. I never thought that weeping could make one so confident. At the play's conclusion, as planned, I dashed over to Crystal's house (mansion), got washed up, shaved and dressed. I still didn't quite have the hang of tying a bow tie, so Crystal did it. I wondered how many male suitors she had done this for: dozens I'd wager. I was, however, impressed with her cheerful mood considering how late we would be arriving at the gala. She looked great, as she could do on occasion. I think social events such as this, brought out all her good hormonal. Instincts-----endorphins, estrogen, etc. Crystal was about my age, although she professed to be several years younger. I wasn't buying that, but she did appear, at the very least, to be aging gracefully. Always being on top of fashion, I suppose, didn't hurt, and her money gave her the freedom to explore the ever expanding possibilities of plastic surgery.

We finally arrived at the club at ten thirty. The crowd had already been fed and watered----especially watered. Yep, a lot of folks already had a load on, and were acting just plain silly. I was surprised that there was enough booze in Amarillo to adequately supply this bunch. Strangely enough, I can't drink; not because I don't enjoy a few cocktails, but any pleasure I derive is nullified by the terrible migraine headache I'm prone to.

Sadly, we missed dinner, which was simply 'fabulous' according to the food connoisseurs Crystal spoke with. We carried on bravely, albeit it with empty stomachs. Dancing was something we both enjoyed, and the band was top notch. And there was great gossip to be heard in every corner of the ballroom. With most of the gang inebriated, tongues had been loosened to the degree that any dirty little secret you wanted to know about certain prominent people about town, was no longer a secret. However, most would probably have alcoholic amnesia for these juicy tidbits by the next morning. Their priority would be to find a way to overcome their miserable hangovers.

Crystal and I left the party early, both of us bored to tears with the whole scene. To be more accurate, I was definitely bored, whereas I think she was too. Crystal was awfully hard to read, and I never really knew when she was truly happy, sad, or just indifferent. She usually had an expression on her face not unlike a deer caught in the headlights, except with a faint hint of a smile: Mona Lisa with a Rolex. The times she really came alive were when she was discussing financial matters with her key advisors----mostly commodity market gurus, since her family fortune had been founded on oil and ranching.

Sex was joyless for her; more of an obligation she felt she owed me for being her 'boyfriend.' And, I must mention her profound hypochondriasis. I think she might have invented this ailment, she was so damned immersed in fearing and avoiding every thing you could imagine. Her paranoia knew no boundaries when it came to her health. Apparently, she was allergic to everything in the air, including, I believe, oxygen. Strangely enough, as a doctor, I never once observed clear-cut physical sign~, just the mental fixation on various phenomena that we would all consider normal in our environment. But she could detect things in the atmosphere that would stump Carl Sagan; and she smelt things that no other human nostril had ever detected.

Air purifiers were distributed all over her mansion. It was strictly verboten for me to have about me any scent, be it cologne, deodorant, soaps, hairspray, or, worst of all b.o. God-forbid if my genitals weren't exquisitely clean and smelling wonderful, although I don't know what the fuss was since her head never got close to anything below my belt.

Yes, Crystal was the very essence of the 'High Maintenance Woman.' There were occasions, however, when I found her company most agreeable. For example, we took a trip to Aspen Colorado, and, since she had lived in Beverly Hills, I was able to mingle with celebrities she knew. We came over on the family jet, another first for me. Not only was that heady stuff, but the skiing, which I hadn't done in twenty years, was pretty darned good as well. By the way, if you ever get offered the chance to fly on some rich gal's private toy, I'd suggest you say yes in a Texas second. We stayed at her favorite spot in Aspen, a grand hotel in every sense of the word. Our suite was elaborate and enormous. Considering the fact that in Aspen I couldn't have afforded a room at Motel 6, I felt privileged, almost to the point of forgetting how poor I really was.

Everything there was frighteningly expensive, and I was on a shoestring budget since my second divorce. Both of my ex-wives made out very well with the settlements for two main reasons: firstly, I had shitty lawyers, and secondly, I was so relieved to get these people out of my life, that I was willing to forfeit almost anything. In retrospect, that, of course, was a terrible mind-set going in to divorce negotiation. With this attitude, they and their attorneys have you by the short ones, and the next thing you know, you're filing for bankruptcy.

Crystal had decide to buy a house in Aspen, and asked me if I would do some house-hunting with her and her realtor. How could I refuse, especially since I was curious about the kind of houses we'd see for a few million bucks apiece. So, one fine morning, we set out to see some 'homes' (read mansions.) Property in Aspen was outrageously valued, but my gal had an unlimited budget to play with. Not that I'm a namedropper, but we did see homes owned by such people as George Hamilton, Martina

Navatilova, Barbi Benton (Hefner's ex- girlfriend,)and many others. Barbi's house was very different indeed. It was built in the round, the master bedroom consisting of one massive, round waterbed. You actually had to crawl through a little tunnel to get to it. Now that's a different kind of foreplay. Looking around at all the pictures of Barbi and her Playmate friends, I'll bet that small crawl space was worth the effort.

I started to get a little anxious when Crystal began referring to potential homes to purchase as OUR home. She also had done a little research into the procedures involved in obtaining a medical license in Colorado. Subtlety wasn't Crystal's long suit, and I suddenly was horrified at even the slightest notion that there would be a permanent arrangement with this woman. My discomfort during this little house tour was the capper for me. Long story short, we parted company shortly after returning to Amarillo.

Chapter 71

And then there was Lizzie (not Borden.) I guess I'm just attracted to pretty, but very neurotic, disturbed women. I've already mentioned her in a previous chapter that time when my second marriage was evaporating. What I didn't talk about was the evening I ended it. Her crazy paranoia finally got to me; it even got to my dick, so you know what bad news this chick was! The capper was that my daughter Ina was present for this momentous occasion. What irony: first, she witnesses my casting her aside, and now, another episode of Mel's ongoing situation comedy entitled "How to Ditch a Woman When One of You is Certifiably Insane!" Ina had written me a letter a few months prior, expressing her desire to put the past behind us. She was anxious to rekindle some sort of relationship with her father. That letter was a shocker, coming out of left field. We hadn't communicated for years, literally, and when we did talk on the phone, it always ended in anger and mutual resentment. As a doctor, I know a little psychology, and I had tried to assess where she was coming from. Unfortunately, no matter how rational and calm I tried to be, my hatred for her mother and what she had perpetrated to distance my children from me, always came to the forefront, and all rationality quickly vanished.

But in this letter, she bared her soul, sounding a positive tone as regards a possible reconciliation with her long-lost father. Also, she indicated a desire to come to Amarillo, not just for a visit, but to stay with me for an undetermined period of time. She wished to attend college here as well, and I was all for that. Wow!

So that's how Ina came to be at the 'Last Supper' with Liz. By this point, we had both had a bellyful of her griping and emotional nonsense. Once Liz started bitching about the menu with the waiter, and began getting on Ina for no particular reason, that was if for me. I told her to shut the hell up, and we'd talk after dinner, but until then, no more babble.

Ina spent about a year with me and, for the most part, I thought it went pretty well: that is, until Debbie entered the picture.

Chapter 72

True Love at Last

I didn't know Debbie Nelson, even though she had worked at St. Anthony's Hospital more years than I. There were momentary sightings, but I did take notice. I also took notice of her wedding ring, so I steered clear. She was and is, a strikingly beautiful woman, with long, wavy brown hair, green eyes, and olive complexion. And what a figure! Men have died for less, but she wasn't available. Unbeknownst to me, however, she had just about reached the end of the trail with hubby number two, and she soon would be single again. What a coincidence since that was my current marital situation. Deb had done solid work at Saints for years, serving competently in many posts. She was finally recognized for her stellar work ethic and competence, when she was asked to help establish a new rehabilitation unit. Her boss, a nice lady name of Latayne, asked for her specifically, obviously aware of her abilities. As it turned out, this would be the coincidence of a lifetime for me.

Grace, the rehab doc, had become a friend of mine and had begun asking me on to cover the unit for her when she was away on meetings or vacations. And that is how Deb and I met. I finally got to see her up close and personal, and she looked better the closer I was to her. But she seemed aloof, almost dismissive of me. Was I that big a joke? Was I that unattractive? Or maybe it was my attitude. One day, the hospital had a charity bake sale, and she asked me to buy a cake. I actually said something like, "why would I want to do that?"

Yes, I was an arrogant jerk! To tell the whole truth, I said really stupid things, like most men, when confronted with a beautiful woman. Men are basically wimps and cowards, even the most handsome, suave guys I have known. We crumble and mumble when we first meet a 'babe.' So this non-relationship continued for a while, until one fine day when Donna, the head nurse on the rehabilitation floor, told me, in confidence, that she knew a gal who really wanted to go out with me. She said that she was very sweet, very pretty, and furthermore, I actually had met her.

"No, I don't think so" I said." I've not been lucky enough to come across anyone who fits that description in a very long time, especially right here in my own backyard. Hey look, just in case I'm totally wrong, if I may, can I get you to tell me her name?"

"Her first names is Debbie, and believe me, you do know her. Look, here's her number. Just give her a call. I promise she'll be thrilled to hear from you."

"Hell, what have I got to lose? I replied. "I'll call her real soon, promise."

"You won't regret it" she said. And boy was she right.

That night, being the cool, calm, I don't- give- a- shit individual as I was, I rang Debra. She sounded just terrific, and as Donna said, she was most receptive to the proposition of a date. I decided to ask her out on the safe brunch, first date thing. Hey, you can't go wrong: its cheap, it's in broad daylight, and you both come and go in separate vehicles. Nothing gained, nothing lost, and no hurt feelings. Also, you avoid stupid, clumsy attempts at a good-night kiss, and all that silliness.

We arranged to meet at IHOP the following Saturday morning. I was getting increasingly curious to see who this Debbie person was. My diseased brain couldn't recall a 'Debbie' encounter, so it remained a mystery. Saturday finally arrived, and I arrived at IHOP first. Damnation, that's a bad move; I'll appear too anxious. I got a booth by the window with a perfect view of the parking lot. My theory there was simple: if she turns out to be a dog, perhaps I can somehow sneak out another exit. On second thought, I couldn't be that mean, so just hope for the best, right?

I sipped on my java waiting, daydreaming about past dreadful experiences with pretty women, which almost made me move my ass on down the road. But then, I saw her pull up in the little Mitsubishi sports car she had described on the phone. I watched with great anticipation as she stepped out of the vehicle and began walking towards the front door. I'll be damned, I do know her!! It was that aloof chick who worked on rehab, the gal I was rude to when she asked me to buy a cake for the hospital charity fund. I never knew her name because we hardly ever spoke to each other, and when we did, it was merely a quick hello-good-bye deal.

My first thought was very basic: my God, she's fucking gorgeous. Don't screw this up Mel. Stay calm and cool, but don't sound snobby or aloof, etc., etc. Well, all my apprehension was for naught. She was not only one of the most physically appealing women I had ever laid eyes on, she was also one of the most delightfully friendly as well. And she had a great sense of humor to boot. I knew right then that there would follow many, wonderful dates. This was finally THE ONE. I was officially smitten and was already planning a New Year's Eve proposal, ring and all. There was one little hitch to this unoriginal, yet very romantic scenario: when I asked her out for the Big Date, she had already made other plans to go skiing with her girlfriends up in Taos. What? I was speechless, and overcome with a mixture of anger, disappointment, and the physical sensation of my heart being ripped to shreds, all in the same instant. This could not be happening----I had it all figured out, and I was certain of her feelings. All I could do was tell her what I was feeling. She was actually a little freaked out about just how agitated I was. That's when I said, "Hey, I love you, and I was going to ask you to marry me on New Year's Eve. Now do you understand why I feel so completely miserable?"

"Mel, I had no idea you would react this way. After all, it was just a couple of days over New Year's. But now I understand. I do love you, you know?"

"Listen Deb, I know this is totally insane to do this over the phone, but I have to just do it. Will you marry me? I love you more than anything on earth, and I can't let this feeling keep churning me up without telling you everything. Skip Taos, okay? let's get engaged-----tonight!!!"

"Okay Mel, but you know you're crazy, right? But I believe that you are the love of my life too, so yes, of course I'll marry you."

"Don't move a muscle Deb, I'm coming right over."

"Me!, it's one in the morning for God's sake!"

"So what? I'm already in the car.".

And so it was that I flew (literally) over to her house that night, and we made sweet, passionate love all night long. We were officially engaged(sans ring of course,) and the rest, as they say, is history.

We were married on January 11, 1995. Since then, the poor girl had been through some horribly down times with me, but to her credit, and my everlasting gratitude, she has hung in there. Even though she is eighteen years my junior, and there is an obvious generational cultural gap, we can relate to most everyday things, the stuff that really matters. Besides, I know that she is far wiser and more practical than I, and our ages don't really matter. I've concluded that women at any age are usually more mature and street-wise than us men.

Thus it follows that Debra and I are an excellent match, for I am immature most of the time, and she is decidedly not. She is wise and practical, which, again, I am not. However, we share one thing in. common that makes this marriage work; we are both good, decent people who mind our own business, and enjoy our little life together immensely. We don't wish ill on anyone, and, like all good Texans, we buy lottery tickets once a week. And we don't interfere with each while at work, and, at home, we observe certain rules of individual privacy.

After almost thirteen years of marriage, I think we've managed to adhere pretty closely to the aforementioned rules of common etiquette and mutual respect, without affecting our deep love for one another. What can I add to that, except to say-to all you single folks out there, good luck. May you be as fortunate as I, after all these years; in finding a mate. And if you fail the first, second, or umpteenth time in your relationships, keep trying. One day, you may be overwhelmed by one incredible human being, ad I was. In that spirit, I've asked Debbie, almost since the day we started dating, to have inscribed on my tombstone, "He never gave up!"

Chapter 73

Not to long after my marriage to Debbie, my daughter Ina, mercifully, put an end to our strained relationship, and went back to Toronto where she belonged. Even though I'm Jewish and was raised in Toronto, I can see through the left wing bullshit of the intelligentsia in the northeast. My daughter was just out of her element being here in the Texas Panhandle, a conservative enclave in most ways. Her departure was the final cleansing I needed of the whole Toronto marital experience. I hasten to add that she never seemed to be of my flesh and blood because she was a one hundred percent carbon copy of her mother, and, in my not so humble opinion, that was the impenetrable barrier to her being a decent human being. Given the inability of either of us to come to some accommodation about our differing points of view on just about everything, we couldn't cut Each other any slack. Accordingly, I've closed that chapter of my life for good. How utterly unfortunate!

Debbie and I set up house at my little 'villa' in Tascosa. This house ultimately led to my second bankruptcy, although there were other extenuating circumstances. There is no substitute for bad luck coupled with bad judgment. That is a killer combination that I have managed to barely escape from before, but I guess I needed to learn the lesson one more time that you can't always be Houdini.

When I separated from my second wife, we had started building a new house. How's that for dumb as shit? At any rate, it was a done deal since I already had bank financing, and the foundation had already been poured. Too bad our marriage didn't have much of a foundation. The bills from all the contractors and sub-contractors were steadily mounting, and I was scrambling to pay these debts. I was using high interest credit cards to help with the payments, never a good idea.

Aside from the house fiasco, there were other disastrous events leading to bankruptcy #2, not all of which were things I could control. I will fess up to overspending on new automobiles, jewelry, tons of clothes for both of us, etc., etc. Unfortunately, back then, we were both shopaholics-----not a good thing when you're inevitably going to be broke.

Even with all this debt weighing us down, I managed to tread water for some time. But there was one more final nail in this coffin, something neither I nor anyone in the Amarillo health care scene, saw coming. My hospital, St. Anthony's, after years of denials that it would ever sell out, did just that. It finally capitulated, and 'merged' with Baptist Hospital across town. But this was not a merger of equals: it was in fact, a buyout by High Plains Baptist of St. Anthony, leaving many of us gasping to catch our breath and maintain our sanity (and our jobs.) Sold down the river by an unscrupulous order of nuns------can you believe this shit?

I need to explain the comment about lost jobs. A year prior to this 'merger', I had made the tragic error of selling my practice to St. Anthony's. I thought, like many other naive doctors before me, that I could have my cake and eat it too, and greed can be oh so unattractive. The notion wasn't idiotic, that is to say, selling your practice for a goodly sum of money, and then coming to a contractual arrangement to remain employed by the buyer to stay on as medical director of said practice. So everyone comes out a winner, right? Hell no! It's not that bloody simple, mainly because your business expectations as a self-employed person, and the new owner's expectations of both you and their new investment, aren't necessarily even close. My termination was a startling event, one I never saw coming.

Nevertheless, one miserable afternoon, an administrative hatchet man name of John something or other, casually strolled into my office, along with his assistant, an unfortunate looking woman named Eileen, and sat his fat ass down. "Dr. Genraich" he said, " Eileen and I are here today to ask you to vacate this office within the next ninety days. Your contract does allow us to terminate you and give you three months notice." He said this so matter-of-factly, that I wasn't at all sure I grasped the full weight of what was occurring, or even if he was at all serious. Maybe it was just a cruel joke. Not bloody likely.

"You mean to tell me that you want me to resign for no particular reason? Don't you have to abide by the letter and spirit of our contract?" I was thoroughly befuddled by this sudden turn of events, and was desperately trying to remain under some control given my fear and panic. This was, after all, 'the last stand' for good old Me! Job opportunities in family practice were very limited in Amarillo, Texas. If you were fifty-two years old, and not board certified, your chances of gainful employment in major urban centers were reduced to the proverbial wing and a prayer.

The suit's reply was chilling: "Doc, you obviously have forgotten the escape clause in your contract that either party could exercise. Didn't your lawyer go over this with you before you signed on?"

"What lawyer" I said, "I just assumed that this was a standard employment contract, binding on both parties, with no hidden, bullshit escape clauses. I just assumed that if you did a good job, as I always have done, the rest would take care of itself."

The suit smiled that wicked, sarcastic little smile of his, and continued. "Think again doc. You know, you doctors always amaze me. I mean, how could anyone go ahead and sign such an important, complicated contract as this one, without getting proper legal advice beforehand. You guys are unbelievable."

I sat there silent for a moment, trying to digest his sarcasm and sanctimonious business advice. I finally managed to as a question: "what on earth has precipitated this decision about my future with this organization, because I know I've given this practice my usual solid effort, and continued to build the business?" I was fighting for my financial life, and I knew it. I was shaken to the core of my being: I wish that I could say that this would be the last time I would feel this way, but it would happen again several more times over the next ten years. I will relate the details of those sad tales a little later on. Doctors have no special protections against the cruelty of the new, money-driven power brokers of medicine.

"Look doc" the suit concluded, "its nothing personal. We simply can't afford you any more, given that you're just not pulling your weight around here. Look at your balance sheet man; you're not meeting any of the goals we had set for this office. We're not an ATM machine, nor are we a charity for doctors who can't cut it. If it makes you feel any better, you're not the only office I'm visiting today with the same message."

"That's really comforting John. Hey, I've put down roots here in Amarillo, and considered this my permanent home; a place to finish out my career. My wife and I have been very happy here, and I have enjoyed the past nine years in practice at St. Anthony's', probably the most enjoyable and rewarding of my professional life. Just when I am feeling this sense of peace and contentment, you walk in here today and destroy all that I have worked for in a heartbeat. How dare you and your rotten company! Get the hell out of my office! My attorney will be in touch. Just crawl on out of here, and take that scrawny bitch with you asshole!"

"Okay, okay-----calm down man. Don't shoot the messenger."

Chapter 74

Oklahoma---Not O.K.

The preceding chapter was brought to you by mismanaged health care everywhere. I didn't know it right at that moment, but, sadly, I was on my way out of Texas. Yes, after a nasty bit of negotiation to settle the matter of my severance package, I was headed for Oklahoma City. I had been recruited by a physician there who was looking for a partner (read slave.) His name was Richard Dickman. How appropriate that name would turn out to be. The hospital where the Dickman worked was, in fact, the party that had hired the recruiting firm that, unfortunately, found yours truly. Their incompetence will be chronicled a little later. As for the 'Dickster,' he was a brash, arrogant, mean-ass little shit, whose sole purpose on this earth was to accumulate wealth. Being abusive to those unfortunate docs who had attempted to work with him as an employee orerstwhile junior partner, was also something I believe he enjoyed. He was a tyrant in his little domain. To me he represented everything rotten in medicine: the greed, corruption, and collusion with a big hospital corporation. Said hospital company, I'm pleased to report, is now (2007) in deep financial poop, so maybe there is some justice in this world after all. The only folks I feel sorry for are the hospital employees, whose 401K plans were invested solely in the stock of this company. What a cruel joke that has become for them, but they had had no choice in the matter.

As for Dickman, I always am *amazed* at how tyrants can command loyalty from the troops. Whether your talking about Hitler, Mussolini, Stalin, Sadam, or Hillary Clinton Oust kidding,) there will always be folks who will follow evil people anywhere to achieve any goal, even if the goal is pure evil; and even if many good people are destroyed should they get in their way.

From the first second I walked into his office, I was treated like a leper. I was, in a word, ostracized----persona non grata. I was thoroughly befuddled since I couldn't figure out what it was that I had done to warrant this abusive treatment. Funny thing about instincts; my wife has a great sixth sense, and she felt an immediate negative aura about the place. She picked up on the frigidity and negativity of the office staff. Later that day, Deb told me how uncomfortable she felt in that environment. I tried to allay her fears, writing them off to the normal amount of apprehension we both felt coming into this new situation. How wrong I was, and how right she was.

Speaking of instinct, or tell-tale signs, when we first crossed the state line into Oklahoma, almost immediately we had a flat tire. As if that weren't prophetic enough, I later discovered that there had been a sign at the border that I hadn't noticed on that first foray into Oklahoma, but on the way out of the state, I did see it. It read "Attention! You...are now entering Hell! Proceed at your own risk." Somebody really does need to put up a sign that says something like that, with the addendum that all medical professionals avoid a certain hospital in Oklahoma City, and certain evil physicians like the Dickman. Someone has to protect these people, and I've made that one of my priorities at this later stage of my career. There's just too much of this shit going on in medicine today. It's enough to make you vote for Hillary and her universal health plan. How much worse can it be?

The situation at the Dickster's office was getting progressively intolerable through no fault of my own. I would certainly own up to any contributions I was making to this debacle, but that simply wasn't the case. Just to clarify that point, when I interviewed for this job, I was totally honest about the fact that I was, in fact, not board certified (read Kosher.) That was critical as it turned out, since many hospitals and managed health care plans were no longer accepting us dinosaurs into their pool of providers. This flat out eliminated many job opportunities for me; thus, I was always mindful of the fact that I must ask the question as to whether or not my lack of said board certification would affect my practicing medicine in a certain location.

"Absolutely no problem" said the recruiter. The hospital administrator was also in full agreement with that statement. Wrong, wrong, wrong you fucking knuckleheads! As I had feared, I couldn't get on any major insurance plans in Oklahoma City, all of which my erstwhile partner was on. He was pissed, but not half as much as I was. Our minimalist relationship then became microscopic, and I was shunned by everyone in the office. My future was non-existent with the Dickman.

In addition to the insurance debacle, the recruiting firm screwed up in another critical way. They had confidently asserted that I could and would obtain my Oklahoma license in just a few weeks after submitting my application. Dead fucking wrong again! The state board only met every three months to review licensure applications, and they had just met a few days before my arrival. I was stranded in the middle of Hell, with no prospects for license to practice, no friends, and soon, no cash.

My lawyer in Amarillo, a rotund, jovial fellow, turned out to be, in a word, incompetent. He failed to negotiate on my behalf, a decent severance package from St. Anthony's. And just to add insult to injury, you should have seen the bill the s.o.b. sent me, in which he alluded to his 'great success' in arbitrating this matter. Shakespeare was so right: "Kill all the lawyers" he wrote. God knows, no one would miss them.

Chapter 75

I bid adieu to the Dickman and company, but we still had some legal matters to clear up (naturally) regarding my contract, and our purchase of charts from a retiring doc. Another brilliant move on my part, but enough said about that accounting fiasco.

Before my departure from that office, I had spoken to one of the twenty vice-presidents of the hospital corporation that had recruited me. He was in charge of outpatient services, and could be useful since they were building a new clinic in Del City, ironically not too far from my home. Somehow, I managed to convince him to give me a shot a getting this new enterprise up and running. I now had the title of clinic director, and was pretty darned pleased with myself for pulling off this little coup. What Mr. Big-wig didn't know, was that I had no alternative; that is to say, I had no other job prospects, and I was desperate. I just couldn't show any vulnerability, or else I was sunk. You know, no one in med school told me it would be this frickin' hard a task to secure employment. I will have to agree with John, 'The Suit,' on his point that doctors are the world's shittiest businessmen.

Del City was a quaint little place, and a refreshing change from the doom and gloom atmosphere I had just left behind. My 'staff' consisted of one nurse, a lovely gal I'll name Grace. She was very kind to everyone, especially to me. She was like a sister really, except I didn't have any sisters, especially of African American descent. The remaining 'staff' was rounded out by a sweet, funny little woman named Sheila. She was married to the medical director of the corporation's clinic in Midwest City, but she never talked about him or business over yonder. Smart girl. Sheila was fortyish, about four foot ten, short red hair, oversized glasses, and, most importantly, she possessed a wry sense of humor. I love a woman with a great sense of humor, even though I've been accused of being humorless by many women in my life. I think I'm terribly misunderstood by the opposite sex, but that's a topic for another day. Suffice it to say, I really do like women, but I digress. I'm pretty sure that Sheila was one of the principal reasons that her husband was such a great success in solo practice. She had the personality, and he had the medical skill; in short, a perfect team. He had made the same mistake as I, selling his fine practice to the greedy fucks that owned the hospital and clinics in Midwest City, and the my new facility in Del City. Now, he was at their mercy, and these folks weren't very merciful. Hell they'd slit their mommas' throats if it meant another couple of bucks for their share price.

So, the three of us plodded on, slowly building a clientele in Del City. I was feeling increasingly optimistic about the future for a change, as was my bride, Debbie. She was working part time at a little boutique near our home, and loved it. We had a small, but swell circle of friends, and our lives were steadily improving. My mood had shifted from utter despair, to a much sunnier outlook. I daresay I was even optimistic for the first time in a year. Oklahoma so far had been a bi-polar experience; just plain psychotic. Our sanity was being vigorously tested, and so far we were maintaining a semblance of rationality: until,. of course, the next catastrophic event.

The company had made the brilliant decision to close our clinic just when it was getting off the ground, and even becoming profitable. Since I was about to get sacked again, and I would be scrambling (again) to finda new job, I thought this would be an appropriate time to give my view of depression as I have experienced it.

Chapter 76

"I have been through some terrible things in my life, some of which actually happened." Mark Twain said that, and it has stuck with me. We all have moments that overcome us with grief, a sense of hopelessness, and a mysterious longing for something better for the future. Hope springs eternal, but in my deepest, darkest moments, that's just a line; another harbinger of false hope, amidst a sea of despair and depression.

Life sometimes thoroughly sucks. You get kicked around enough times by ex-wives, ex-employers, and ex-children, and all your reserves of good will and charity towards your fellow man, are, in a heartbeat, gone--- at least temporarily. Even those who love you and care the most seem to be indifferent and cold, but that's your distorted perception when you're really down. I have felt that way from time to time, and you just want to cry when you are that sad and frustrated. I have felt completely alone in my own little world of financial catastrophe and emotional bankruptcy, and no one seems to give a damn. I usually snap out of this morass after a few miserable days (or even weeks,) of self-inflicted purgatory. I wished I could understand why this happens. It's certainly not rational, but I do have a theory, which is that the burden of life's occasional sorrows and misfortunes is simply too much to bear, and my only reaction is to withdraw. I have to give in to those feelings for a while, and hit rock bottom, before I can start back up again and face the realities of this world.

I'm quite certain that the above described syndrome is not just peculiar to me. I have known many people, from close friends to family members, who, at one time or another, have felt exactly the same. My only conclusion is that everyone, at some point, suffers from depression, but when it persists for a great length of time, then professional help is needed. But, for the vast majority, depression is a fleeting, unwelcome visitor which usually leaves as quickly as it arrives. I like to call it my 'Dark Stranger.' I'm not a Christian, (I'm reconsidering that position,) but I would imagine that my 'Dark Stranger' would be interpreted as a visit from Satan, whose purpose is to drag me down to his subterranean level.

One more thing about depression: a guy just can't get a hard-on if your stupid life depended on it, another cruel side affect of the 'downs.' There's one surefire way I have for measuring my level of depression, and that is how good or bad an erection I can get, and how long I can maintain it. Never fails, that one; accuracy to within one inch, more or less. But when the depression begins to lift, so does my dick. In other words, the dick to depression ratio slowly improves, until you can once again stand at attention. In the interim, thank God for Viagra, the depressed man's holy water.

Chapter 77

The 'Doc -Boss'

I need to discuss people in medicine like 'The Dickman.' First of all there's just too many of them. They're everywhere I go it seems, and, just my luck, I manage to get involved with too many of these assholes. My first job in Toronto was a great experience, but I still had to learn to tolerate my bosses. Individually they were reasonable, decent people, but, collectively, they were one big 'Dickman.'

Then, in Lubbock, Texas, I had the misfortune to run into a heathen name of Gerald Hillbilly. He may be the worst doc-boss I've ever known. He was a crazy, motherf-----ing tyrant, and probably the meanest person I have ever met in medicine. Now that's quite an honor, considering all the evil aliens I've encountered. Like most tyrants, he was paranoid, and sadistic, especially when it involved money. He'd kill his momma if he thought she had stolen a penny from him.

He was looking for a doc to round out his roster for a new family practice clinic he was establishing, and, just my luck, he found me. There were four of us plus Gerald, but he didn't have a clinic practice. He owned and operated an ambulatory care center (minor e.r.) in the hospital next to our building, and also owned a similar facility in San Angelo. All these guys (and a few gals) are entrepreneurial, and I have nothing against that. It's how they function to acquire their wealth that I abhor. They will do every rotten, low-down, mean-assed thing, to achieve their goals. That includes a rigid scope (sans lubricant) up the bottom for anyone who is stupid enough to get in their way.

Dr. H. scheduled me to work in his walk-in center (minor e.r.) half of the time, and the other half was in the new clinic. As per his instructions,

I was to build my practice by referring new patients I saw in the walk-in center, to follow up with me in the clinic. By new patients, I am referring to folks who were not accustomed to using Gerald's operation as their source of regular general practice care. This arrangement was quite alright with me, satisfying our mutual needs. Several months passed, and my practice was beginning to take off, thanks in large part to my work in the walk-in center.

My second wife and I went on vacation to Mexico. We were both spent and had to get away from work. When I returned, I felt rested and relaxed, and I foolishly had this optimistic notion that things were good and soon to get better. I had barely stepped foot inside the house, when the phone rang. It was Gerald, and he sounded seriously pissed. He didn't talk when he was angry, he growled in low, ominous tones. To my shock and disbelief, he said he was firing me, the main reason being that I was 'stealing' his patients. His walk-in clinic was suffering, he claimed, because of the loss of volume and revenue, which he attributed largely to me. I quickly deduced that I was to be the scapegoat for his financial woes, and I wasn't ever going to win this argument.

"But Gerald, I thought that I was just following your plan. How could I misunderstand your instructions when they were so crystal-clear, right from your own lips? Any patient that came into my practice was, as you had stated, a new patient, who hadn't seen you, or your outpatient facility before. Besides, every patient of mine has been instructed, on every visit in fact, to use your clinic for any and all minor emergencies, so I'm at a loss to see how I could be the main reason you're numbers are not up to your expectations. I can't see where I am to blame."

"You are" he replied, raising his decibel level considerably. "I want you out as soon as possible!"

Once again, after doing nothing more than following the doc-boss's instructions to the letter, I was fucked. How can you reason with someone so irrationally greedy and paranoid? He was fashioned from the same mold as Dickman, and too many other I've encountered, but he was more sinister. I concluded that he really was someone to fear, someone capable of doing anything to further his own cause, even if it included something criminal. As rotten as others have been to me, I never felt that I was in any physical danger, and that's how Gerald H. made me feel. Being and elder in the Church of Christ, I should have known better. Watch out for holy rollers-----they'll roll right over you alright.

My wife Bevin actually got on the phone and told Gerald off, and, being from a similar religious background as he, advised him in the strongest terms that he was going straight to hell. That was one of the few times I really was proud of her, showing some gumption for a change.

"Well" I said to her, "I guess we're screwed. I'll have to scurry around and find some work a.s.a.p. I need to get the word out that, at the very least, I'm available for part-time work until something permanent comes along. God knows where though. Lubbock is sewn up tighter than Twiggy's butt by docs like Gerry. Trying to establish a new solo practice here is out of the question."

"Damn it" wife number two said. "Just when I'm settled into a new job that I like, with people who like me, you get sacked. Why can't you blend in and get along with folks like everyone else? All our plans, and our new home, are all up in smoke. Isn't that just dandy?"

"Oh, you think I was given a choice? The man just fired me and I didn't do a damned thing wrong. How could I have avoided that, given how crazy this motherfucker is? Another insane doc-boss on a power trip, and he finds me to prey on. You just don't know anyone anymore until it's too late."

"Just try to find something one time that's secure enough to keep us from having to move again, okay?" she said.

"All I can do is my best" was all I could muster. I was spent and couldn't talk anymore. I was also still in shock. I needed tome to regain some semblance of sanity and composure. The one thing I did know for certain however was that Lubbock was caput!

Chapter 78

Before I chronicle my next few missteps, I have to stop for a minute and just talk about how naive doctors were and still are in business. When I first went into practice back in the stone age of 1971, things were still relatively innocent. Yes, you could hang up your shingle and start a solo practice. Yes, you could get on staff at most any hospital because you had successfully graduated from a great medical school and completed an internship. Imagine that! No hassles with a Board of Family Practice since it didn't fucking exist, thank God almighty. No hassles from local docs since there was enough work to go around for everyone. And if you wanted to do minor surgery, or obstetrics, or emergency room work, or anyone of a million other things not governed by some dumb ass board or government panel of nitwits, you bloody well could! Ah, those were the days----or were they?

This sounds too good to be true, and a lot of what I have described was. But I know now, even in my most nostalgic moments, that all was not sweetness and light. For example, my first job was run by doc-bosses who weren't quite as obviously mean and greedy as, for example, the Dickman; but they still were watching the bottom line like a hawk. If you couldn't pull your weight, you weren't going to hang around too long.

As for hospitals, yes, getting on staff wasn't a big deal like it is today, but that doesn't mean you could behave in an unseemly fashion. Bad language and sexual harassment weren't quite the litigious items they have come to be, involving even the federal government in the form of the EEOC, but you could still be in a spot of trouble with administration. And you could choose to be multifaceted in your practice, but that doesn't mean that there was absolutely no governance. There still had to be some degree of quality assurance to protect the public from fools who bit off way more than they could chew.

I must say that billing and reimbursement were a joke compared to what has happened today. Of course in Canada (Ontario) there was only one payer source by the time I left for America, the provincial government. And you were, indeed paid for everything you did that was a legitimate service. The problem was that the pay was so paltry, that a lot of what you did wasn't worth the time and energy expended by you, the physician. So, was that better than today's confusing system of reimbursement in the good old U.S.A.? My answer is yes, because, as the old adage goes, ignorance is bliss. We didn't know any better, so how could we bitch? It was a more innocent time, and, in many ways, a gentler time for docs, especially family practitioners. You just weren't hassled as much, especially by government, insurance companies, and lawyers, God bless them all.

Chapter 79

I'm still so pissed off about this next event, that I'm inserting it, inappropriately, here and now. What happened to me is just one example of how our health care dollars are wasted in this patchwork of a medical system we like to think has some rationale, but doesn't.

I had a benign lump removed from my upper back a few weeks ago. I had called my good friend, Joe the Surgeon, and asked him to perform this minor procedure in his office. However, he felt it best to have me go to an outpatient surgical center in Lubbock. Okay, fine, what the hell? I've got good health insurance, so why should I care where it's done? Well, I found out pretty darned fast why I should have cared.

First, upon my arrival that morning, I had to fill out an elaborate history form. I counted five pages. It was thorough to a fault, leaving me wondering why it didn't ask for my penis size and sexual preference. Next, a pleasantly efficient nurse arrived on the scene to review my history, ask a few more questions, and run an electrocardiogram. Fine, routine stuff I thought, but way beyond obsessive-compulsive for removal of a small benign tumor. I was almost amused at all the fuss, but in my heart I knew it was all bullshit to justify the humongous bill that the center would generate for all the unnecessary services rendered on my behalf. I decided to just go along with the little game I was witness to, and just get the damned thing over with as soon as possible.

The real shocker came when Dr. Anesthesiologist walked in to discuss my 'conscious sedation' and I.V. fluids. Now this was more than just a fucking joke! Conscious sedation for a minor procedure that I, a humble g.p., do in my own office all the time------bullshit!!!!! But did I offer any objection? Hell, no! I was just like anyone else in an intimidating medical environment: in other words, a pussy. So I actually let them stick an I.V.

in my arm, and then wheel my stupid ass into an operating room. I should have stopped this train right there, and said something like, "what the fuck do y'all think you're doing? Are you completely mad? I just have a tiny lump on by back, damn it. let me get the hell out of here before you kill me!"

Unfortunately, I didn't say those things. What a jerk was I-----another lamb led to another slaughter. I would have made an ideal holocaust victim, quietly accepting my fate. In the operating room, I saw my friend Joe. I did go so far as to say to him, "Joe, don't you think this is a bit excessive for such a minor procedure?"

"Better to take all precautions and do it this way Mel" he said.

Next thing I knew, Mr. Anesthesiologist was wielding a giant syringe filled with a frothy, white substance called Fentanyl, which is used to sedate large humans and small cows. I managed a feeble "Is this really necessary doc?"

"Better to be nice and relaxed and comfortable, so don't worry about a thing----you won't even remember the procedure" said Dr. A. Why did he think I would worry, or not be relaxed?

Even in my increasingly dream-like state, as he injected the sedation, I could smell a rat. My God, what was all this nonsense going to cost me for this one act play? Everything went fine, as I was later informed by Joe. I will admit that the whole thing was almost worth it just for those few minutes of heavenly bliss I experienced, under the affect of the Fentanyl. God I was happy! The world and everyone in it was perfect. I was perfect. Life was perfect. Happy, happy, happy! Unfortunately, that euphoria passed all too quickly, and soon I was headed home, chauffeured by my lovely wife, Debbie.

The lesion was, indeed, benign. Great, but here's the rest of the story. I received bills for this incredibly complex procedure, as follows:

Hospital- -- --$2700.00

Dr.A.-- - - --.- -$400.00

Joe-- - ------ --$450.00

We have here a grand total of thirty-five hundred and fifty dollars for a procedure I would do in my office for a hundred bucks! No, we have no reason for a health care crisis in this country. Everything is just as it should be, as I have tried to illustrate with my little surgery. I'm sure we can all agree on the following points: first, we are all getting billed up the rear for unnecessary bullshit; second, our insurance premiums are going through the roof because of said bullshit; third, reimbursement for inconsequential procedures like this, is bloated out of all proportion; and finally, outpatient facilities should not be allowed to bill outrageous sums of money for minor procedures.

What a nightmare! And this is just one example of our so called medical care system in action. Give me a physical break---we have no goddamned system in this country, just a patchwork affair at best. There has to be a better way, but I'm not ready to *cede* to the Clintons and Obamas of the world just yet.

Chapter 80

After my Oklahoma debacle, I was recruited to come to Monahans, the proverbial West Texas 'Hicksville.' Sure, there were a lot of rich oil dudes and dudettes there, but they were still hicks. They had about as much culture as an oil slick on the highway. When I first came to this hellhole, I was given the 'grand tour by the local Chamber president, after which I was justifiably horrified. This place was as far removed from civilization as any place I'd ever laid eyes on. How could I, a cultured, worldly, highly intelligent and sophisticated human being, possibly thrive in the middle of nowhere? I guess the answer to that is to never underestimate the power of human instinct to survive and adapt.

My first week there I stayed at the proverbial 'roach motel,' the Silver Spur. It was run by a fine western family of Pakistani descent. Maybe they were from West Pakistan. Mentally, I was a wreck being alone in this dump, separated, of necessity, from my dear wife. She was still back in Oklahoma cleaning that mess up as best she could. Compounding my dismal outlook, I contracted a nasty case of stomach flu, which led to severe dehydration.

Alone, sick in a dump of a motel, the last straw completing this tragic scenario, was the discovery that I was working for two absolute maniacs. Billy the M.D.,and Gary, the D.O. You know, I've been a doctor for thirty plus years, most of it in the good old U.S.A., but I still don't know exactly what a D.O. is. In Canada, there was no such thing, just M.D., medical doctor. The only other doctor was a PHD, or doctor of philosophy. What the hell was with this D.O. crap? When's the last time you heard a little kid say that he or she wanted to be a D.O.? Give me a royal break! This is just nonsense, and Gary epitomized the wannabe -a- real doctor syndrome exhibited by most D.O.s I've known. He was a pompous jackass, but that was just his cover for a lot of insecurity. However, he was the quiet enforcer of these two Mafioso docs. They ruled their little domain with an iron fist---no velvet glove here.

Billy was one sick fuck! He was an unscrupulous liar, philanderer, and a greedy bastard if ever there was one. And those were some of his better qualities. I'm ashamed to admit that he was a fellow Canadian, he being from Nova Scotia and I from Ontario. In other words, he had been an asshole in two countries. He was thin wisp of a man, standing about five foot seven, and weighing no more than one hundred and thirty on a good day. You sometimes need confirmation that there is a God, and you know it when he visits upon someone as rotten as Billy, a rare condition that makes it difficult for him to keep his eyes open. He had to go to Houston every few weeks for Botox injections in his eyelids. Yes Virginia, there is a Santa Claus. Aside from that specific physical quirk, Billy was the spitting image of a malevolent Howdy Doody. Nonetheless, he fancied himself quite the ladies' man. Unfortunately, the ladies didn't share that sentiment, but that didn't stop our boy from trying to force himself on many a young thing. Ironically, his fourth wife was not altogether unattractive, and, superficially, seemed a very pleasant soul. Go figure, eh? As for Gary, he was working on his third and probable third imminent divorce. For a guy who fancied himself quite the stud, he sure had an ugly wench at home. Together they looked just like Mutt and Jeff. She stood no more than five feet fall to his six-feet five inches. She could have easily passed for his pet poodle, except poodles are cute. B. and G. had the good cop-bad cop routine honed to perfection, with Billy being the hard-ass enforcer, and Gary seemingly the benign, quiet one. Hey, snakes are quiet too, right? These guys were filthy rich in spite of their individual domestic issues. They ran four weight loss clinics (read scams) in the region, which were a cash cow of undeclared earnings. I don't know how many sets of books old Billy-boy kept, but in a former life he had been an accountant and banker, skills which he had utilized to perfection. Witness the fact that these guys had never been audited, which doesn't speak too well for the crack investigative teams at the Internal Revenue Service, Medicare, Medicaid, or private insurance companies.

Incredibly, they rejected those patients who couldn't afford to pay, even though their legal mandate as a Rural Health Clinic was to see anyone who walked in the door, regardless of ability to pay. They got away with if, and the clinic was indeed a money factory: grind 'em in and grind 'em out as fast as possible. They knew just how much to bill to which payer source.

If was so slick that I almost admired their prowess as crooks. And I was working my ass off in this setting, although I didn't have much ass left after my bout with gastroenteritis. I was however, gaining a large, faithful following of patients, while, at the same time, trying my best to adapt to these two strange personalities who employed me. If was a real juggling act to fit in while appearing not to be trying to outshine the boys.

Debbie was back in Choctaw trying to sell our soon-to-be ex-house, and having no luck at all. Our financial situation was desperate, and ultimately we were forced to give it back to the mortgage company after foreclosure proceedings were initiated. Just prior to the actual legal proceedings, we actually had a buyer for the house, but we couldn't sell it. Do you want to know why? Because the dumb fucks who held the mortgage, along with their attorneys, wouldn't allow it to happen, that's why! It was a combination of greed and stupidity: greed on the lawyers' part in their attempt to prolong the process and thus pad their bill; and stupidity plus clumsy beaurocracy on the part of the lender, who, in my opinion, got exactly what they deserved.

Chapter 81

My shock finally wore off, and I slowly regained some semblance of rational thought. I was thoroughly exhausted. My beleaguered brain struggled to come up with an alternative plan. It was now obvious that these two assholes wanted me out, even- at the risk of a lawsuit over the contract. They felt invincible, immune to potential litigation because, as I later learned, many others before me had traveled the same road through their office, suffering a similar fate. And the boys remained legally unscathed. Amazing!! Maybe its time their perfect record was spoiled. I plotted, schemed, and agonized, thinking about how I could exact my revenge. This was much too demanding, physically and mentally. What a waste of time and energy, perseverating about these two criminals. I had to take a different tack: the best way to get even with people like this was to get a better job in the same town. In other words, achieving success in their town and once again enjoying life, would drive them crazy, especially if they lost patients to the new doc. Brilliant! At least now I had a plan, and I knew just who to approach with my brainstorm: one, Joe Wright, the CEO of the local hospital. I think he hated these pricks even more than I, and, given my current state of mind at his time, that was saying a mouthful.

Joe and I met the next day, at my invitation, for lunch. We quickly came to a verbal agreement which consisted of 'my taking over the medical directorship of the rural health clinic, a country owned facility. The clinic's name was 'Sandhills Family Clinic,' and I couldn't have come up with a If J crappier name if I tried for years. It doesn't even have the word 'Medical' but you get the idea----the name doesn't work; and neither, for countless years, did the clinic. The place was, in fact, a long- running joke in town, and also, among my colleagues. Professionalism was completely in absentia, while inter-office gossip was the order of the day.

The worst doctors imaginable had passed through these doors, usually leaving town as fast as they had arrived. Two Professional Assistants, one LVN, along with two clerical staff, comprised quite the crew. It was party time, with a smattering of medical practice thrown in just to keep up appearances, which kept the paychecks coming. This was going to be, one hell of a challenge, whipping this bunch into a professional medical office team, but I was up for it. I decided right off, that anyone who didn't fall into line and become a team player had to go----simple as that.

To make a long story short, with mostly new personnel who had a smidgeon of professionalism in their collective attitudes, the clinic became a smashing success; so much so, that it was providing significant degree of competition to Mutt and Jeff.

Chapter 82

So, inevitably, the bankruptcy proceedings arrived. It actually went pretty smoothly, but the real pain of it doesn't sink in until much later when you suddenly become acutely aware of how your lack of credit forces you to grovel for everything you need, such as a house and automobiles. Most importantly, the ability to loan money when you really need it is gone for quite a spell. In other words, you're fucked for at least seven, long, miserable years. One of the great ironies, at least to me, is the fact that folks who can least afford it, get charged the highest interest rates on everything, especially credit cards. This is your punishment for having the audacity to do a Chapter 7. Maybe I'm crazy, but that seems ass backwards. lower interest rates would help us get out of our financial bind, and allow us to secure necessities. That's too damned common sensicall reckon, what was I thinking?

Back in Monahan's, the only good time to be had was when Debbie came to stay with me on weekends at my new, luxurious one bedroom apartment that I had found to replace my palatial surroundings at the Silver Spur. Having already secured a rental duplex in Odessa, only thirty miles away, it was easy for her to commute, and be with me when I was on call at the hospital. The rental in Odessa was a cozy, perfect little place for the two of us, and we loved it. We wanted to remain there indefinitely, however my new employers insisted that I move to Monahan's and become a visible presence in the community-----you know, public relations and all that nonsense. God help me, for we acquiesced to their demand, and eventually found a suitable home in Monahan's which met our needs, but without a fraction of the charm of our duplex. The only real bright spot in this, if that's the right term, was that the boys had to co-sign the bank note in order for little old bankrupt me to secure the property. This could prove to be an interesting bargaining tool on that inevitable day that I leave this town. Houses priced over ninety-thousand dollars don't exactly sell like wildfire in Hicksville, Texas, thus, having the boys cosign the note might be a saving grace when we eventually head back to civilization. But leaving Odessa was particularly hard on my dear wife. She had grown to love our little domain, and she enjoyed what Odessa and Midland had to offer.

In Monahan's, the locals were decent enough, but, like they say, small minds think alike. The main recreational activity, as far as I could tell, was watching flies fornicate. Second to that excitement, was going to church. That was fine for all the decent, Christian folk, but, being a heathen Jew from the great northeast, I had to find my own 'church.' I did find something that fit the spiritual bill: the local municipal golf course. living in the bible belt, I had to show my spirituality, so I went to my church at every given opportunity. I've always loved being in my own private sanctuary. It nourishes my spirit and clears my mind. I always feel energized and fulfilled by a visit to my church, especially when the good lord sees fit to keep me on the straight and narrow------the fairway of faith, so to speak.

One of the last times I played golf in Monahan's was on a peaceful Friday afternoon. I had a habit of leaving work early when things slowed to a crawl, and would make a hasty retreat to my 'church.' What a beautiful afternoon it was, sunshine, blue sky, green fairways, and, best of all, not another living soul in sight: just me and my thoughts.

After playing ten holes, it suddenly dawned on me that I was shooting one of the best rounds of my entire life. Every putt ended up in the cup as if guided by a laser beam. Almost every drive split the fairway, and when it didn't, the recovery shot was perfect, landing right in the heart of the green. A feeling came over me that I was unfamiliar with in recent times---something bordering on euphoria, but much more spiritual than that. For the first time in years, I felt complete peace and gratitude just for being alive. All my worries disappeared. It was so quiet, I could hear my heart beating, and felt my blood flowing to every part of IT!Y body. I carried this feeling with me to the last hole, a demanding par five. And just as I addressed the ball on the tee, I backed away, staring at God's handiwork. A magnificent monarch butterfly had landed on the ball, and remained there for what seemed an eternity. When he finally took flight, I hit my drive, long and straight just as all the other drives had been this day. As I walked down the fairway, the strangest thing happened; I began to cry like a baby. It suddenly had dawned on me that the butterfly was not a coincidence, but rather, it was a message from above. God was watching over me and He would never abandon me in difficult times such as these. I was bursting with emotion when I arrived home.

I told Deb about my wondrous afternoon, and she too felt that a spiritual force was at play. I know this sounds corny, but I'll never forget that afternoon. That was the moment when I realized, despite all my skepticism of the past, that there was, indeed a God. And He cared about me.

Chapter 83

The apocalyptic event in Monahan's, came crashing down on all around me in late August of '99. My contract with Mutt and Jeff (Billy and Gary) called for an automatic raise in salary of fen thousand dollars after six months on the job. This was not based on productivity, and was nonnegotiable. Unbeknownst to me, the boys didn't particularly believe in contracts (or the law in general for that matter,) and sure enough, when I got my first paycheck after this initial six months of employment, it was for exactly the same amount as I had been receiving. Naturally, I thought that this was just an honest mistake, so I took the matter up with the office manager, 'Big Momma." She was obviously embarrassed by this situation, and did her best to avoid eye contact with me. I could tell that she was winging it when she attempted to explain away the lack of an increase in my check. There was no real attempt at clarification, other than to say that the check was, in fact, correct, and she was just doing her job as prescribed by her bosses. My first thought was that, once again, I had been taken out back of the woodshed, and given a thorough beating without any means of self-defense, sort of, but I was getting accustomed to this treatment.

After I had regained a little composure, I went to Bill's office and asked for a private chit-chat. He got up, closed the door, and sat down, staring at me with his half-closed eyes. I got right to the point.

"What's the deal with this check Bill? You know it's supposed to reflect my raise as per my contract, so can you tell me what exactly happened here."

"Well Dr. Genraich," he said, avoiding eye contact just like Big Momma. "Gary and I have decided that we just can't afford to pay you any more at this time. Sorry."

Stunned, I replied "But this is a legal contract! There are no ifs or buts. You have no loopholes here. It's as straightforward as any provision in a contract can be."

"Now you listen to me" snapped Billy, "we don't think you're pulling your weight around here, so the raise isn't justified anyway."

"What the hell do you mean 'not justified?' I've been working my butt off for you guys, generating excellent billings. I have their numbers from your office manager to back that up. Look Bill, you simply have to keep your legal obligation to me."

Bill was getting more agitated by the second, and, in the ugliest tone imaginable, replied "no raise Me!, and that's it! I don't want to hear any more discussion on this matter, understand?"

I bravely pressed on, "well then Bill, tell me this-------when do you anticipate that you can afford to honor this contract, and give me my raise?"

"Probably never" he shot back. "This meeting is over. I'm going to lunch; you just do whatever it is you think you have to."

I was thrown into a state of catatonia by this little shit. A strange, tingly-sensation came over me, and I felt otherworldly. Maybe I'd get lucky and have a fatal heart attack, putting me out of my chronic misery. This really did happen, didn't it? My stopover in 'Nowhere' on my way to 'Somewhere' suddenly wasn't going too well. I walked to the bank to deposit my paycheck, still dazed, but also getting more pissed off with every step. I couldn't believe it. After my Oklahoma experience, how could this happen again? Why was I doomed to run into evil pricks like this time after time? Why God, why? That question reverberated in my fragile little mind for hours and days thereafter.

The vacancy created by my departure from the deadly duo's clinic, was filled by one mid-level practitioner, and a J-l visa doc from India. Their salaries combined were close to what I had been earning. As if that weren't enough, another P.A., Chuck Speed (I swear I didn't make that name up) was also brought into the fold by the boys. I'll admit that Chucky didn't come cheaply, but he could generate six or seven times his salary; so he was actually a bargain. Chuckles and Billy had been close buds and confidants even before this unholy union, and both share certain proclivities. I can't say more because I hate lawsuits, especially when they're directed my way, but one thing I can say: I was living in fucking Peyton Place and didn't know it. God, how long can I survive here?

Chapter 84

Things in Monahan's we're getting a bit dicey. The same old problems were cropping up with the rural county clinic I was supervising, the main one being a severe shortage of money to effectively serve the locals. Monahan's was dying economically, slowly but surely. I felt the possibility of making progress had passed us by as surely as the rain we so desperately needed had passed us by. Old money, old thinking, rigid conservatism, profound greed and selfishness had, in effect, choked off most prospects for growth. They could have had a Wal-Mart, a large prison, a nuclear waste site, and other job creating enterprises. They ran off all the potential employers, and sabotaged the future of this town and county.

As for the clinic, after the poorly informed citizenry had voted down a hospital district which would have provided a decent revenue base for the hospital and clinic, we were back to square *one, under* the control and tender mercy of the county commissioners' court and its judge. The hospital board was our other warden, and neither the court nor the board got it. By that I mean that they didn't take into account the positive economic force the clinic had become, and what great potential there was to increase its cash flow. With expansion of the clinic would come more employees, and thus, more tax revenue for the county, not to mention more retail dollars for local merchants. This would be a win-win for the hospital/ clinic, and the community; economics 101 so to speak. I'm no frickin' professor of economics, but I know some common sense business practice, the best example of which is how one dollar paid out to a new employee, reverberates around a community and benefits everyone.

Well, common sense got pitched out the damned window, and the financial squeeze was on again. We lost a nurse we desperately needed, and she was not replaced. Our illustrious new *CEO* of Ward Memorial

Hospital, one Dicky Clueless, didn't deem it a priority to have the clinic adequately staffed. Unfortunately, Dicky had the board eating out of his hand, and all the county court cared about was staying under budget, instead of caring about the quality of health care given to all its citizens. The demise of the clinic and, most likely, the hospital as well, was, in my view, inevitable and imminent. Given how strongly I felt about the future of health care in Monahan's, I had to resign. I had recently received an offer, literally from out of the blue, to work in Levelland, and I jumped all over it. How ironic that I would be replaced by the doc who was fired as the medical director at the community health center I was going to in Levelland. I heard later, after assuming my new position, that this fellow was a real pill. He had alienated the staff, and left patients and their families literally in tears with his crude, insensitive comments and opinions. I was left speechless at hearing of his cruel ways. I couldn't fathom any doc thinking and behaving in this foul manner.

So, he ended up in Monahan's. I'll be damned. And to think that just one phone call from Brother Clueless, or anyone on the board to check this guy's employment record out, and they would have had a clue as to what they were getting. How careless and stupid can you be, especially in the business of hiring a doctor for your community? But, then again, this happens all over rural Texas since they're so desperate for docs (and nurses, P.A.'s, *etc.*) More often then not, they check credentials and background only half-heartedly, if at all. Hell, even I can get a position almost anywhere in the 'boonies' of rural Texas, and I'm not even Board Certified in Family Practice (Kosher.) I'm on the move once again. I couldn't leave Monahans fast enough even though I wasn't exactly sure what I was getting myself into in Levelland. Time will tell.

Chapter 85

Let me give you another example of petty politics and bigotry in today's wonderful world of medicine. First, let me bore you with some ancient personal history.

I graduated from med school in the Stone Age, 1969 to be exact. That was five years or so before the advent of a new residency program for family practice, which would lead to a doctor gaining 'Board Certification in Family Practice.' In other words, he was then officially Kosher. I took the only route available to me back in the day, which was to do a one year internship following med school. After that, I decided to go forth into the real world, as a g.p., rather than specialize. The words 'Family Practice' were foreign to me since everyone who wished to be in primary care in my era, was a 'General Practitioner.' This was not a specialty, and, in my opinion, it still isn't.

So, what happened here? How did this come about, this bastardization of General Practice? Well, here's what went down. A group of insecure, academic types among our g.p. colleagues, came forth upon the land to elevate their ego-challenged status to gain the title of 'Board Certified.' Thus, they concocted this horrific scheme to cheat medical graduates who wished to be generalists, out of another three years of their lives. They now had to enter into a residency program to become 'family practice' specialists, which meant, for most, more years of poverty toiling in a stinking hospital, sucking up to staff nitwit physicians who had now anointed themselves 'Professors' and 'Associate Professors' in 'Family Medicine.'

Isn't that just dandy? These idiots just arbitrarily do that, and, p.s., don't tell the poor bastards who are already out in practice that someday their livelihood will depend on whether or not they are 'Board Certified.' Hey, that's not bloody fair, is it? Somebody went and changed the rules in the middle of the goddamned game! A bunch of folks, mostly men I might add, were trying to fuck with my ability to earn a living, and, to this day, I have resented the hell out of it.

What with all the mergers and acquisitions in medicine, plus the increasing penetration of managed care (no pun intended,) the complicity has come full circle. By that I mean that the propaganda machine from the American Academy of Family Practice and the big university medical hot shots, have propagated the myth that Board Certification, by definition, increases one's I.Q. and stature in the medical community. And the payers (insurance companies) have bought it, have all the major urban hospitals and clinics in the land. So let's just relegate these pre-family practice residency freaks like me, to working in underserved, rural areas where they bloody well belong. How's that for petty political chicanery and prejudice? I, and my 'boomer' brothers and sisters, have been relegated to second class citizens, unfit to practice in the big, important places in our tidy little medical world. Give me a break!

This is but a small example of the bigger picture, but it happens to affect me now. Nonetheless, I persevered, and found myself in a managerial position in little old Levelland, Texas, a dot on the West Texas map. I was the medical director of a community health center, and somehow I secured admitting privileges at the local shit-hole hospital, in spite of great resistance to approving me. They fucked up legally, by giving me temporary privileges under the existing by-laws, which did not differentiate between board certified, or non-board certified family docs. They had, indeed, forgotten to change them to prevent vermin like me from getting on staff. So they were compelled to let me pass through their pearly gates, much to the charging of most of the staff docs. Chalk up one for the good guys against prejudice and bigotry!

To sum up: Board Certification in Family Practice-------nonsense! And to all those boomers like me who have been caught up in this travesty of justice I say, hang in there; someday we will get our long overdue retribution against those academic fucks who would relegate us to the scrap heap and then hope we won't speak out to defend our rights. Time will vindicate us, and I will do all I can to make it right again, even if I have to rent the Jumbotron in Times Square, and yell and scream from the highest rooftops "Give us Justice!"

Chapter 85

After my departure from Monahans, I came to serve as medical director of a community health center in Levelland, which was, in a word, a mess: no morale, no teamwork, no leadership----in short, a train wreck with default just around the corner.

I made some notes of things to attend to, and tried to prioritize the various problems I saw. However, so much was so wrong, that I had to address almost everything simultaneously. I took me months to orient myself so as to understand how this machine was supposed to run, both clinically and financially.

Most of our funds came from the federal government in the form of a grant, the rest coming from a rapidly diminishing state grant, private donations, and revenue from the clinic. The clinic revenue was mostly nominal payments from the poor, uninsured, huddled masses (otherwise known as mostly illegal Hispanics and poor white trash.) Okay, that's a generalization, but the truth hurts sometimes. But I never thought I'd live to see the day when Medicare and Medicaid patients were actually coveted. Being a federally granted community health center, our reimbursement from both Medicare and Medicaid was astounding, much higher than urban areas. I guess that was the government's way of thanking us for living in Hicksville, where few of my colleagues wished to reside. Ah, but as I saw it, we were the few, the chosen, the prosperous, and the urban docs were eating each other alive, competing intensely for fewer and fewer insured patients. Why, its gotten so desperate, I heard a radio spot the other day by an ophthalmology group in Amarillo offering free cataract surgery to poor folks that 'qualified' for their assistance. Unbelievable: you know things are bad when greedy pricks like these dudes will do ANYTHING pro bono!

Meanwhile, back at the CHC (community health center,) I had been studying our payer mix, and, in a word, it sucked. Over two thirds of our patients could barely afford transportation to the clinic, let alone pay for the office visit. Expecting remuneration for things like X-ray and lab, was a dream. Obtaining services from the local hospital for our mostly uninsured folks, was impossible. Of course, the hospital billed itself as 'not-for-profit,' but we all knew what a joke that was. By the way, that goes for any hospital in the land that makes that claim. They're just as greedy and avaricious as any private institution that operates purely for profit, but at least those folks are honest about their motivation.

How about medication, you ask? That is our one claim to fame, because we can provide generic and name brand drugs for a nominal sum through our Patient Assistance Program, and our stock of generics. Most of the big Pharmaceutical companies provided us with many expensive drugs as a charitable contribution to many Federal CHC'S. Were if not for our pharmacy program, our patients would go largely untreated.

So I guess you could say that we're doing our bit for our fellow man, but that's just partially true. Let's be honest here: my colleagues and I in these organizations still want to make a good living for all our efforts, which I don't consider hypocritical if you weigh the good we do against our compensation. I think it's a fair tradeoff: living in the sticks with little cultural stimulation) few dining out choices and last but not least, living as a minority (white) in a largely Hispanic community. Now I know how the other half has always felt, but not really since I am not poor, nor am I struggling to support my seventeen children and relatives that all live within a block or two of my double-wide.

I was going to get into a long-winded dialogue about illegal immigration, but I'll just leave that to the politicians. What I will say, however, from the standpoint of healthcare dollars, is that these folks are bankrupting our already strained medical system in this country. Hell, we can't afford to pay for our own indigent and uninsured population, let alone Mexico's.

Chapter 86

I was at a TACHC (Texas Association of Community Health Centers) meeting in San Antonio in the fall of '02. There was a gala the last evening honoring several members to TACH for their efforts over the years. One middle-aged, Hispanic man was given a great honor for his long service, followed by one incredible acceptance speech in which he went on ad nauseum about his ancestors' struggles to get started in America. He also threw in a comment about how he personally had endured prejudice, and overcome the many hurdles put in his way by the 'gringos' who run this country. I beg your pardon?! I could hardly believe the crap I was hearing from this jerk.

Let me tell him about my ancestors, and their struggles to get out of Europe in the early 1900's to escape certain death. The Russians, Germans, French, Polish, Hungarian et ai, just couldn't get enough of Jewish blood. Once they had a taste of it, like a grizzly bear, nothing else could satisfy their appetite to kill. That, my friends, is 'prejudice' and 'hurdles.' And let me tell Pablo about my grandparents' arrival in Canada, with absolutely nothing, as' legal Immigrants' (refugees.) I ask you, are Mexican immigrants refugees, fleeing from an oppressive, cruel regime that persecutes, tortures and kills, like Stalin or Hitler? No, they are simply illegal aliens with nothing but the shirt on their back and their basic labor skills.

My mother's parents settled in New Brunswick, and my grandfather did any menial job he could find to support his family----without complaint. They eventually ended up in Toronto, where he continued his labors, finally catching a break when he and his three sons bought a grocery store. After many twenty hour days and nights, the store began to flourish, and it provided a comfortable living for four families for a long time---over forty years in fact. The grocery store had been bought in a package deal with a small apartment building above it, and an empty space beside it of substantial size. That space became a hardware store that my Uncle Morris ran. No one got rich here, but they survived and were comfortable; that's all they wanted----to be good providers for their families, and they were. And they never bitched about how hard their lot in life had been like our friend Pablo.

Chapter 87

My current predicament concerns my contract. Unfortunately, the payer mix I've previously outlined had a great deal to do with one important part of my contract. Collections for hospital admissions comprised twenty percent of my annual stipend, which, in any other situation, would be reasonable, but I worked for a clinic that served the poor and uninsured
.

Okay, I know what you're thinking, "why should II give a rat's ass about another rich doctor's six figure contract?"

Just hear me out on this, and maybe you can relate to the general topic of honesty and fair play in the process of securing a fair contract of employment in any occupation. Oh, and let me add right here that most doctors are far from rich nowadays, so just abandon that notion before I go any further. Thanks.

As I was saying, the 20% for hospital services initially seemed reasonable. What I didn't know then was just how poor and uninsured our clientele was. Billing and collecting this amount would therefore be impossible, so the 20% was unattainable and just nonsense from the get go. My *CEO,* a chunky, trailer trash gal name of Miss Donna Lee, said that she had warned me about this in our final negotiation. Hell no, she didn't! My wife happened to be present during that meeting, and she sure as hell can't recall any 'warning.' To add insult to injury, the contract was subject to annual review and 'possible salary adjustments' depending on productivity (or lack thereof.) Contracts such as this are just a disaster waiting to happen. Please don't be like me---get a lawyer to review your contract. Doctors, including me, are too naive in business matters to negotiate anything important without legal assistance.

Donna Lee Crump, the aforementioned *CEO,* had offered me this job, and in that interview, I now know why she seemed so desperate to obtain my services: no one else wanted the damned position. This was one tough undertaking, as I have outlined. Shaping this place up was going to be an achievement of a lifetime. Not being one to shrink from such a Herculean task, I accepted. Unfortunately, I signed that contract which, predictably, would prove disastrous. As I should have expected, in my second year of employment, my salary was cut by over twenty percent. I couldn't deliver the hospital numbers I needed to for reasons I have explained previously. Because of this drastic cut in income, I had to once again, look to the emergency room to provide me with the shortfall. Oh joy, back to twelve fun-filled hours in heaven, my not-so-favorite moonlighting chore that was a financial necessity.

I will say this for Ms. Crump, aside from the fact that she was a liar: she had obviously done her homework, and, indeed, knew who I was and what I was capable of achieving for her. NO! Just kidding-----she didn't know shit about me. She was just desperate to find a warm body to fill this position; someone to share the blame when the whole thing imploded! Not to forget also that the Feds were demanding that she find a medical director stat, and, no Federal money = no clinic= no jobs for anyone. Just how much the board knew of her dealings with contractual matters such as this, I had no idea, but I suspect they wouldn't have been too thrilled with her methodology for obtaining new providers-----making promises that could not be kept, for example.

But Ms. Donna Lee was cunning, and resourceful, with a good working knowledge of how to use the legal system to her advantage to keep her job. I guess it ran in the family, since one of her sisters was a lawyer. I hate to be mean, but these gals were clear-to-the-bone ugly, and they knew it. I think that's why Donna Lee was so clearly unhappy, while at the same time, she was as dictatorial as she had to be to survive, which she had done for some twenty years. That was a miracle, given the turnover in community health centers among the administrative staff. She certainly knew how to get rid of board chairmen she disliked, or who posed a threat to her. For example, she sued one gentleman for sexual harassment, and he promptly resigned. He had a spotty reputation with the ladies, but I can't imagine any self-respecting male making a pass at Miss Donna Lee. Also, a prominent professional gentleman in our town had been a board chairman, and he too left the post. To this day, no one knows what old Donna had on him, but she undoubtedly had a hand in that one too. I heard rumors that he had the information on her he needed to sway the board into finally taking the steps to fire her, but he resigned before action could be taken. A born survivor, that's our Donna Lee.

Did I mention that Donna was also involved in one of those pyramid schemes like Amway? Yep, there ya' go; another brilliant entrepreneur is born. She enlisted several of her underlings in administration to take part in this venture, but I think it was more coercion than a benign offer to participate. And all of these shenanigans were on company time! No wonder the board was kept in the dark by D.L. That would be immediate grounds for dismissal, but no employee ever called her on it, or reported these goings on to the board. And I'm no heroic figure in all this either. Did I report her to any board member? Hell no----I treasured my job too much, at least until this whole contract mess raised its ugly head.

So here does all this leave me? I had three choices: first, as I said before, accept less pay and work ER to make up the difference; secondly, resign after locating another job; or third, negotiate a compromise contract and forget everything else I know about Donna and her past dealings in deceit and general mischief. Being a pragmatist after all my misfortune in the past five or six years, I'm leaning towards option three. Hell, I can't see us moving again----that might be the death knell of our marriage, not to mention what's left of my sanity. Besides, I rather liked Levelland and Lubbock, in spite of the dry, dusty, windy climate.

It still beats the shit out of places like Houston, where I was perpetually drenched in sweat for eight years. I can still wake up in a cold sweat after having a Houston nightmare----what a hellhole! Summertime in Houston was like winter in Canada: you must stay indoors to survive. Oklahoma City was pretty much like Houston, with the added bonus of tornado season. Yippee!

I should probably take back that trailer trash label I pinned on D.L. After all, I might very well have ended up in a stylish, upscale double-wide myself the way my luck had been running. Maybe I've overlooked the 'glass is half full' line of thinking. After all. less money would finally force us to live within our means. For example, selling our expensive house would remove a huge financial burden, and help keep us out of perpetual debt. The same goes for spending less on frivolities like clothes we don't need, high-priced restaurants, and almost any recreational activity that involves laying out significant bank. I was feeling better just thinking of all these savings we could achieve.

Chapter 88

Donna Lee and I have to go to Denver as leaders of a new collaborative project on cardiovascular disease. It would be just the two of us, alone, with no buffer zone of other team members. This promised to be a gloomy, if not disastrous journey, given my feelings for Ms. Donna Lee. Her incompetence and dishonesty about my contract were bitter pills to swallow, but I had to, if only to preserve my sanity.

Ever the optimist, I thought of every scenario that could end in tragedy on this junket. I perseverated in this negative mindset for weeks, until I had finally grown so sick and tired of myself, that I just had to let it go. As the 'twelve steppers' say, "Let go and let God." Easier said then done, but I did pray for divine intervention and guidance, a huge step for me, the ultimate cynic. Desperation will overwhelm cynicism any day of the week, and you'll do anything, even pray, to relieve the stress. And you know what? Damned if it didn't work! What a novel concept-----prayer actually helps solve problems! And there weren't any harmful side affects such as I have experienced in the past using tranquilizers. What with prayer being free, who says there are no bargains to be had anymore? That's as close to a religious discussion that I will ever get into, since I find that trying to verbalize my spiritual essence to others is infinitely boring for them and me.

The contract issue will never be resolved to my satisfaction, I know that now, but at least I'm finally over it, and I can breathe freely again. As for the meeting, my worst fears were never realized, and it actually turned out to be productive. Donna Lee and I remained cordial to a fault, but we would never be friends, that was a certainty. How can you befriend anyone that you could never trust?

Chapter 89

During my second year as medical director of South Plains Community Health Center, a new 'doc' came on board, one Timothy Gross, D.O. I'll resist the temptation to take another pot shot at the osteopath thing just because I'm a nice guy. Besides, I've given what little information I could glean on this bunch of so-called doctors, so I'll leave it at that. Tim was a new graduate, a former chief resident in family practice at Hole-in the Wall Medical Center, and he was a giant of a man. Standing about six foot three and tipping the scales at well over two-hundred and eighty pounds, the name lumpy comes to mind, except that lumpy ('leave it to Beaver') was much better looking. When Tim laughed, the whole damned building shook right along with his multiple layers of adipose tissue (fat.) He had a Miss Piggy nose, two or more chins, and a high fashion buzz cut. His pants were always riding up on him, and he couldn't seem to keep his butt crack free from attack by his own clothing. He was a real mess of a human being. On the surface, he seemed a jovial, harmless sort of dude, just trying to get along and settle into his first job outside of school. At first, everyone, including me, rather enjoyed his high spirited antics, and even his whining, which was mildly amusing in its seeming innocence.

But soon little things began to surface, and he slowly evolved into something quite different-----irritating and disturbing at the same time. His 'humor' became increasingly sarcastic and edgy. It was rapidly becoming apparent that he was using the guise of back-slapping, good boy humor, to hide his true, malicious, devious intent. His agenda was light years removed from his apparent persona. The bottom line was that Tim was one hell of a shit disturber, reveling in others' misfortune, which somehow made him feel better about himself. I found it sad that anyone's ego needed that much massaging.

Poor Mrs. Gross, I don't know how she managed with three children----a little boy and girl, and Tim. Typically, the wife was even larger than her slovenly husband. One had to assume that she had sought comfort in food. We all have our addictions to try and help us through the dark times, and I would surmise that her drug was food-----Illegal, but still potentially deadly. How else could she stay married to this jerk, unless of course I misjudged her as well, and her jolly, chubby exterior masked something sinister? Hell, at least she snagged herself a doctor, even if he was a D.O. I wonder if, to her, that made up for all the crap she's put up with. I've seen them together many times, and his behavior towards his wife was rude, obnoxious, demanding, whiny, verbally abusive, self-absorbed, and above all else, selfish. And these were some of his better qualities. But hey, she's got a doctor!

So what was Tim's real agenda? Keeping things in a constant state of turmoil served two purposes: first, it made him feel more important to raise cane and keep people off balance; and second, it undermined my authority as medical director/which he believed brought me down to his level. Basically, he wanted to make all of us look stupid so that his brilliance would shine through. All I can say to that if he was so damned brilliant, why didn't he go to Harvard instead of Podunk u. to become a D.O. Someday I believe I'll have to ask him that question, but in the meantime I'd just have to tolerate his nonsense up to a point. Beyond that point, he would be gone as far as I was concerned. My advice to Tim was to grow up fast, and in the process, find another agenda to follow. As we all expected, Tim finally did himself in. One fine day we were checking out what were to be our exam rooms in our new clinic building, and when Tim was shown where his would be, he had a fit. He confronted our CEO, who had decided where each doctor's exam rooms would be located. He was pissed off because he had already made his choice on this matter. She stood firm on her decision, which infuriated him to the point where he imploded, throwing a fist in her general direction. It missed her, fortunately for him, but he put a large hole in the drywall near where she was standing. Tim was fired on the spot by Donna Lee, who had witnessed the last scene in this tragic one act play. I'm not sure what in God's name the chief financial officer was doing choosing rooms for doctors, but that's beside the point I suppose. Tim had a wicked temper, the crowning glory of all his other psychopathic issues, and it did him in.

The only moral here, really, is that in any business, there has to be some code of behavior. For a 'doctor' to behave this way, no quarter could be shown. We all have to bite our tongue sometimes, no matter how righteous we feel our cause is, but this was so pathetically petty, this argument over who gets what rooms. I should have known Tim would go out with a whimper, not a bang, over something trivial to everyone but him.

Chapter 90

You know that old saying 'watch out what you wish for, it might just come true?' That is precisely what happened to me at South Plains Rural Health Center. I had hoped and prayed for Donna lee's departure for so long, I could almost taste it. In spite of the fact that my professional life was actually going along fairly well, being firmly ensconced in my job as medical director with a thriving practice, I still was foolish enough to think things could somehow be better with another *CEO* And then, it finally happened. The board got a wild hair to fire her, and they did just that. That was about as ugly a situation that night as I have ever experienced. As much as I had my personal disagreements with Donna lee, I couldn't help but feel badly for her given the way she was treated at that meeting. It was as if, after twenty years of loyal service, she was suddenly the villain, and the main reason for all our problems. The board members behaved like a pack of wild animals, circling in for the kill, and they couldn't have been more demeaning and cruel. This was a personal vendetta, not an objective search for truth.

After this crucifixion, the clinic leadership, including myself, was stunned. Who was next? After witnessing this debacle, we felt the board could throw anyone of us out the door and not give it a second thought. These were mean-assed people! Ignorance and cruelty are a bad combination----does the name Hitler ring a bell? The folks around me, including the clinic manager, Ida, and the pharmacist, John, threw a couple of names out as a possible replacement for D.L., including, of all people, me! Of course I declined to consider such a possibility, especially since I was about as busy as a person could be, what with my clinic duties and emergency room work as well. But, after a while, the notion of being the big cheese struck a chord deep in my soul, and it felt right. I hadn't given it a moment's thought until these folks suggested it, but, as time went on, I knew I could balance my clinical duties with this leadership role. If a salary could be negotiated that allowed me to discontinue my emergency room moonlighting, then there was no real obstacle to making the change.

It was all making sense to me now: I had traveled a long, winding road, with many tough breaks along the way, but it had allied me to this place at this time---my real destiny had finally made itself known. I was to be the leader of a community health center in Levelland, Texas, and this was how I would finish out my career. Perfect! But (there was always a but), there was someone else who desperately wanted this job, and she was quite a presence-----all four-hundred pounds of her. It had probably been twenty years since she could *see* her feet while in a standing postion.

One of Donna lee's last acts as executive director was to hire a pediatrician, Ms. Luby McDonald, thinking this would help our bottom line considerably, given how much Medicaid reimbursed for pediatrics in a rural setting. That was sound reasoning if you pick the right doc, but that was not to be the case. Miss. Luby was as lazy as she was gigantic. To put it another way, her lack of motivation to *see* patients and put in a decent day's work was patently obvious, and her only raison d'etre, was to become the new director as soon as she found out that Donna lee had been terminated. So there it was, I had a rival for the position I now coveted, and I was not a happy camper.

We both had interviews with the board, an opportunity to make our case for ourselves. I felt that I gave an excellent accounting of myself with my presentation, and left the meeting feeling rather confident. Boy was I wrong. I didn't get the job, not because of the board's perception that I couldn't do it, but because I was the number one doctor in volume of patients seen, and they felt they couldn't jeopardize the clinic's current success by taking me away several hours a day, from my post as a clinician. I was a victim of my own success as regards building a big practice for myself and the clinic. I had foreseen that the board might look at things that way, and had addressed it at my interview. I told them that I was willing to work longer and harder to do both jobs well, and could do so if I didn't have the added burden of doing a twelve hour shift in the ER once a week. Obviously, my argument, sound as it was, fell on deaf ears, and Miss. Luby won out. Her dream came true-----she now had an excuse for sitting on her fat ass all day, shuffling papers and playing on the computer. My dream, conversely, was dashed, and, I feared, so was my future with this company. After running such a hard campaign for the position that she had won, I knew in my gut that, as her chief rival for the top post, Luby would find a way to dispose of me, even though I was the one provider that was keeping the clinic afloat.

I'll spare you the boring details of how I lost *yet* another job, but that's what happened. Just prior to my formal dismissal, I was offered another job as clinic physician in Morton, a little oilfield town twenty-five miles west of Levelland. Ironically, it was for more pay and less hours, so I accepted with no hesitation. My only other option was full-time emergency work, which didn't appeal to me at all, so Morton it was. So, once again I circled the wagons, and gathered up my things to head west. My quest for the perfect job was still very much in play. For the first time in my life, I had serious doubts that such a thing existed, but I will never give up the search for this holiest of grails.

Chapter 91

I need to inject a final word about federally granted Community Health Centers before moving on, and here it is------bullshit! Given that the mission of these clinics is to serve those who would otherwise go unserved, most of you would consider us to be filled to the brim with the milk of human kindness: true charitable spirit by the whole clinic team. Wrong, wrong, wrong; that couldn't be further from the truth. These places are no different than 'for profit' institutions, striving to milk the last possible cent from patients and donors alike. Survival is paramount in every business, and this was no different, with the exception that the feds pretty much guaranteed our survival, so long as we met certain benchmarks that we actually set for ourselves each year.

What I am getting at here is that we weren't special in any way just because we were supposed to be more charitable than the rest of the 'for profit' medical world. People are the same in any clinic or hospital: the same pettiness, jealousy, greed, and selfishness. It didn't feel any different than many other places I had worked in, which was disappointing. Not to be a complete hypocrite, I had my own ambitions and personal greed issues as well, but at least I've been honest about it. I will say too that I enjoyed the work and the appreciation that was shown by the patients. They made me feel that this was one of my more worthwhile endeavors of a long career.

As of this writing, I am sad to say that the clinic is not doing well at all, thanks to the incredible stupidity of a board that knows nothing about medicine as a business, and to Dr. luby and her little band of merry maids, who are working hard to figure out how to not work hard and still keep the clinic open. Sour grapes you may say, but that is not the case. I just think it's a damned shame to see this project go down the crapper given that, in the final analysis, I did buy into the mission wholeheartedly.

Chapter 92

Once the ascension of Miss. Luby to the executive director's throne at South Plains Rural Health Center was a certainty, I knew my ass was about to be kicked into the next county. That being the case, I decided to accept an offer to work, just by sheer coincidence, in the next county just west of Levelland, saving everyone a lot of bother, and saving me from a very painful ass-kicking.

Just by chance, the main doc-honcho in Morton, another shitty little West Texas town, lived in my neighborhood. One fine night, he and his wife were walking down my street when I happened to be completing my evening walk with my faithful Chihuahua, Katie. He said hello, and introduced himself, asking me how things were going for me as medical director at the community health center. After I related to him just how things were not going, he actually offered me a job------his! Seems he was looking to retire in the next year, and Morton was looking for a doc to replace him. Hell, I was all over that offer. When I told Debbie, my long suffering wife, what had transpired, she urged me to look into it, given how miserable we both were about my current job prospects.

And look into it I did. I called the CEO the very next day and set up an interview. He sounded like a kind, receptive man, excited at the prospect of finding an experienced physician without having to pay a search firm thirty or more thousand bucks. I was a screaming bargain for God's sake. And within a month, I was firmly ensconced in the rural health clinic in Morton, the largest 'city' in Cochran Country. With a grand total of perhaps two thousand souls, being dubbed largest city is a dubious honor at best.

This hospital, and this clinic, were over fifty years old, and looked every day of it. What a relic. The distinct musty, dusty odor that old buildings have, hit my sinuses like a hammer every morning I walked into this dungeon. This had to be the most depressing atmosphere of any hospital or clinic I had ever experienced, which is saying a hell of a lot given all the crappy places I have seen and worked in. The saving grace was the people that worked there. They were kind and· generous to a fault, especially my good friends, nurses Ernestine, Betty, Linda, and, of course, my faithful and devoted nurse from Levelland who followed me over to Morton, Diana D. She was and is a peach of a gal, a warm and loving human being who has been as loyal as one-person can be to another. That quality has no price, and is not for sale anywhere. Yes, there were great people in Morton, but the monotony of doing very little work was starting to get to me. And, after six months of sheer drudgery in a tiny, dark, dingy office, the capper came when the soon-to-be-retired doc decided that, guess what, he wasn't going to retire after all. Gee, my luck is holding. As the old saying goes, if it weren't for bad luck, I wouldn't have any at all. Of course this meant that, sooner or later, the county and its hospital board, would, of necessity, have to let me go. They couldn't afford to pay two docs' salaries, and I understood that----it wasn't their fault.

I did, eventually, have my say with the doc who had recruited me to replace him. I didn't exactly give him the tongue lashing he deserved for going back on his word; it just wasn't worth the effort to state the obvious. Besides, I was used to this sort of treatment at the hands of my colleagues, the 'doc bosses' as I have labeled them, so why should I be surprised and upset. I did, however, tell him near the end of my stay there, that he should remember one thing from this debacle: his actions had serious consequences for two other human beings, me and my wife. Perhaps he should think things through a little more before he decides to fuck around with folks who are anxious to believe that the best situation has just fallen into their laps.

I have to admit, however, that he did buy me one year of time to catch my breath after Levelland, and, at the same time, collect a decent pay check. As far as I know, he is still in command at Cochran Memorial command central, and bully for him!

In Conclusion.

So you wake up one morning and you are sixty-two years old, and you are amazed by the fact that you are still living. After three marriages, two bankruptcies, numerous job debacles and run-ins with wretched human beings like 'The Dickman' et ai, damned if you're not here. I never much thought about survival until I turned sixty, and, during the past eighteen months, until I lost both my parents. I had no idea how traumatic and depressing it felt to be an orphan, regardless of one's age.

Oh for the carefree years of medical school, ha -ha! Can you believe that anyone would call med school carefree? Now I can. Those were incredible, wondrous years, topped off by a journey of epic proportions through Europe and Scandinavia. I wish more than my mind could be transported back to a long-gone era when my only worry was how to make five bucks last a day, and where would I sleep that night. Those days can never be repeated in this dangerous world, and today's young students shouldn't take the risk. How sad, that the innocence of four decades ago couldn't survive. It is a cruel and brutal world overseas, and it has reached these shores as well. Our innocence has been forever lost.

And so too it is with the world of medicine: lost innocence in so many ways. Where once we could converse with our patients of either sex, and not have to measure our every word for fear of a lawsuit, today that is not the case. In fact, when I was just a young pup in my first solo practice, I examined women all alone----no female nurse in the room, and neither of us felt that this was amoral or unusual in any way. Today, that would be tantamount to sexual misconduct by a physician. My one –employee office suited my finances just fine, and we operated an efficient, mildly profitable shop. Today, the solo doc is all but dead. Big hospitals and insurance companies, with their diminishing reimbursement plan for all docs, especially in primary care, have seen to that. Whether it's Medicare, Medicaid, Blue Cross, or whomever, they have colluded to kill off as many solo family docs and Internists as possible-----the rotten bastards. So, while overhead has gone through the proverbial roof, payment has gone through the floor.

The thought that I would go through five jobs in ten years, was unimaginable. Back in the day, a doctor usually had the same office and staff for his whole career, and retired at a respectable age, still young enough to enjoy the fruits of his labor. Not so for many of us boomers today, as we bounce from job to job, evil doc-boss to evil doc-boss. I never dreamt that there would be so many rotten people in my profession, screwing the whole damned thing up. Currently, I work for an occupational medicine outfit owned by a married couple who happen to be physical therapists by trade, and would-be entrepreneurs in their dreams. That's not a bad thing, unless your lust for money is so profound that it obscures all traces of humanity you one might have once possessed. These folks, especially the husband, remain glued to their office desks, plotting their next big financial move, and, at the same time, obsessively counting every penny in their rather sizable bank accounts. The employees and the doc (moi) are forced to work like dogs for their meager paychecks. Volume, once again, takes center stage. That is the only thing that matters, that, and how much you can rape workers' compensation insurance for. Words fail me in describing this pathetic scene in this old, musty-dusty clinic building---people-scurrying about, rushing clients in and out as quickly as humanly possible, with absolutely no control of volume flow. If we die right there on the spot, I'm sure that we will be unceremoniously carted off, and another miserable soul will be there in moments to replace us. So goes the cycle of 'life' in this rat-hole.

Okay, so perhaps you think that I have portrayed myself as to much the victim, but that is not so. We are all victims of evil, corruption and greed on the part of these territorial, monolithic hospital corporations, the insurance industry, and the increasingly impersonal treatment from mega-clinics, and doc-in-the -box shops. Grind 'em in, grind 'em out, that's all they give a shit about----volume, more volume, instead of individual human beings. One on one time with a patient has disappeared; it's now a laughable concept. Everywhere you turn, you find this new landscape of medicine bereft of good-will, or even a trace of the Hippocratic Oath. I, for one, long for the good old days that we will never see again. Yes Virginia, Dr. Welby is dead.

Chapter. Dr.G.'s Top Ten list of Medical Rip-Offs and Pet Peeves.

1. Unquestionably, the holistic (alternative) medicine craze ranks atthe very top of the list. This is a billion dollar industry that is so multifaceted that it is hard to categorize all the elements involved. This new public obsession could have its very own top ten list. let's begin with health food stores, such as GNC. To me, most of what they sell is just over-priced junk. Vitamins are just vitamins after all, and can be purchased for pennies at Wal-Mart for example. And no one, not even Linus Pauling, has shown that mega-dosing with any vitamin is beneficial, and, indeed, could be harmful. Other products, such as anti-oxidants and various herbs and spices, similarly have no basis in scientific fact. There are virtually no controlled studies to back up the outrageous claims made for these substances. They may just as well sell this useless crap out of a medicine wagon, using a traveling snake oil salesman to make the pitch. I like nostalgia as much as the next guy; I just don't like to pay a high price for it.

2. Alternative medicine also encompasses procedures such as acupuncture, hypnosis, chelation, hyperbaric oxygen chamber, *etc.* The result with any of these 'therapies' is largely disappointing, not to mention very expensive. Unfortunately, the most vulnerable in our society, the elderly, are being ripped off all the time by the vultures who hard sell them these 'cures'. And just who protects these citizens from the charlatans?

No one, especially in the legitimate medical world: not the AMA, not state medical boards, not peer review committees of hospitals and large clinics, not even the vaunted AClU protects the citizenry from this junk science. In short, self-policing in medicine is almost non-existent, and private organizations that purport to protect us are just blowing hot air up our bottoms.

3. Weight loss clinics----one of my all-time favorites. Yes Virginia, they're still are privately owned clinics raking in the big bucks for doing very little more than prescribing diet pills. I've even been to a meeting sponsored by the National Association of Bariatric Physicians. There actually was some decent information on new treatments on the horizon, including less invasive surgical techniques, but mostly, it was smoke and mirrors, theoretical balderdash. I heard some discussions on new diet regimens that I believe were conceived on another planet. I don't think I'll ever aspire to be a 'bariatrician.'

4. Pain Clinics: now this is a painful topic, especially financially. Most pain docs are anesthesiologists who got lazy and found God, who In turn, led them to the promised land---that is to say, the means to churning out much more money in a faster and easier way .. When other docs have thrown in the towel because they either don't have a good working knowledge of all the medication options, or they don't want to be involved in using controlled drugs for a multitude of reasons, they refer their patients to these guys and gals. In many cases docs won't participate in using pain control meds for cultural and even religious reasons. I can't relate to any of this rationale, especially since a doctor's number one mandate is to relieve pain and suffering. Perhaps some cultures have such reverence for pain that they prefer to allow it to go untreated. And I think that any doctor, regardless of background, should not be allowed to practice in this country if they are unwilling to relieve their patients' suffering. Getting back to the pain docs, their number one procedure is the ESI, or epidural steroid injection. A very long needle is inserted into the patients' spine, containing a sizeable dose of steroid (cortisone) medication. Usually, these injections are of little help, and if they do help,

it is for a very short time. And they are very costly, a windfall for the doctor and a pain in the wallet for the patient. Two things always cause me to scratch my head: first, most of the insurance companies will pay handsomely for repeated shots of this sort, and secondly, the patients will go along with this treatment for quite a while before realizing what a complete waste of time and money this is. The procedure takes just a few minutes, and the doc can do dozens of these a day, raking in thousands for a minimal amount of effort. I don't know anyone doing this 'work' that is anything but filthy rich; and the system allows this rip-off to continue with virtually no criticism by the medical establishment. I should have considered being a pain doc, but, in all good conscience, I can't participate in areas of medicine that I find to be, at best, suspect.

The only other function served by the pain specialist, is to prescribe inordinate amounts of narcotics. Someone has to do this, but is it always justified since most patients just don't need unlimited amounts of dangerous controlled substances. Again, there is very little oversight by anyone in authority with regards to these prescriptions. It's as if they're prescribing candy, for God's sake. Does the name Anna Nicole Smith ring a bell?

5. Chiropractors: I come from the traditional side of medicine that is based in legitimate science, so the things I have seen and heard for myself concerning this 'profession' lead me to believe that what you have here is nothing more than glorified physical therapy, with a few twists (pardon the pun), some of which I have found to be dangerous to the patient. Just as one example of potential danger, I have had patients with serious spine issues, such as herniated discs, who have been subjected to rigorous 'manipulation' by chiropractors, the end result being more pain than prior to this 'treatment.' But catastrophe could have also been the result in the form of permanent weakness or even paralysis of an extremity.

I find manipulation to 'pop' someone's back, a frightening prospect at best. Just what the hell are they trying to accomplish here? I have no clue, since the spine cannot be anatomically changed unless you go ahead and fracture it, or require an operation. Another thing a lot of these folks do is engage in the same sort of nonsense as the health food stores, pushing vitamins, minerals, herbs, etc. as being effective in healing muscles and joints. A few have even gotten into weight loss, applying staples in the patients' ears to serve, supposedly, as an appetite suppressant. And people flock like sheep to these creeps, again, because they are desperate to try anything. I hate to be a cynical truth-monger, but there still is no substitute for hard work and determination when it comes to permanent weight loss. I have spoken with hundreds, if not thousands, of people over the years who have blown thousands of dollars on bogus gimmicks for rapid weight loss, when all they really needed to do was spend a few bucks on a couple of visits to their local Weight Watchers branch office, and buy a pair of good walking shoes. I've stopped giving out advice like this because it almost always falls on deaf ears. I hate that glazed eye look when I tell patients the facts of life ----they hate the unfettered truth and end up resenting me, which doesn't serve any purpose other than to discourage new patient referrals to my practice. Honesty is just not in these days, at the least when it comes to weight loss.

6. Cardiology. Once upon a time, long, long ago, there was a kindly, skilled specialist in cardiovascular disease, who used his clinical acumen to evaluate the needs of his patients. He was prudent in the tests and procedures he ordered, taking into consideration the costs of unwarranted tests to the patient, as well as the potential for side affects with some of the tools at his disposal. Well, you can kiss those days' good-bye folks, because cardiology has become a huge financial windfall. You see, what has happened here, as with many specialties, is the death of the solo practitioner, which has resulted in the formation of large clinics read (factories) where patients are processed like cattle. Each and every patient, regardless of his or her symptoms, or ability to pay, will, without question, get a . nuclear stress test and an echocardiogram (ultrasound of the heart.) It goes without saying that these procedures

are very lucrative indeed. And add to that the 'routine' lab studies everyone gets, plus the cost of the consultation with the cardiologist, and you have quite a windfall for the clinic. Imagine generating close to two-thousand dollars for every person seen daily in any business situation. Now multiply that by a factor of twenty (or more.) Wow! Along with all this, there still remains in the wings the cardiologists' true bread and butter, the angiogram (heart catheterization.) Unless you walk or run quickly away from the center, many of you undoubtedly will have an angiogram. Why is that you ask? Because the other tests you have already had and paid for may very well prove to be inconclusive, and thus the gold standard of cardiology, the angiogram, is your only hope of clearly defining the problem, if indeed there is a problem at all. God knows, there are a boatload of angiograms done in this country every day that are completely uncalled for----no overpowering reasons other than to pay for the doctor's new Mercedes. The nuclear stress test and the echocardiogram have become the standard of care for every single patient who sees a cardiologist. The only way to curb health care costs on procedures like these, that in many cases are unwarranted, is, as previously stated, for the big insurance companies, including Medicare and Medicaid, to require from the physician a clear-cut indication for performing them. This will probably never happen in my lifetime, but one can .always hope that common sense will someday prevail. Universal health care should fix this, right Mr. Obama?

7. The cardiologists have done a brilliant job of mimicking the financial success of the large, Multi-Specialty Clinics, which have had decades to perfect the art of the wallet biopsy. As soon as the patient hits the door, he is subjected to a dizzying array of specialists, procedures, and lab/x-ray studies. To me the main reason for a group of docs getting together in business is to save money on overhead, but it has evolved that this is no longer the raison d'etre. The one and only reason now is to generate more money for everyone in the partnership. It certainly has nothing to do with the welfare of the patient. They don't get better care just because they're in a big, fancy

building. What they do get is a bigger bill since they've been processed through the clinic 'program.'

8. Television Scams.

These scams are among the worst cases of fraud perpetrated on the American public. At first, I found them amusing, but, the more I hear and see them, the more disgusted I get. The old saying that 'if it seems too good to be true it probably isn't,' is still the unvarnished truth. Some of my favorite infomercials concern topics such as male (penile) enhancement; hair restoration; diets (of course,) skin rejuvenation without surgery; and the incessant chatter about holistic cures for a wide range of disease states. There are weekly half-hour programs, usually on Saturday or Sunday morning, that try to come across as legitimate medical discussions, but are really just vehicles for pushing junk products. There must be a fortune to be made because a ton of money is being spent for television time. For sheer entertainment value, I'd rather watch some of those old Oral Roberts faith healing programs------at least no one is hurt, and it seems like a fun way to spend a Sunday morning.

9. Doctor Hypocrites.

Have you ever been hi this situation as a patient? Your doctor walks into your examining room after your annual checkup, and tells you that all your tests are normal, and, in the short term you should be alright. You ask him what the heck he means by 'short term.' The reply from Dr. Hypocrite goes something like this: "Well Mr. Smith, even though I can find no major health issues at this time, there still is one overriding risk factor that you have---obesity. Sooner or later, this will prove to be a significant issue for you, especially in terms of cardiovascular disease and diabetes." let me stop right there and describe for you the good doctor's physical presentation. He stands about five foot six inches, weighs two-hundred and eighty pounds, give or take a pound, has bad breath, body odor, and a five o'clock shadow at ten am. His lab coat is in desperate need of a cleaning, he has two chins, one enormous abdomen, and beads of sweat on his forehead and upper lip. He wears bifocals half-way down his nose to create an air of distinction and credibility. On the other hand, you are five foot eleven, weigh one hundred and ninety pounds, and go to the gym regularly. You ask how in the world he can label you 'obese' given your current state of good health and your almost nonexistent weight problem. Here is his comment: "Sir, in my opinion you are a walking heart attack waiting to happen. You must change your lifestyle drastically if you hope to have a normal lifespan. You must change your eating habits, get plenty of exercise, and most importantly, quit smoking." "But doc" you say, "I told you that I quit smoking seventeen years ago, remember? And as for exercise, I go to the gym at least three times a week, running on the treadmill two miles each time. My diet is vastly improved in recent years, with much less -earbs and fat. What else can a guy do to be healthy?" Dr. H. has no snappy retort in response to Mr. Smith because he's been busted. Yes, Dr, H.'s little game of 'let's play doctor' has not impressed his patient, and he was called on it. The only thing that would have been better would have been. a diatribe by Smith that would go something like this: "Listen Dr. Casey, you fat fuck; you haven't the first clue just how good or bad my health really is. You know how I know this? Just by looking at you, Charles Atlas! And you're telling me how to live a healthy lifestyle? First, let's examine your pathetic life: first thing you'll do tonight when you leave the office is stop at the nearest deli and feed your fat fucking face with a corned beef sandwich dripping with fat because that's the way you ordered it. Don't forget to add a Big Gulp of coca cola to your meal; you need the extra calories you stupid bastard. Then you'll go home (with some takeout of course,) sit down on your big fat ass, turn on the television, and vegetate for the next five or six hours. Finally, you'll cap off this evening of exuberant health activity, by falling asleep in you Laz-Boy. If you're lucky, you'll survive another night of sleep apnea, and wake up the next morning. Your wife won't wake you up because you're too grotesque to have a wife."

For the record, there really is a Dr. H. came to know him in my Amarillo days. He was an internist and was, in fact, morbidly obese, which didn't stop him from running a weight loss clinic out of his office. The obvious question that arises out of this is how can anyone, male or female, take advice on losing weight from a doctor who has no control of his own habits? This is actually a very common phenomenon: doctors doling out sage pronouncements on patients' failures when they themselves are shamefully inadequate in maintaining even a semblance of a healthy lifestyle. I think you should get your own house in order, my fellow physicians, before lecturing your patients on their shortcomings. How can anyone take you seriously------ you're just a joke if you can't set an example for your folks.

10. Physician Incompetence.

Last, but certainly not least, is my all-time favorite pet peeve, the epidemic of incompetence that exists among today's family physicians. In spite of the fact (or because of it) that most are board certified, there is no assurance that your doc is any more competent than the old time general practitioner who, although not boarded, had a tremendous amount of practical skill and knowledge. This topic is so complex and multi-faceted that I could write a book about this subject alone. I'm not saying that I'm the greatest primary doctor that ever came down the pike, but, after over thirty-five years in practice without any major litigation, I am good enough to recognize who knows what and who's full of shit.

One of the major components of incompetence is just plain laziness. A lot of docs are terminally lazy! I don't know where this originates since to make it through medical school you can't goof off----ever. The words 'lazy' and 'medical school' are incompatible with reality. Most students I knew in my med school days were type triple A personalities, but a rare few got through being more laid back most of the time. They could gear up to an A when exams were imminent, and, afterwards, settle back into their type B mode. But, when internship and residency came along, even the B's had to pick up the pace and work hard; they had no other choice. How they did that, given their predisposition to be slackers, I can't say, but somehow they mustered the will and energy for those few years.

Once out in practice, certain specialties lent themselves to a more relaxed pace. Some examples would be dermatology, psychiatry, pathology, or staying in an academic environment and teaching or doing research, or both. There can be no laziness in any surgical specialty, emergency medicine, critical care intensivist, cardiology, pulmonology, etc. However, in primary care, especially family practice, you can work as hard or as little as you wish depending on how much money you want to earn. And, if you have a government job, such as in a V.A. hospital, or Community Health Center, you can work fewer hours with far less intensity. Conversely, if you are in private practice, either solo or in a group, you must, of necessity, work hard and see many patients to generate a decent income.

But incompetence is much more than just laziness. For example, there are many medical students who are brilliant in school: so long as they have a book to memorize, and an exam to ace, they are very impressive. But, put them out in real world situations as a physician, and they fail miserably. They can't transform their academic skills into common sense-Clinical solutions. They are, in fact, clueless when faced with the real thing.

Secondly, many of our doctors who are foreign grads are just not up to snuff. There are several reasons for this, such as lack of communication skills, cultural variances, and second-rate education from certain medical schools, either overseas, or offshore (Mexico or the Caribbean.) I've known many foreign grads, and, in my experience, the chief problem is lack of understanding of the average American patient. Most of these folks lack the English skills, patience, and empathy that their American colleagues possess. In terms of empathy, certain cultures don't seem to deal with the issue of pain with the appropriate understanding and sympathy for the patient. They rarely, if ever, prescribe strong analgesic medication in spite of the merits of the case. In short, it doesn't seem to bother many of these folks if the patient suffers, which is ignorant and cruel in my opinion, but this attitude may be perfectly acceptable in some cultures, where tolerating pain is expected of an individual. What they seem to have forgotten, is that in this country, we take an oath to relieve pain and suffering. They shirk their primary duty as a physician by ignoring the main reason the majority of us chose to practice medicine.

Another major issue with foreign grads is compulsory service in rural areas, a requirement to for permanent licensure and resident status (green card.) In general, I would say that they are just playing out the string without a lot of effort put forth to practice a high standard of medicine. This isn't universally true, but, in my experience, for the majority, this is the case. Once they have served their time in the boonies, invariably they head for the big cities, where the real money is to be made. What they don't realize is that for primary care today-the big bucks are in the rural areas, not urban centers. Even though they are desperately needed in small town America, they prefer the city life, even if it means a lower standard of living. I can't see the reasoning there, but who am 11Regardless of where they practice, the same level of incompetence follows them. Its like the old saying 'everywhere you go there you are.' Practicing in a big, fancy clinic in the city doesn't confer great clinical ability, and sooner later, the patients figure this out and move on to other physicians with more compassion and competency. I don't in any way mean to imply that the majority of foreign grads are bad doctors, but the minority that I've described, are blatantly unworthy of holding a license to practice in this or any country.